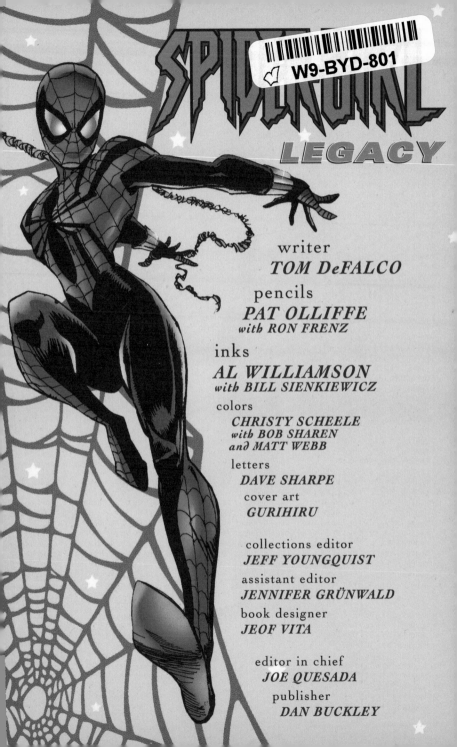

SPIDER-GIRL
LEGACY

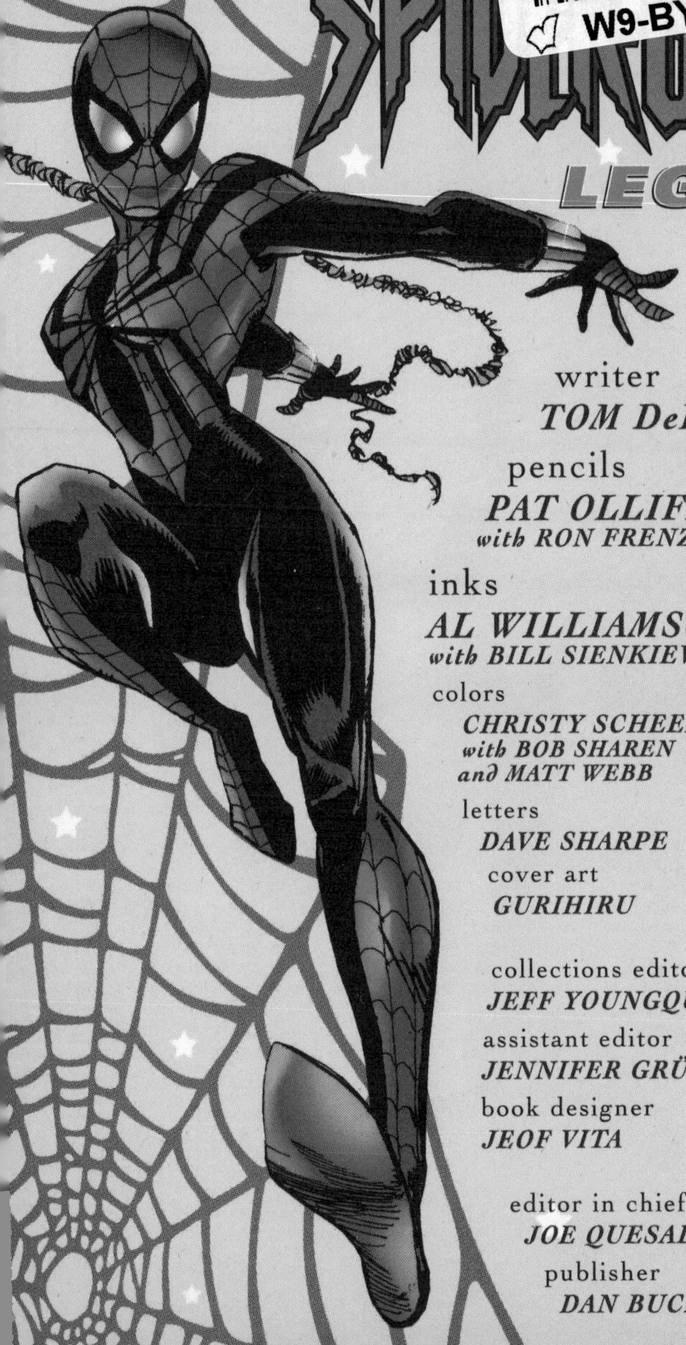

writer
TOM DeFALCO

pencils
PAT OLLIFFE
with RON FRENZ

inks
AL WILLIAMSON
with BILL SIENKIEWICZ

colors
CHRISTY SCHEELE
with BOB SHAREN
and MATT WEBB

letters
DAVE SHARPE

cover art
GURIHIRU

collections editor
JEFF YOUNGQUIST

assistant editor
JENNIFER GRÜNWALD

book designer
JEOF VITA

editor in chief
JOE QUESADA

publisher
DAN BUCKLEY

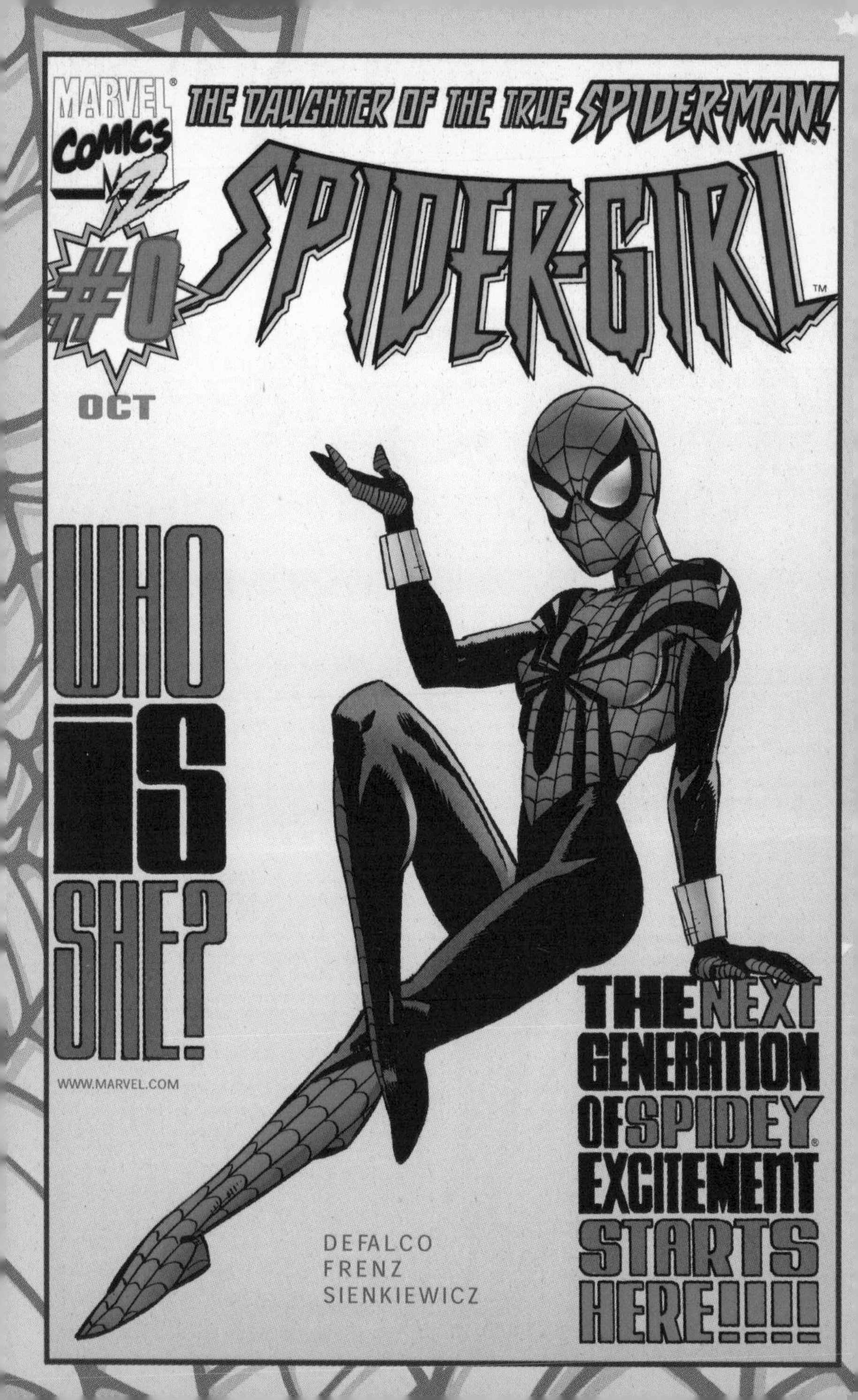

MARVEL COMICS 2
THE DAUGHTER OF THE TRUE SPIDER-MAN!
SPIDER-GIRL
#0
OCT
WHO IS SHE?
WWW.MARVEL.COM
DEFALCO
FRENZ
SIENKIEWICZ
THE NEXT GENERATION OF SPIDEY EXCITEMENT STARTS HERE!!!!

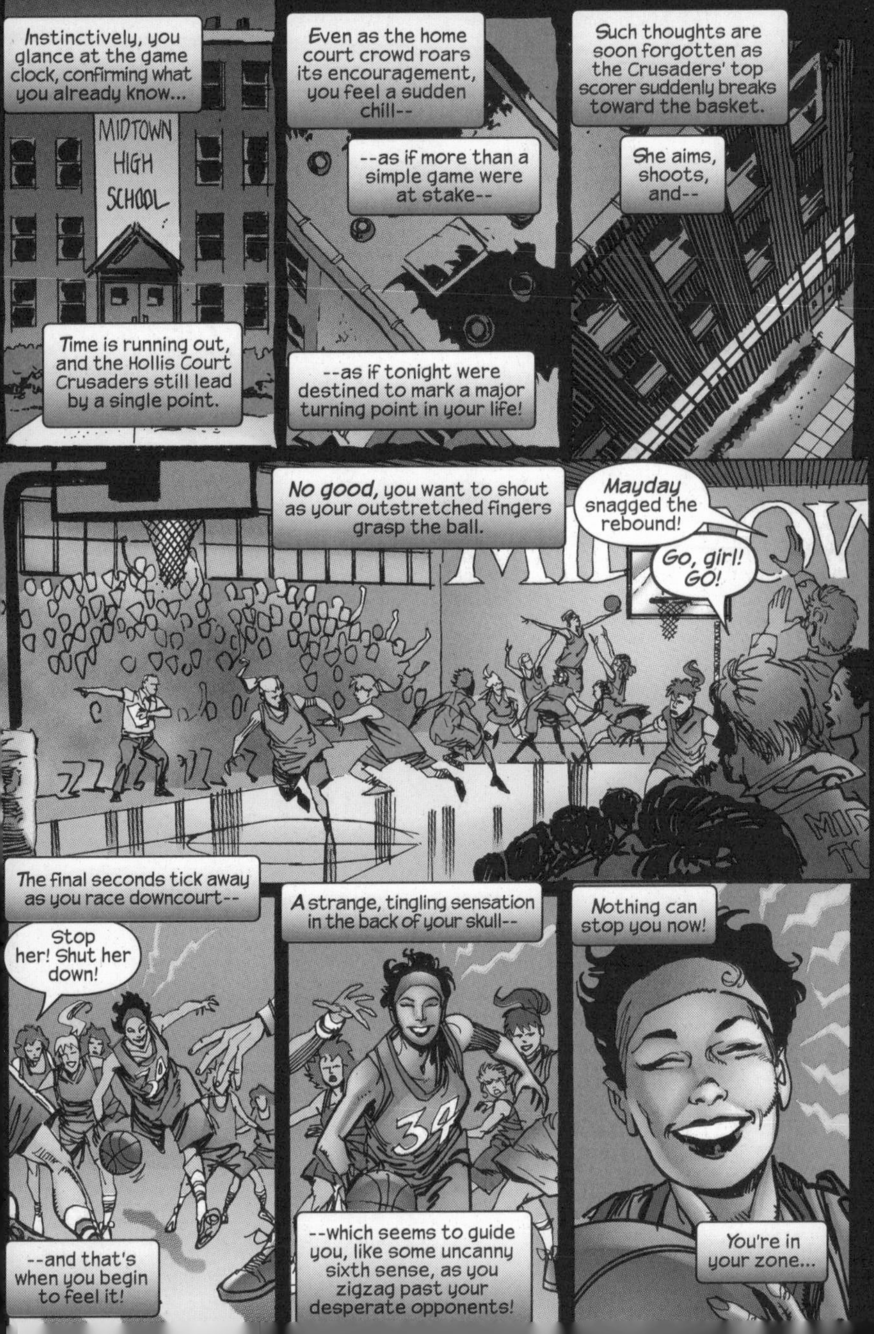
Instinctively, you glance at the game clock, confirming what you already know...
MIDTOWN HIGH SCHOOL
Time is running out, and the Hollis Court Crusaders still lead by a single point.
Even as the home court crowd roars its encouragement, you feel a sudden chill--
--as if more than a simple game were at stake--
--as if tonight were destined to mark a major turning point in your life!
Such thoughts are soon forgotten as the Crusaders' top scorer suddenly breaks toward the basket.
She aims, shoots, and--
No good, you want to shout as your outstretched fingers grasp the ball.
Mayday snagged the rebound!
Go, girl! GO!
The final seconds tick away as you race downcourt--
Stop her! Shut her down!
--and that's when you begin to feel it!
A strange, tingling sensation in the back of your skull--
--which seems to guide you, like some uncanny sixth sense, as you zigzag past your desperate opponents!
Nothing can stop you now!
You're in your zone...

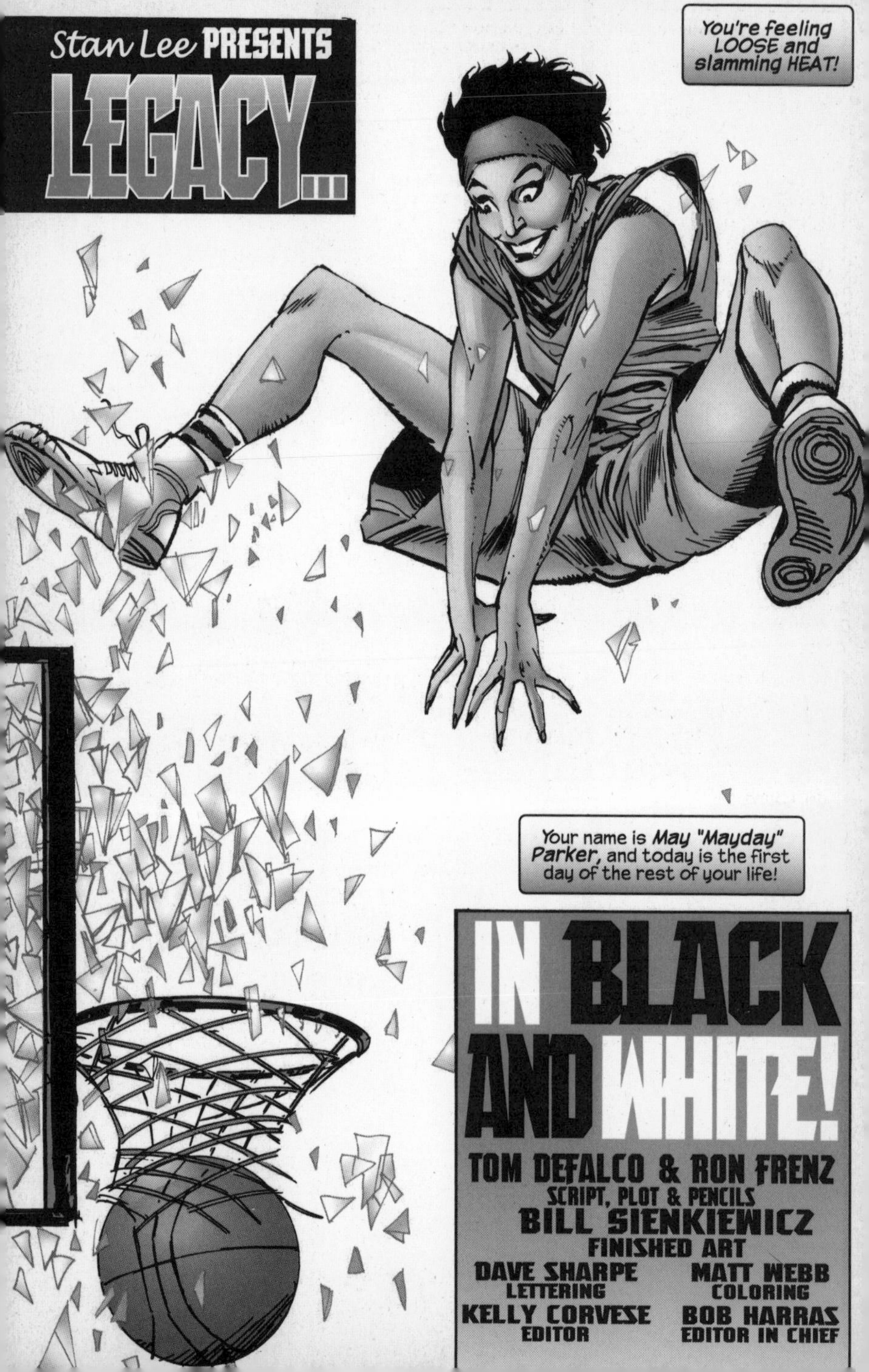
Stan Lee PRESENTS
LEGACY...
You're feeling LOOSE and slamming HEAT!
Your name is May "Mayday" Parker, and today is the first day of the rest of your life!
IN BLACK AND WHITE!
TOM DEFALCO & RON FRENZ
SCRIPT, PLOT & PENCILS
BILL SIENKIEWICZ
FINISHED ART
DAVE SHARPE
LETTERING
MATT WEBB
COLORING
KELLY CORVESE
EDITOR
BOB HARRAS
EDITOR IN CHIEF

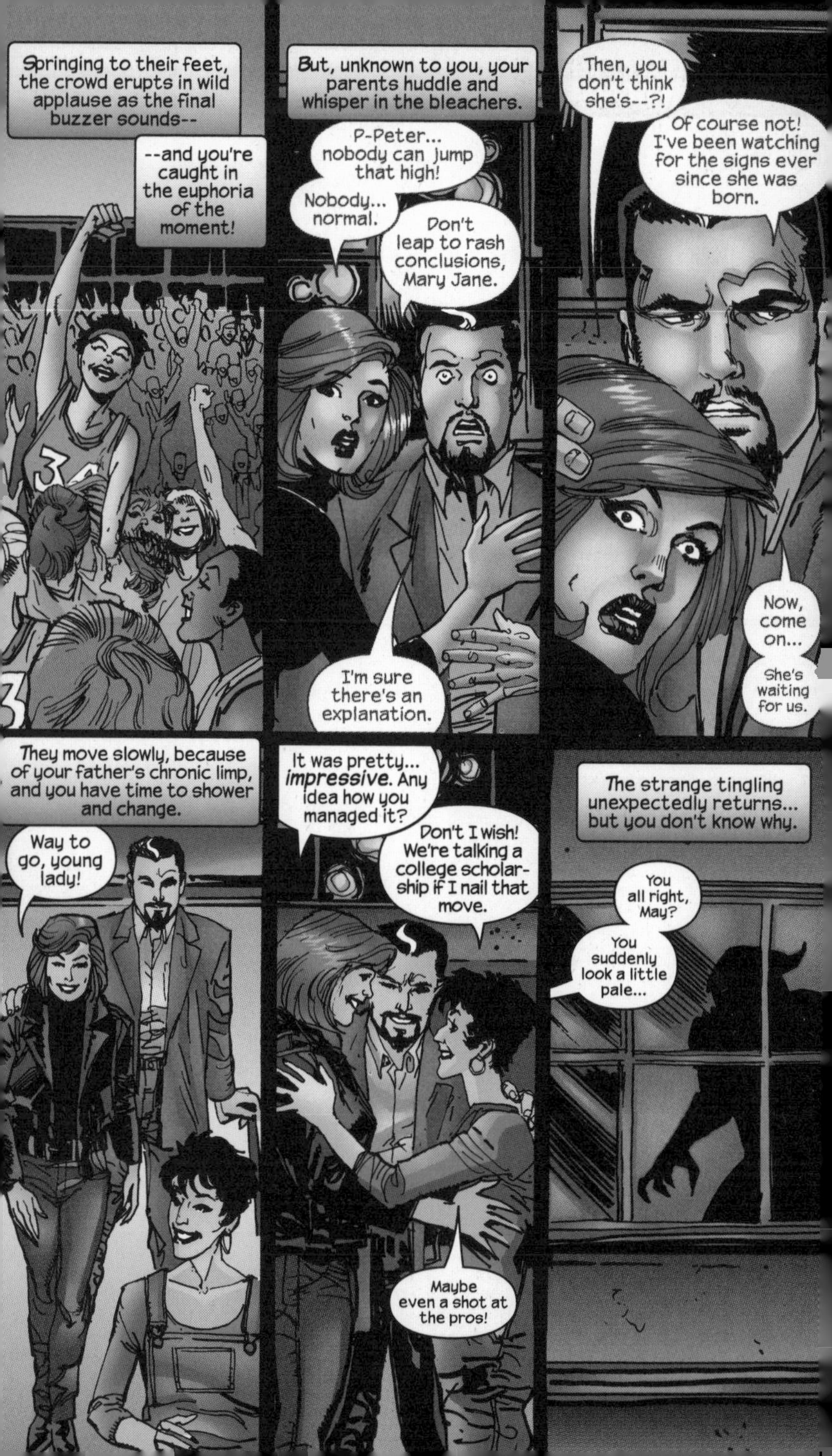

Springing to their feet, the crowd erupts in wild applause as the final buzzer sounds--
--and you're caught in the euphoria of the moment!
But, unknown to you, your parents huddle and whisper in the bleachers.
P-Peter... nobody can jump that high!
Nobody... normal.
Don't leap to rash conclusions, Mary Jane.
I'm sure there's an explanation.
Then, you don't think she's--?!
Of course not! I've been watching for the signs ever since she was born.
Now, come on...
She's waiting for us.
They move slowly, because of your father's chronic limp, and you have time to shower and change.
Way to go, young lady!
It was pretty... impressive. Any idea how you managed it?
Don't I wish! We're talking a college scholarship if I nail that move.
Maybe even a shot at the pros!
The strange tingling unexpectedly returns... but you don't know why.
You all right, May?
You suddenly look a little pale...

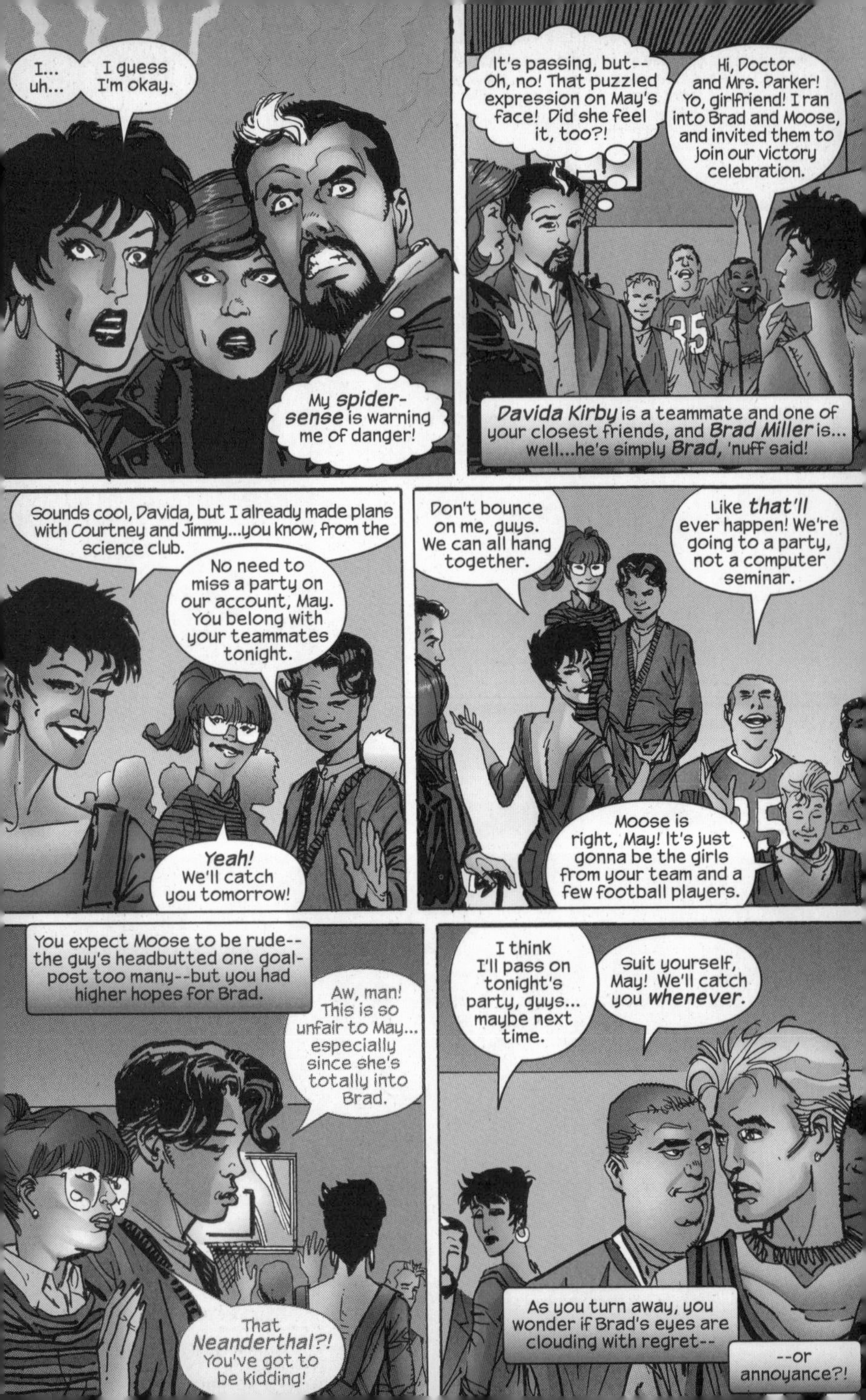
I... uh...
I guess I'm okay.
My spider-sense is warning me of danger!
It's passing, but-- Oh, no! That puzzled expression on May's face! Did she feel it, too?!
Hi, Doctor and Mrs. Parker! Yo, girlfriend! I ran into Brad and Moose, and invited them to join our victory celebration.
Davida Kirby is a teammate and one of your closest friends, and Brad Miller is... well...he's simply Brad, 'nuff said!
Sounds cool, Davida, but I already made plans with Courtney and Jimmy...you know, from the science club.
No need to miss a party on our account, May. You belong with your teammates tonight.
Yeah! We'll catch you tomorrow!
Don't bounce on me, guys. We can all hang together.
Like that'll ever happen! We're going to a party, not a computer seminar.
Moose is right, May! It's just gonna be the girls from your team and a few football players.
You expect Moose to be rude--the guy's headbutted one goal-post too many--but you had higher hopes for Brad.
Aw, man! This is so unfair to May... especially since she's totally into Brad.
That Neanderthal?! You've got to be kidding!
I think I'll pass on tonight's party, guys... maybe next time.
Suit yourself, May! We'll catch you whenever.
As you turn away, you wonder if Brad's eyes are clouding with regret--
--or annoyance?!

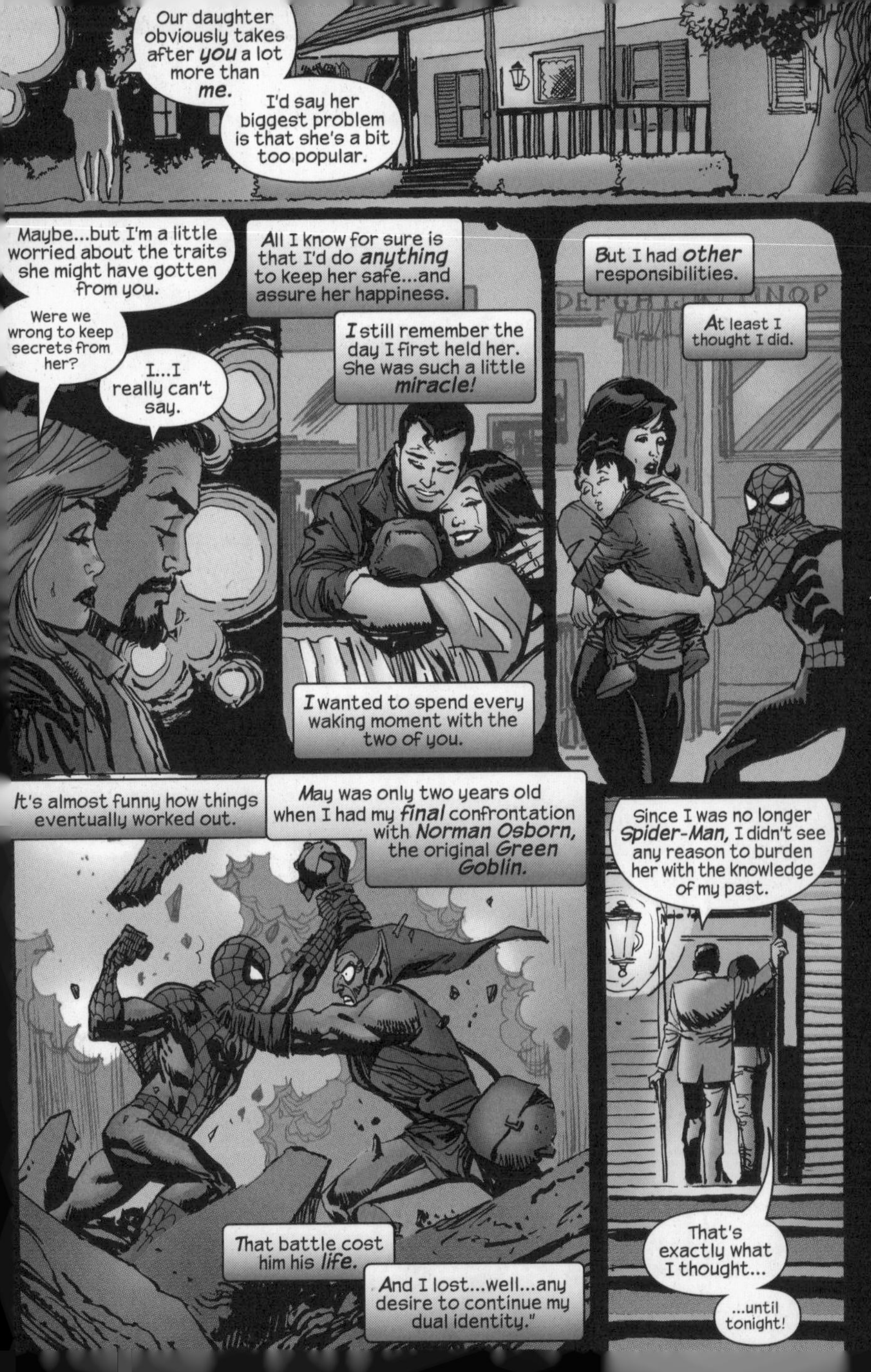
Our daughter obviously takes after *you* a lot more than *me.*
I'd say her biggest problem is that she's a bit too popular.
Maybe...but I'm a little worried about the traits she might have gotten from you.
Were we wrong to keep secrets from her?
I...I really can't say.
All I know for sure is that I'd do *anything* to keep her safe...and assure her happiness.
I still remember the day I first held her. She was such a little *miracle!*
I wanted to spend every waking moment with the two of you.
But I had *other* responsibilities.
At least I thought I did.
It's almost funny how things eventually worked out.
May was only two years old when I had my *final* confrontation with *Norman Osborn,* the original *Green Goblin.*
That battle cost him his *life.*
And I lost...well...any desire to continue my dual identity."
Since I was no longer *Spider-Man,* I didn't see any reason to burden her with the knowledge of my past.
That's exactly what I thought...
...until tonight!

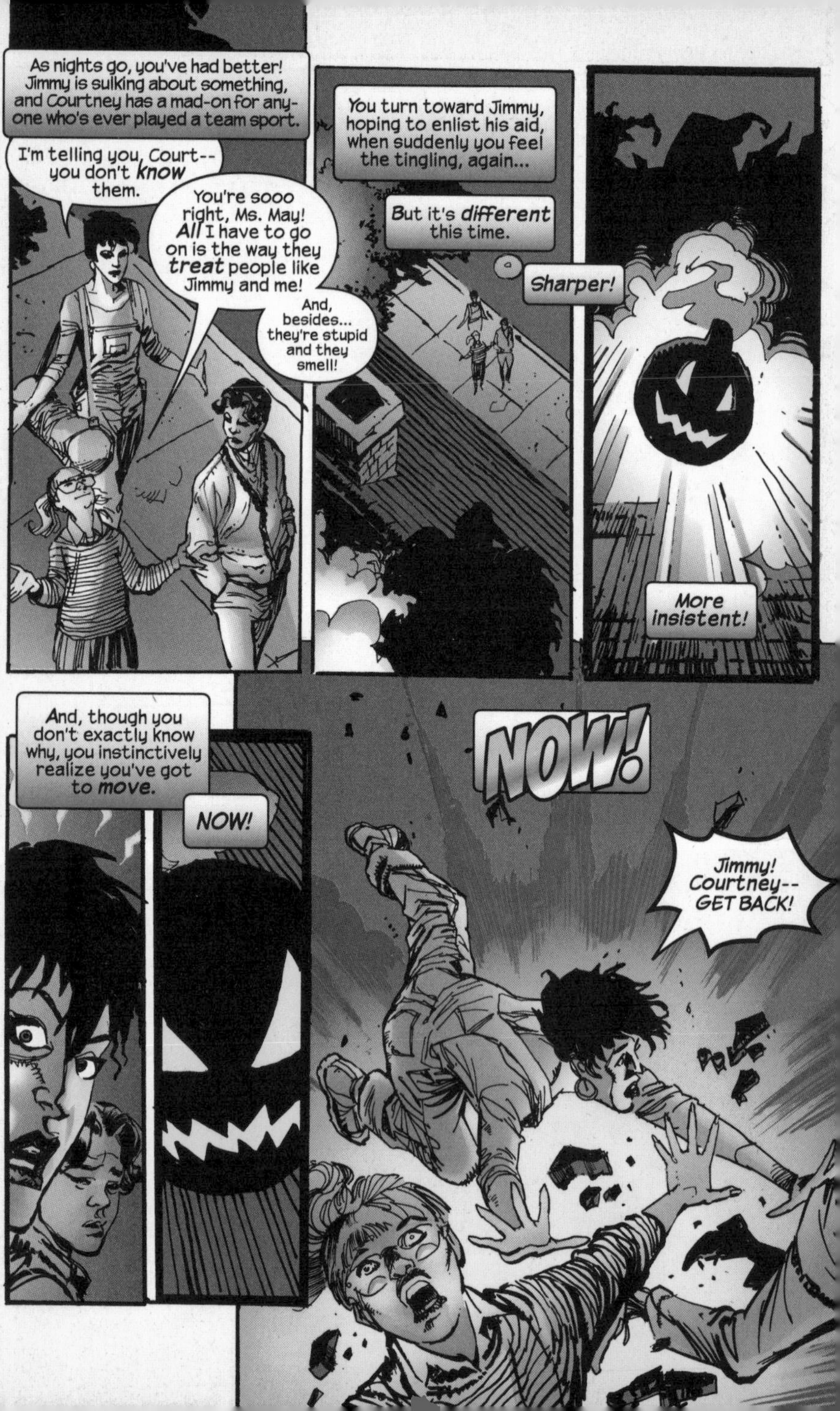
As nights go, you've had better! Jimmy is sulking about something, and Courtney has a mad-on for any-one who's ever played a team sport.
I'm telling you, Court-- you don't know them.
You're sooo right, Ms. May! All I have to go on is the way they treat people like Jimmy and me!
And, besides... they're stupid and they smell!
You turn toward Jimmy, hoping to enlist his aid, when suddenly you feel the tingling, again...
But it's different this time.
Sharper!
More insistent!
And, though you don't exactly know why, you instinctively realize you've got to move.
NOW!
NOW!
Jimmy! Courtney-- GET BACK!

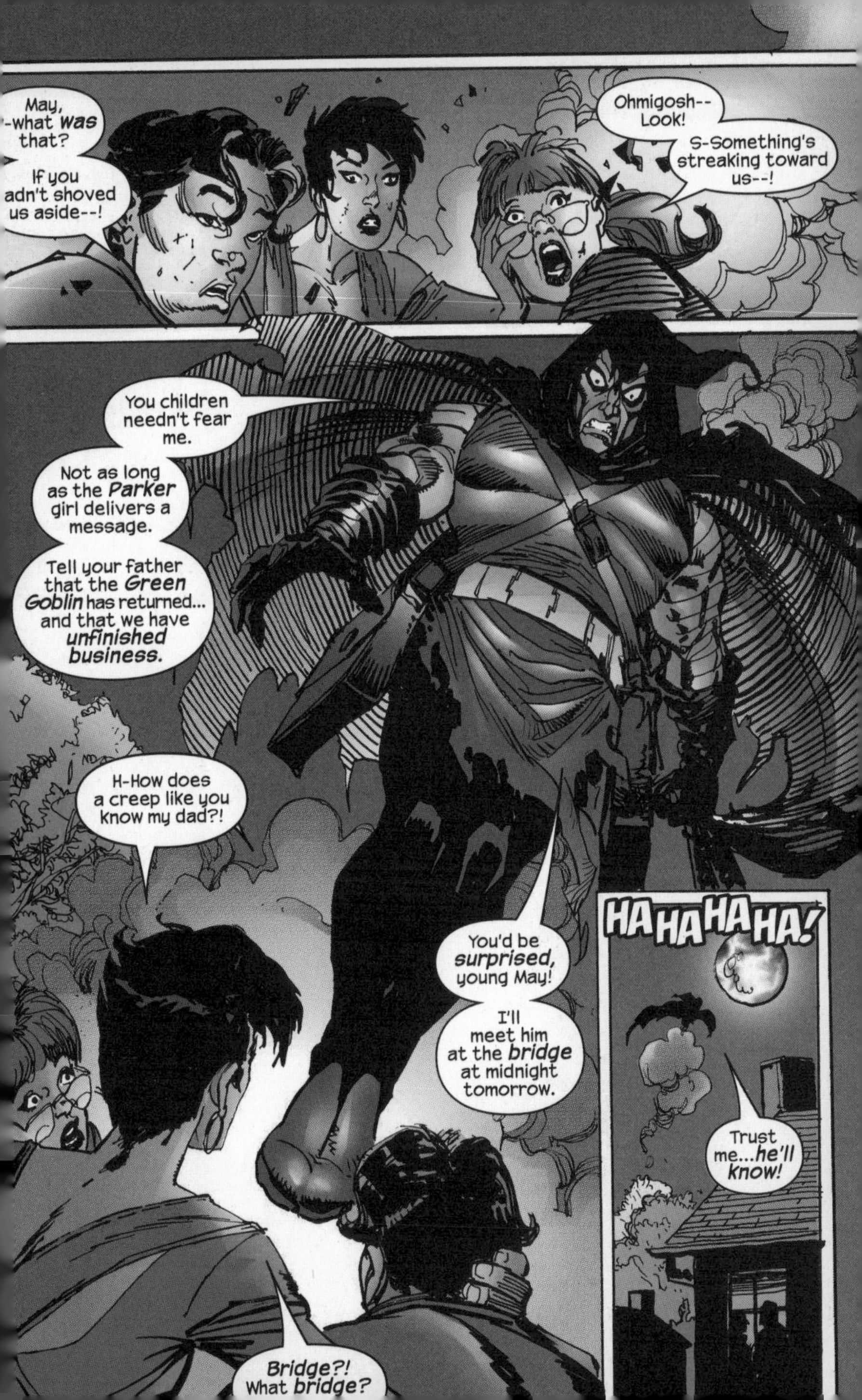
May, --what was that?
If you hadn't shoved us aside--!
Ohmigosh-- Look!
S-Something's streaking toward us--!
You children needn't fear me.
Not as long as the Parker girl delivers a message.
Tell your father that the Green Goblin has returned... and that we have unfinished business.
H-How does a creep like you know my dad?!
You'd be surprised, young May!
I'll meet him at the bridge at midnight tomorrow.
Bridge?! What bridge?
HAHAHAHAHA!
Trust me...he'll know!

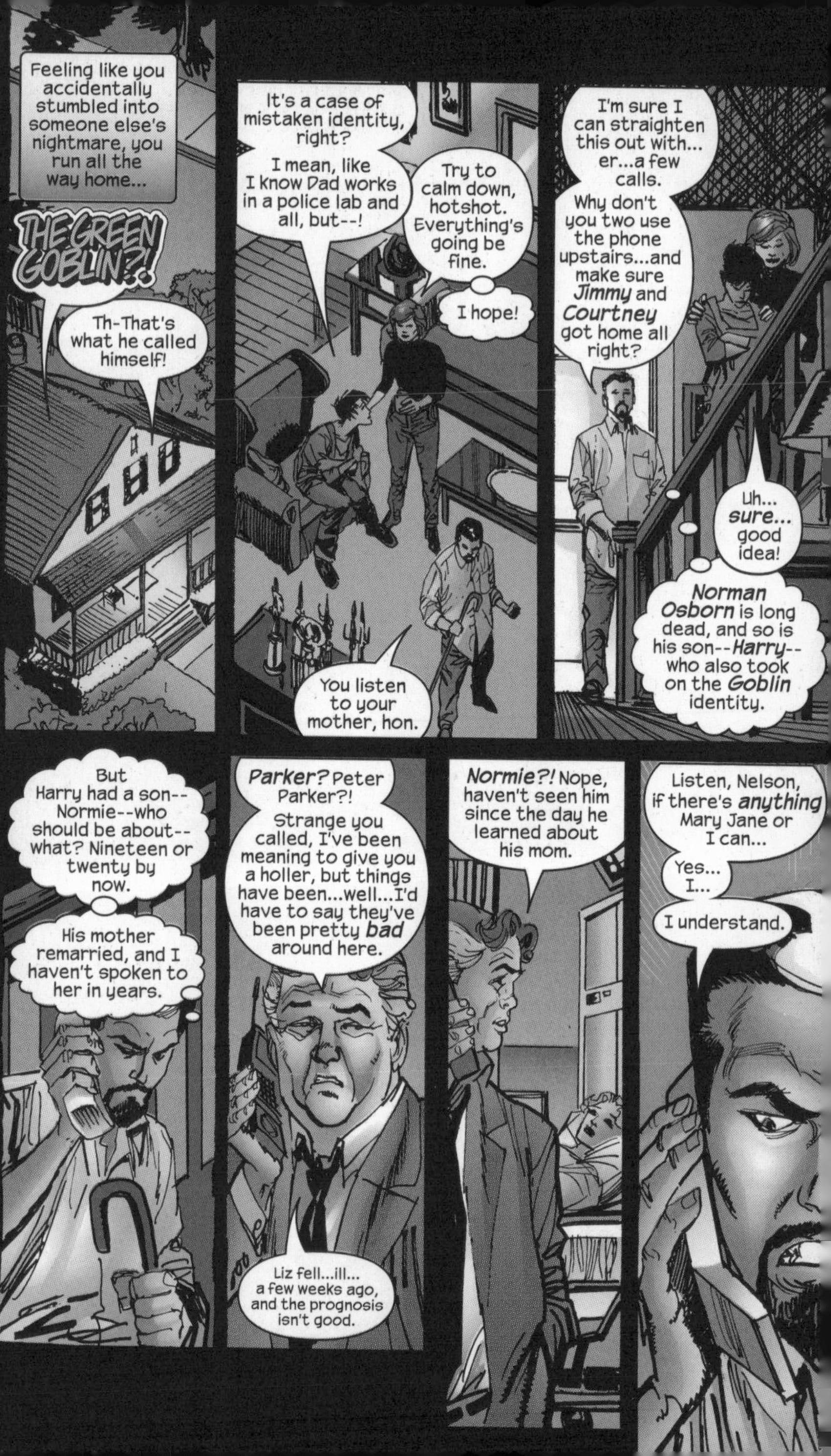

Feeling like you accidentally stumbled into someone else's nightmare, you run all the way home...
THE GREEN GOBLIN?!
Th-That's what he called himself!
It's a case of mistaken identity, right?
I mean, like I know Dad works in a police lab and all, but--!
Try to calm down, hotshot. Everything's going be fine.
I hope!
You listen to your mother, hon.
I'm sure I can straighten this out with... er...a few calls.
Why don't you two use the phone upstairs...and make sure Jimmy and Courtney got home all right?
Uh... sure... good idea!
Norman Osborn is long dead, and so is his son--Harry--who also took on the Goblin identity.
But Harry had a son--Normie--who should be about--what? Nineteen or twenty by now.
His mother remarried, and I haven't spoken to her in years.
Parker? Peter Parker?!
Strange you called, I've been meaning to give you a holler, but things have been...well...I'd have to say they've been pretty bad around here.
Liz fell...ill... a few weeks ago, and the prognosis isn't good.
Normie?! Nope, haven't seen him since the day he learned about his mom.
Listen, Nelson, if there's anything Mary Jane or I can...
Yes... I...
I understand.

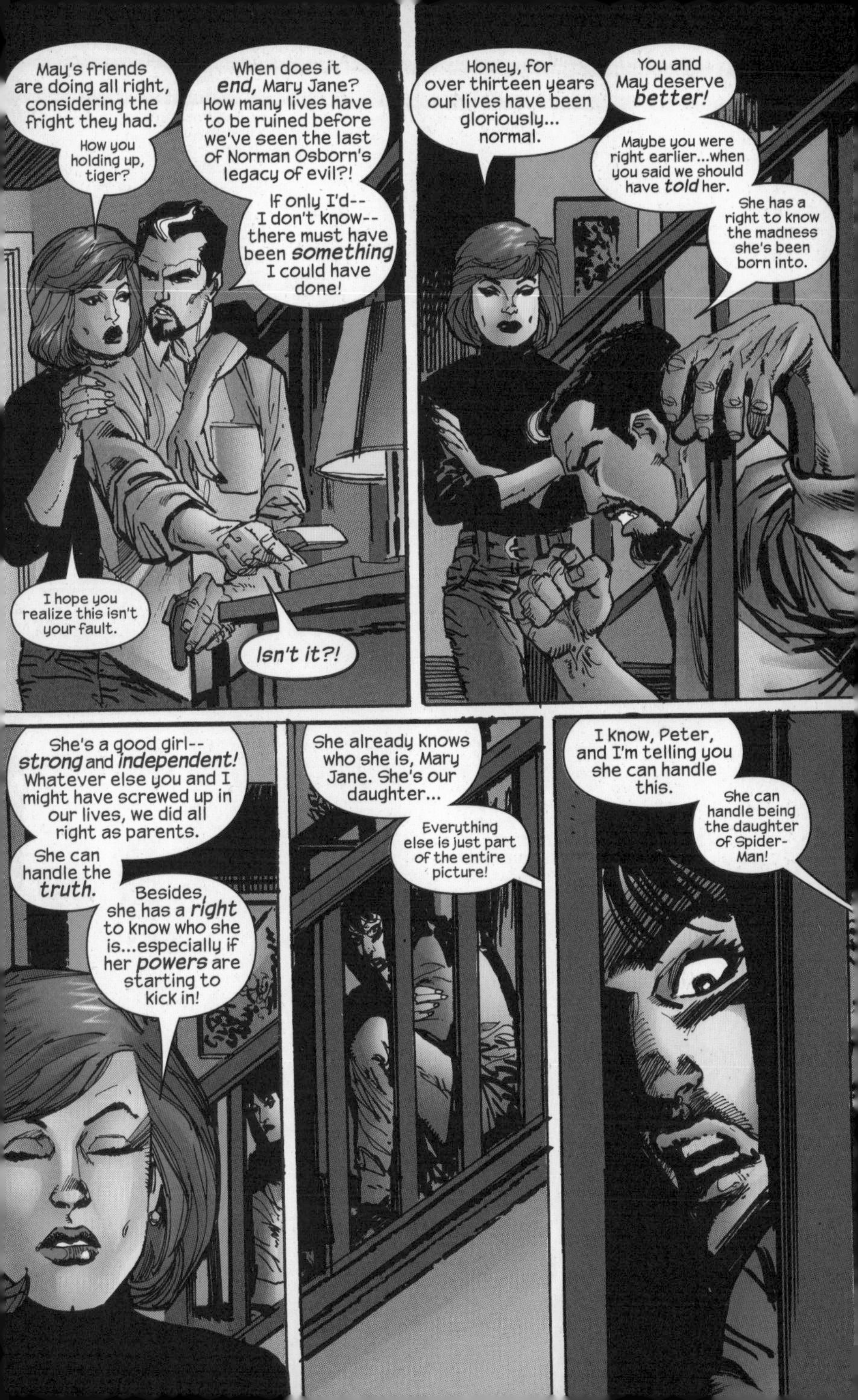
May's friends are doing all right, considering the fright they had.
How you holding up, tiger?
When does it end, Mary Jane? How many lives have to be ruined before we've seen the last of Norman Osborn's legacy of evil?!
If only I'd-- I don't know-- there must have been something I could have done!
I hope you realize this isn't your fault.
Isn't it?!
Honey, for over thirteen years our lives have been gloriously... normal.
You and May deserve better!
Maybe you were right earlier...when you said we should have told her.
She has a right to know the madness she's been born into.
She's a good girl-- strong and independent! Whatever else you and I might have screwed up in our lives, we did all right as parents.
She can handle the truth.
Besides, she has a right to know who she is...especially if her powers are starting to kick in!
She already knows who she is, Mary Jane. She's our daughter...
Everything else is just part of the entire picture!
I know, Peter, and I'm telling you she can handle this.
She can handle being the daughter of Spider-Man!

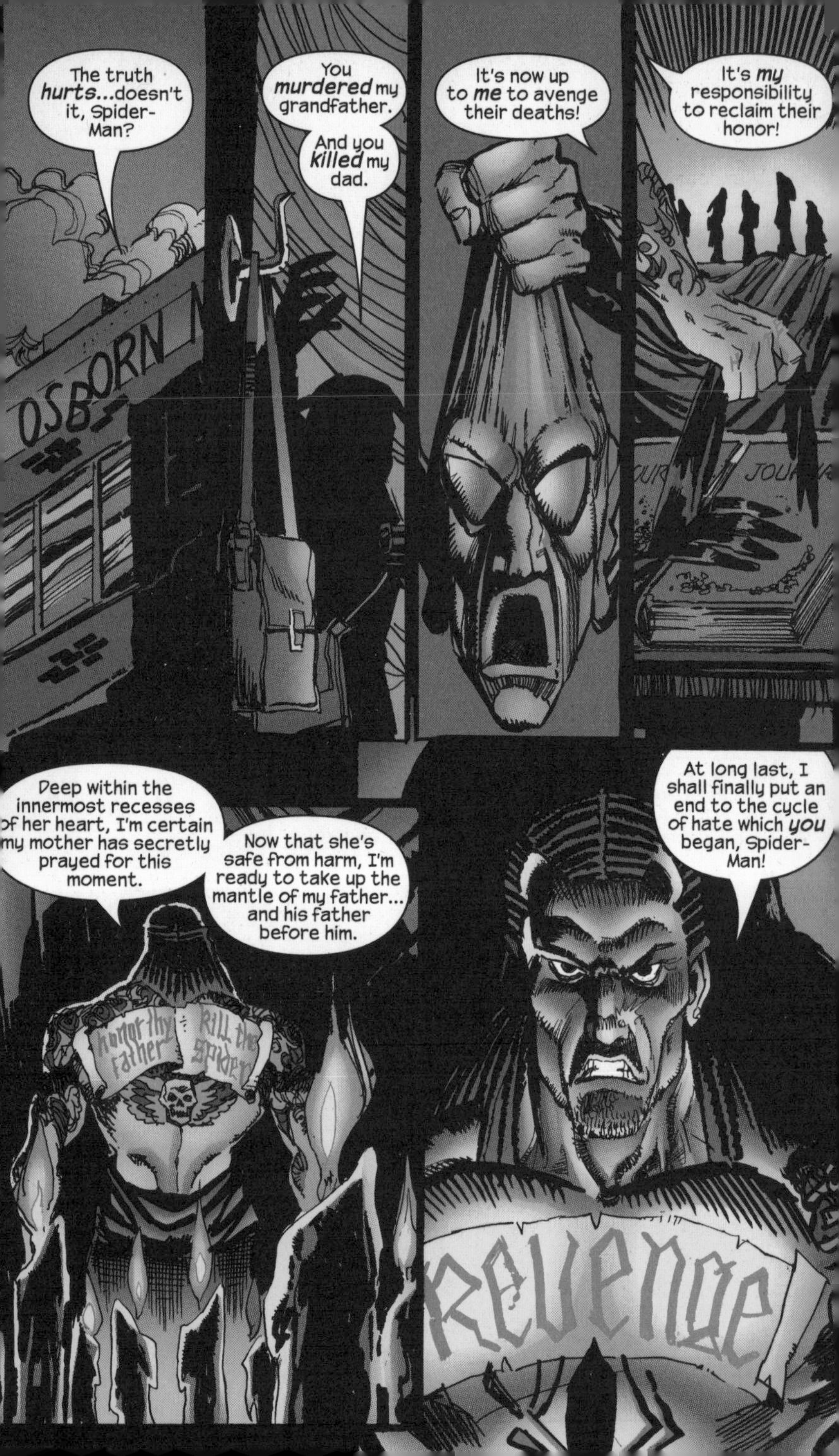

The truth *hurts...*doesn't it, Spider-Man?
OSBORN
You *murdered* my grandfather.
And you *killed* my dad.
It's now up to *me* to avenge their deaths!
It's *my* responsibility to reclaim their honor!
Deep within the innermost recesses of her heart, I'm certain my mother has secretly prayed for this moment.
Now that she's safe from harm, I'm ready to take up the mantle of my father... and his father before him.
honor thy father
kill the spider
At long last, I shall finally put an end to the cycle of hate which *you* began, Spider-Man!
REVENGE

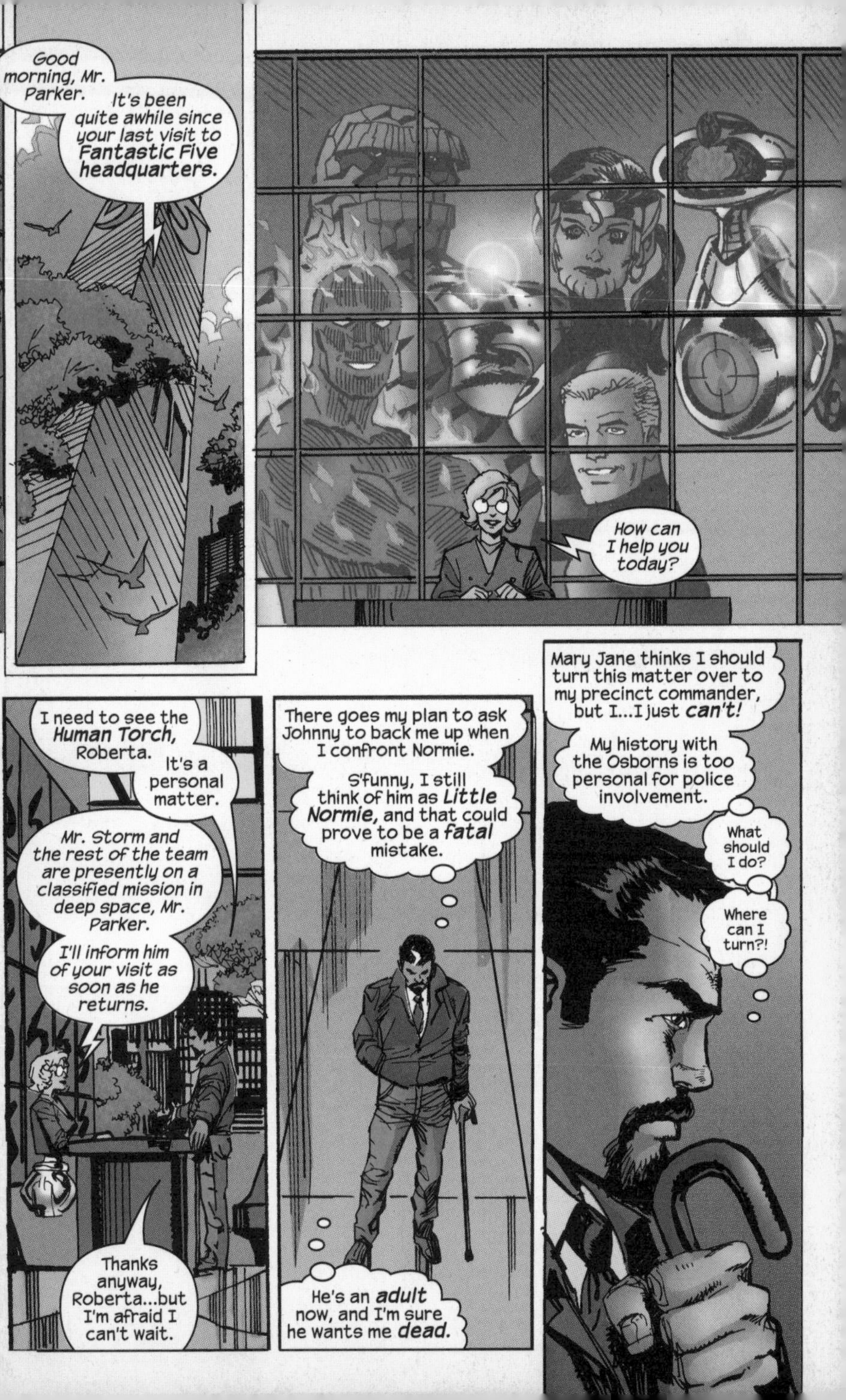

Good morning, Mr. Parker.
It's been quite awhile since your last visit to Fantastic Five headquarters.
How can I help you today?
I need to see the Human Torch, Roberta.
It's a personal matter.
Mr. Storm and the rest of the team are presently on a classified mission in deep space, Mr. Parker.
I'll inform him of your visit as soon as he returns.
Thanks anyway, Roberta...but I'm afraid I can't wait.
There goes my plan to ask Johnny to back me up when I confront Normie.
S'funny, I still think of him as Little Normie, and that could prove to be a fatal mistake.
He's an adult now, and I'm sure he wants me dead.
Mary Jane thinks I should turn this matter over to my precinct commander, but I...I just can't!
My history with the Osborns is too personal for police involvement.
What should I do?
Where can I turn?!

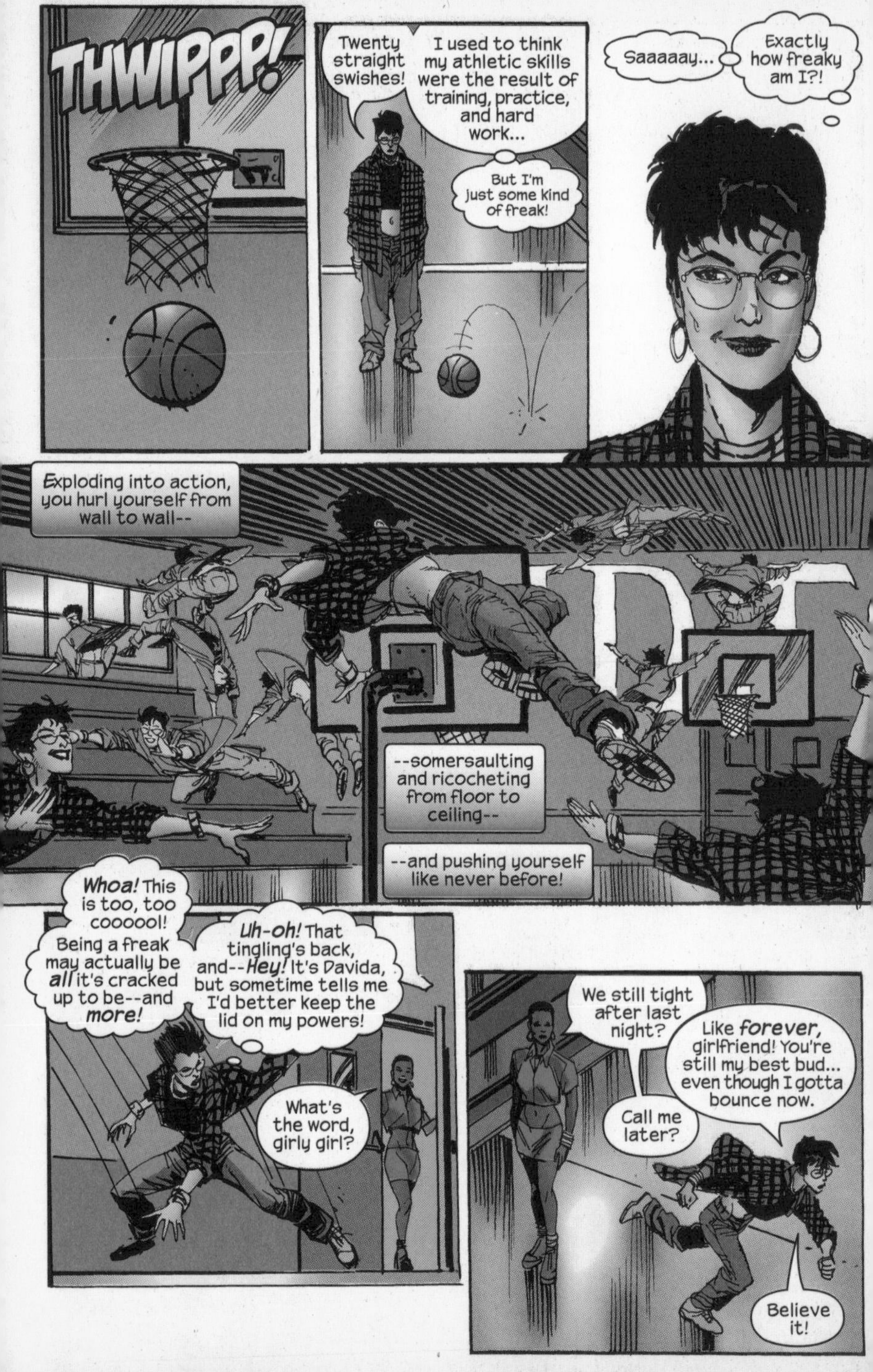

THWIPPP!
Twenty straight swishes!
I used to think my athletic skills were the result of training, practice, and hard work...
But I'm just some kind of freak!
Saaaaay...
Exactly how freaky am I?!
Exploding into action, you hurl yourself from wall to wall--
--somersaulting and ricocheting from floor to ceiling--
--and pushing yourself like never before!
Whoa! This is too, too coooool! Being a freak may actually be *all* it's cracked up to be--and *more!*
Uh-oh! That tingling's back, and--*Hey!* It's Davida, but sometime tells me I'd better keep the lid on my powers!
What's the word, girly girl?
We still tight after last night?
Like *forever,* girlfriend! You're still my best bud... even though I gotta bounce now.
Call me later?
Believe it!

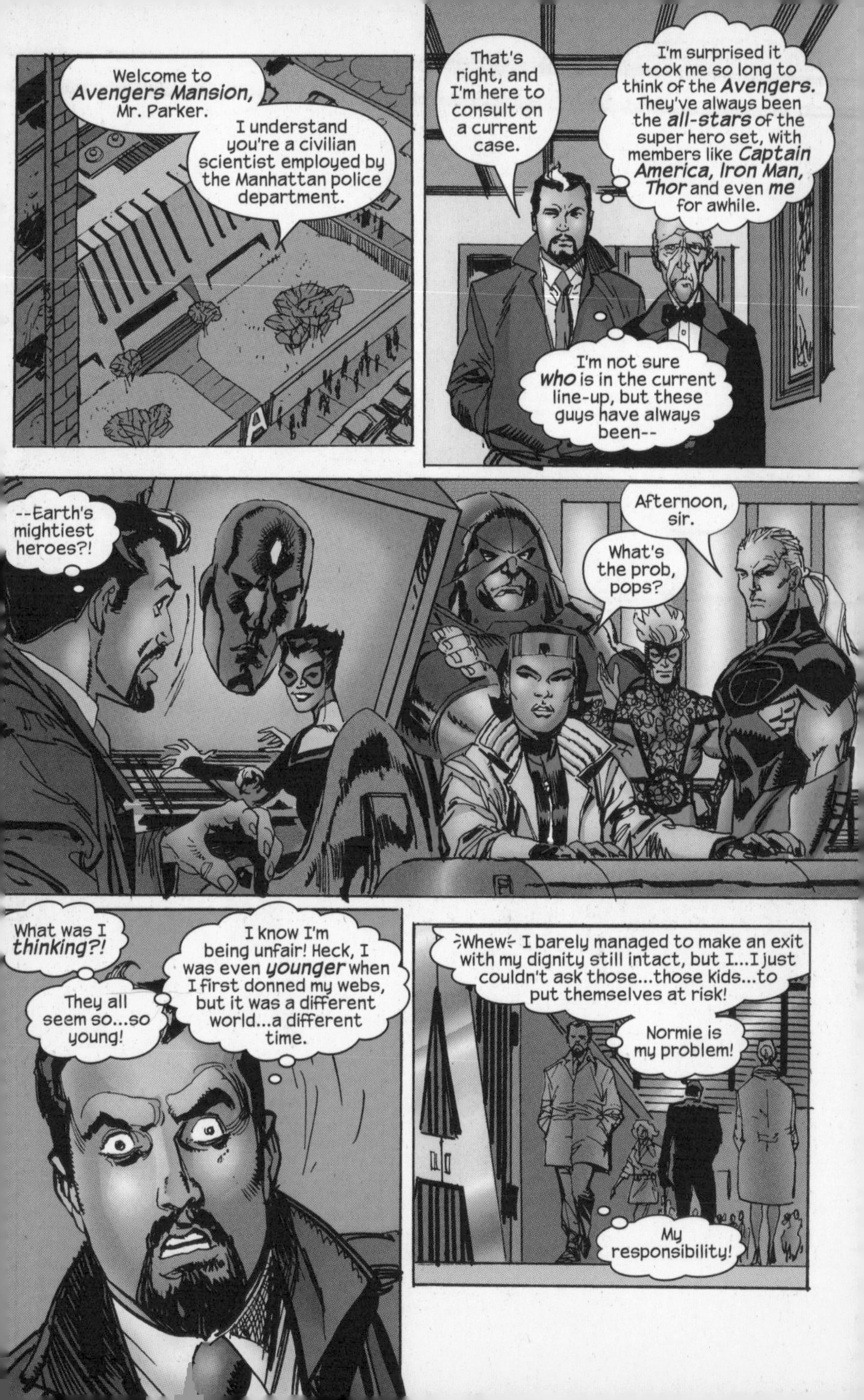
Welcome to Avengers Mansion, Mr. Parker.
I understand you're a civilian scientist employed by the Manhattan police department.
That's right, and I'm here to consult on a current case.
I'm surprised it took me so long to think of the Avengers. They've always been the all-stars of the super hero set, with members like Captain America, Iron Man, Thor and even me for awhile.
I'm not sure who is in the current line-up, but these guys have always been--
--Earth's mightiest heroes?!
Afternoon, sir.
What's the prob, pops?
What was I thinking?!
They all seem so...so young!
I know I'm being unfair! Heck, I was even younger when I first donned my webs, but it was a different world...a different time.
Whew I barely managed to make an exit with my dignity still intact, but I...I just couldn't ask those...those kids...to put themselves at risk!
Normie is my problem!
My responsibility!

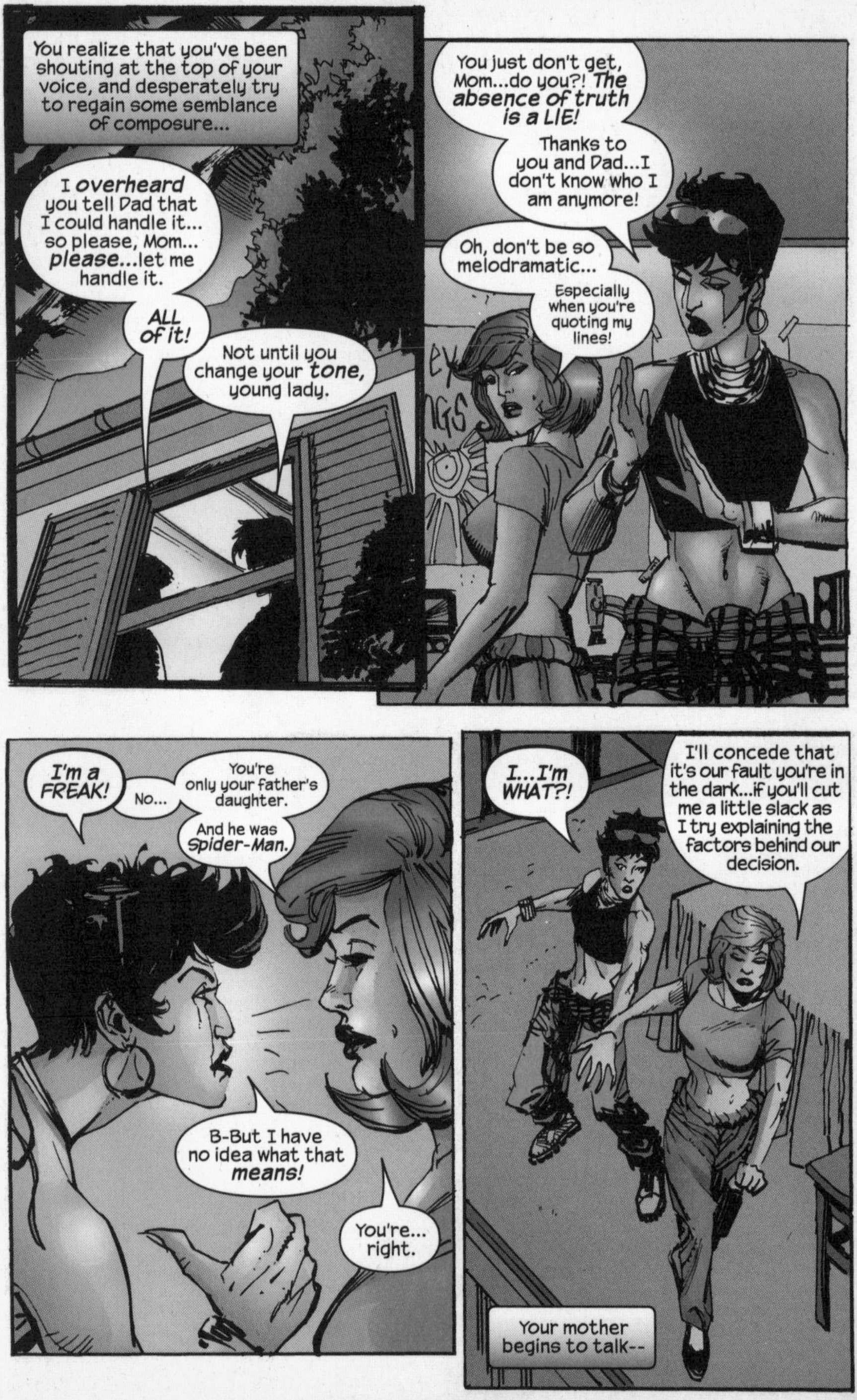

You realize that you've been shouting at the top of your voice, and desperately try to regain some semblance of composure...
I overheard you tell Dad that I could handle it... so please, Mom... please...let me handle it.
ALL of it!
Not until you change your tone, young lady.
You just don't get, Mom...do you?! The absence of truth is a LIE!
Thanks to you and Dad...I don't know who I am anymore!
Oh, don't be so melodramatic...
Especially when you're quoting my lines!
I'm a FREAK!
No...
You're only your father's daughter.
And he was Spider-Man.
B-But I have no idea what that means!
You're... right.
I...I'm WHAT?!
I'll concede that it's our fault you're in the dark...if you'll cut me a little slack as I try explaining the factors behind our decision.
Your mother begins to talk--

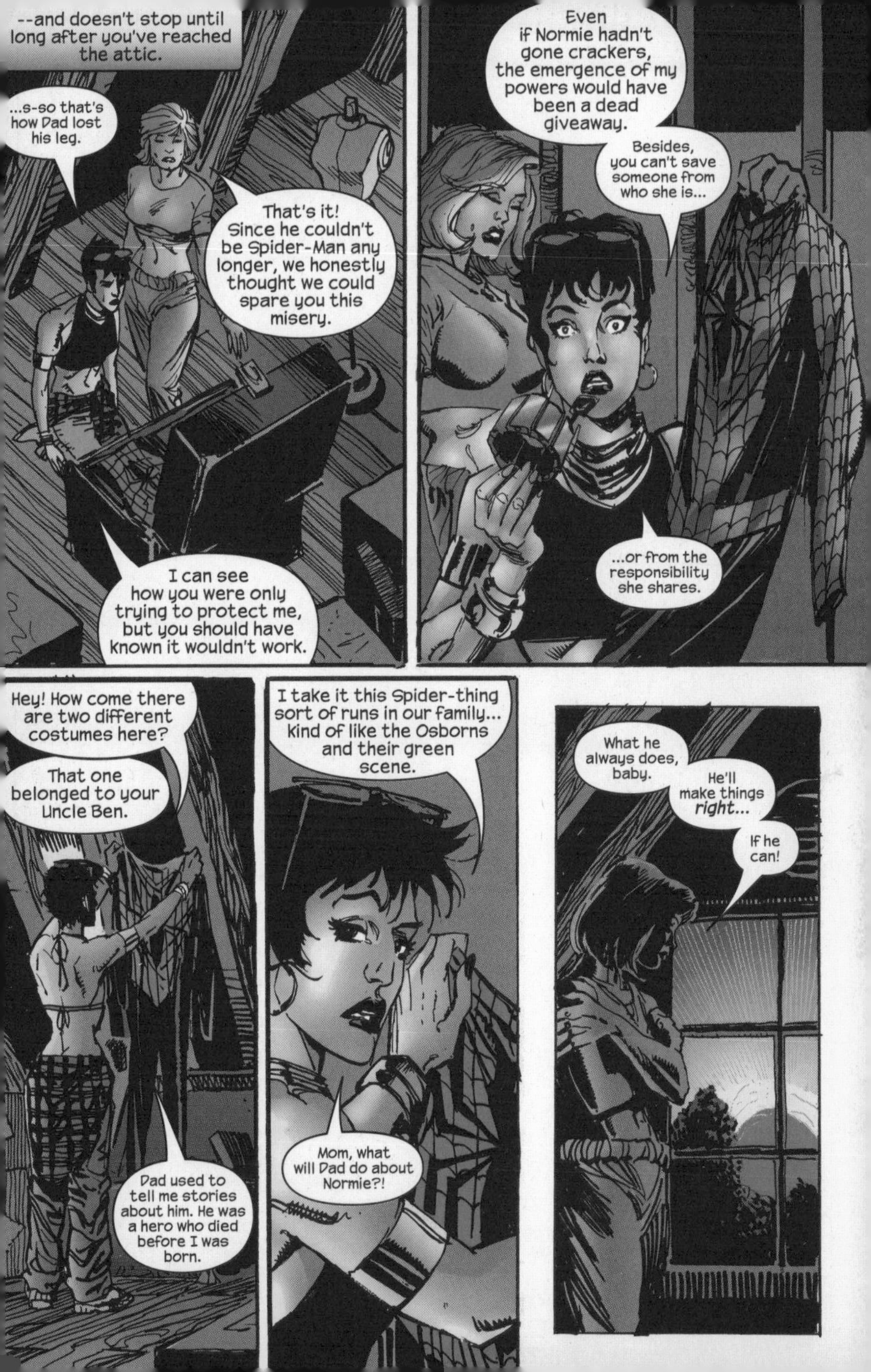

--and doesn't stop until long after you've reached the attic.
...s-so that's how Dad lost his leg.
That's it! Since he couldn't be Spider-Man any longer, we honestly thought we could spare you this misery.
I can see how you were only trying to protect me, but you should have known it wouldn't work.
Even if Normie hadn't gone crackers, the emergence of my powers would have been a dead giveaway.
Besides, you can't save someone from who she is...
...or from the responsibility she shares.
Hey! How come there are two different costumes here?
That one belonged to your Uncle Ben.
Dad used to tell me stories about him. He was a hero who died before I was born.
I take it this Spider-thing sort of runs in our family... kind of like the Osborns and their green scene.
Mom, what will Dad do about Normie?!
What he always does, baby.
He'll make things *right*...
If he can!

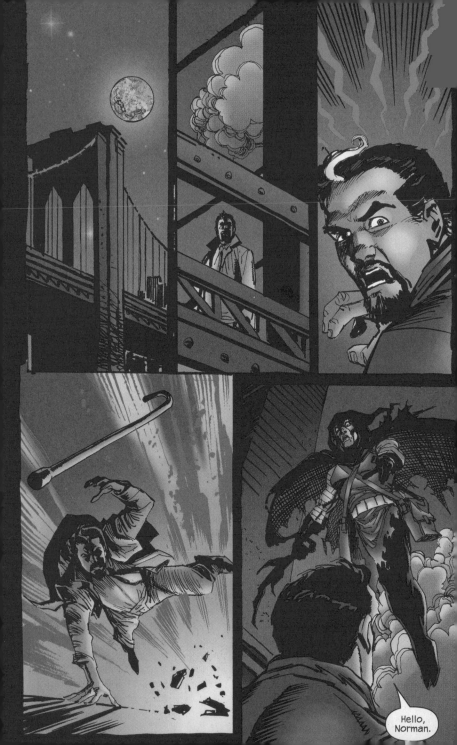

Hello, Norman.

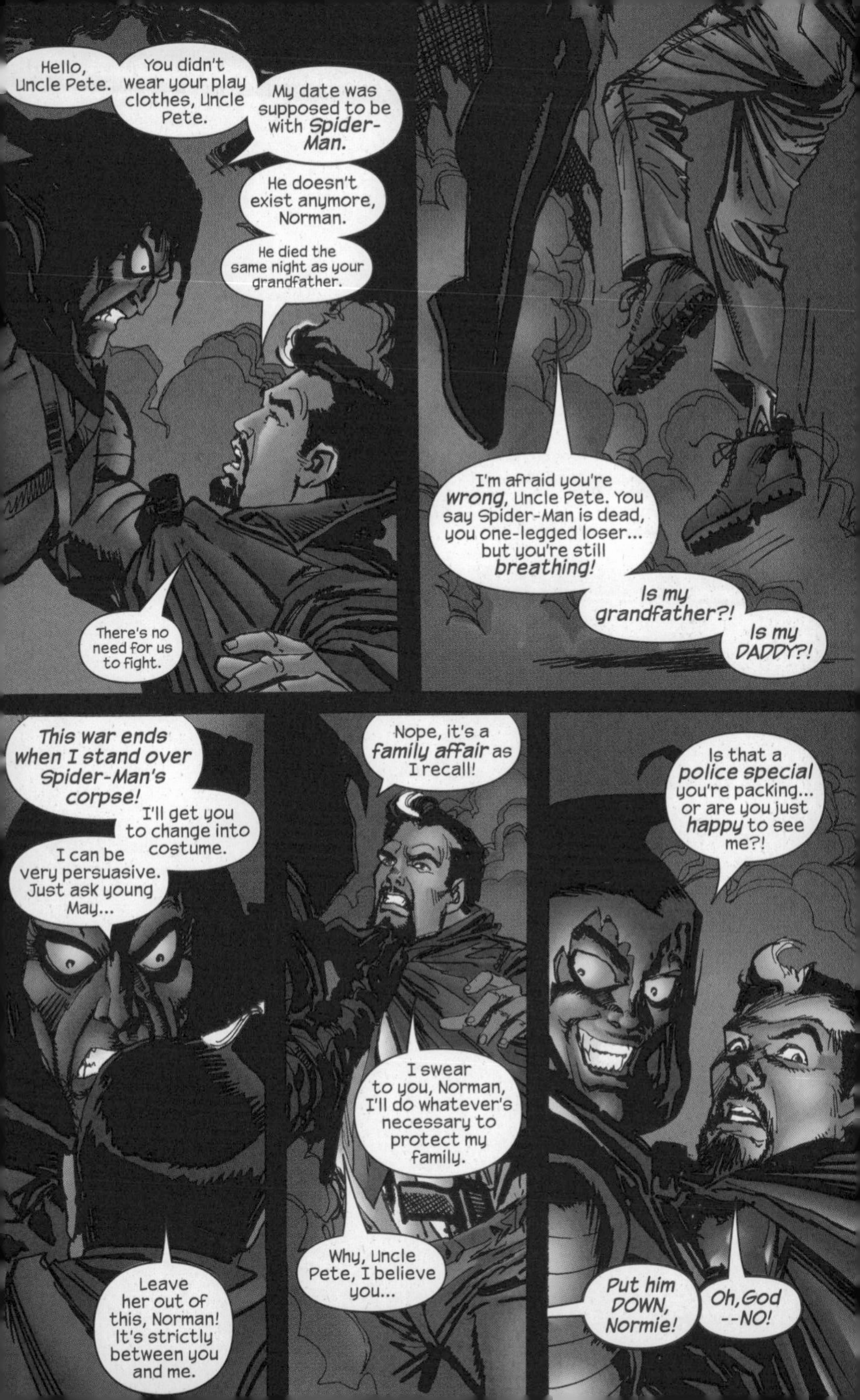
Hello, Uncle Pete.
You didn't wear your play clothes, Uncle Pete.
My date was supposed to be with Spider-Man.
He doesn't exist anymore, Norman.
He died the same night as your grandfather.
There's no need for us to fight.
I'm afraid you're wrong, Uncle Pete. You say Spider-Man is dead, you one-legged loser... but you're still breathing!
Is my grandfather?!
Is my DADDY?!
This war ends when I stand over Spider-Man's corpse!
I'll get you to change into costume.
I can be very persuasive. Just ask young May...
Leave her out of this, Norman! It's strictly between you and me.
Nope, it's a family affair as I recall!
I swear to you, Norman, I'll do whatever's necessary to protect my family.
Why, Uncle Pete, I believe you...
Is that a police special you're packing... or are you just happy to see me?!
Put him DOWN, Normie!
Oh, God --NO!

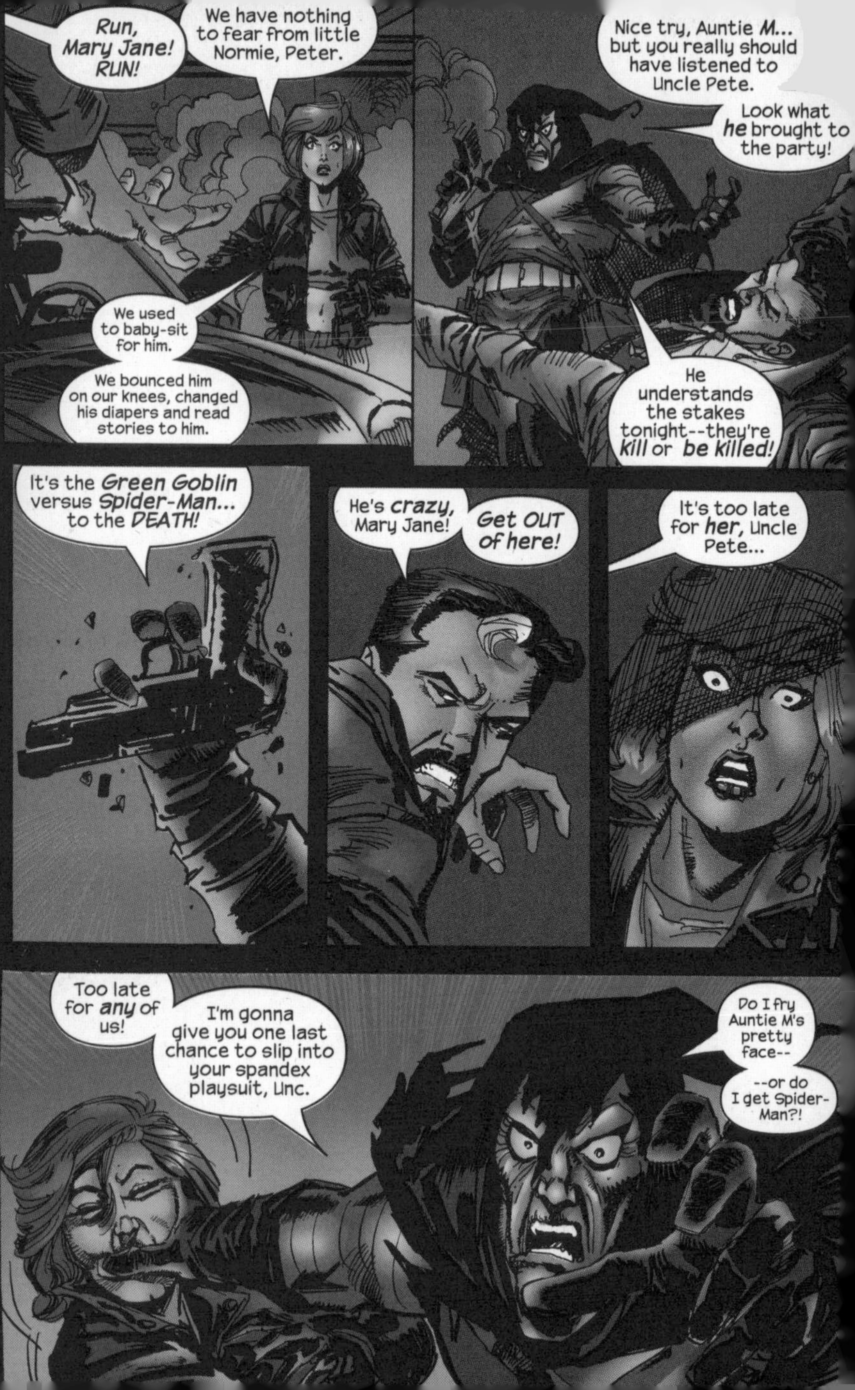
Run, Mary Jane! RUN!
We have nothing to fear from little Normie, Peter.
We used to baby-sit for him.
We bounced him on our knees, changed his diapers and read stories to him.
Nice try, Auntie M... but you really should have listened to Uncle Pete.
Look what he brought to the party!
He understands the stakes tonight--they're kill or be killed!
It's the Green Goblin versus Spider-Man... to the DEATH!
He's crazy, Mary Jane!
Get OUT of here!
It's too late for her, Uncle Pete...
Too late for any of us!
I'm gonna give you one last chance to slip into your spandex playsuit, Unc.
Do I fry Auntie M's pretty face--
--or do I get Spider-Man?!

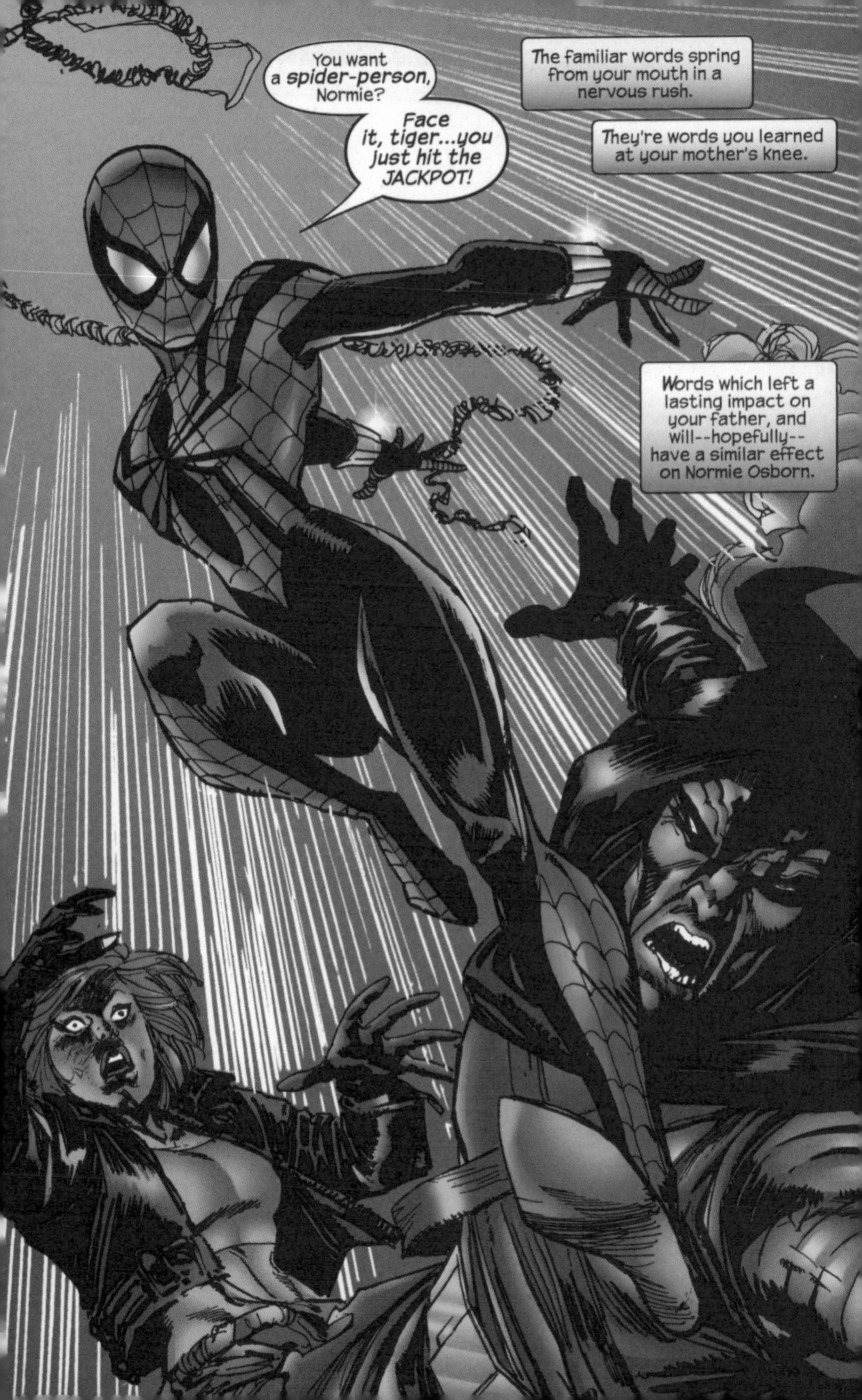
You want a *spider-person,* Normie?
Face it, tiger...you just hit the JACKPOT!
The familiar words spring from your mouth in a nervous rush.
They're words you learned at your mother's knee.
Words which left a lasting impact on your father, and will--hopefully--have a similar effect on Normie Osborn.

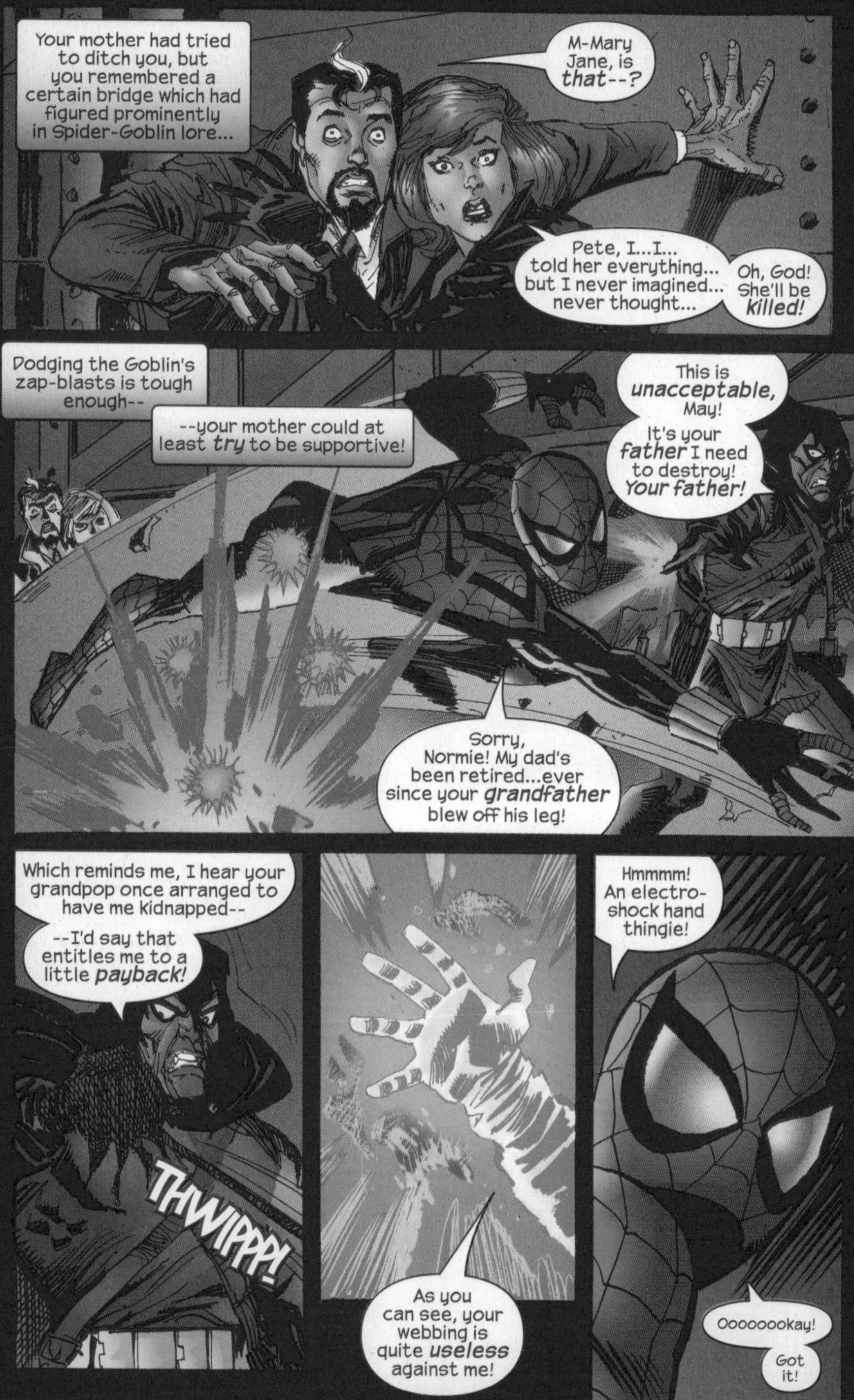
Your mother had tried to ditch you, but you remembered a certain bridge which had figured prominently in Spider-Goblin lore...
M-Mary Jane, is *that*--?
Pete, I...I... told her everything... but I never imagined... never thought...
Oh, God! She'll be *killed!*
Dodging the Goblin's zap-blasts is tough enough--
--your mother could at least *try* to be supportive!
This is *unacceptable,* May!
It's your *father* I need to destroy! *Your father!*
Sorry, Normie! My dad's been retired...ever since your *grandfather* blew off his leg!
Which reminds me, I hear your grandpop once arranged to have me kidnapped--
--I'd say that entitles me to a little *payback!*
THWIPPP!
As you can see, your webbing is quite *useless* against me!
Hmmmm! An electro-shock hand thingie!
Oooooookay!
Got it!

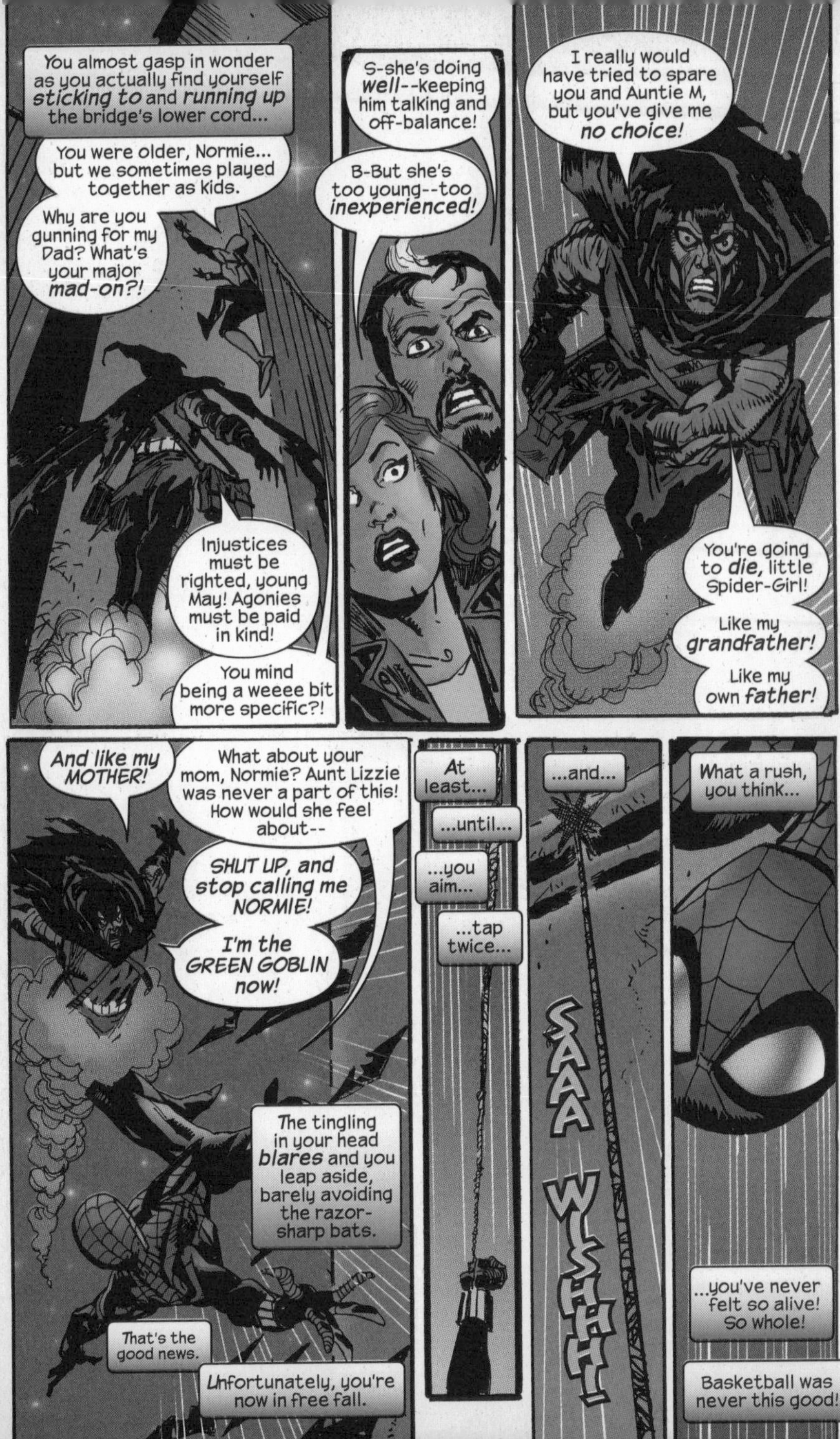
You almost gasp in wonder as you actually find yourself sticking to and running up the bridge's lower cord...
You were older, Normie... but we sometimes played together as kids.
Why are you gunning for my Dad? What's your major mad-on?!
Injustices must be righted, young May! Agonies must be paid in kind!
You mind being a weeee bit more specific?!
S-she's doing well--keeping him talking and off-balance!
B-But she's too young--too inexperienced!
I really would have tried to spare you and Auntie M, but you've give me no choice!
You're going to die, little Spider-Girl!
Like my grandfather!
Like my own father!
And like my MOTHER!
What about your mom, Normie? Aunt Lizzie was never a part of this! How would she feel about--
SHUT UP, and stop calling me NORMIE!
I'm the GREEN GOBLIN now!
The tingling in your head blares and you leap aside, barely avoiding the razor-sharp bats.
That's the good news.
Unfortunately, you're now in free fall.
At least...
...until...
...you aim...
...tap twice...
...and...
SAAA WISHHH!
What a rush, you think...
...you've never felt so alive! So whole!
Basketball was never this good!

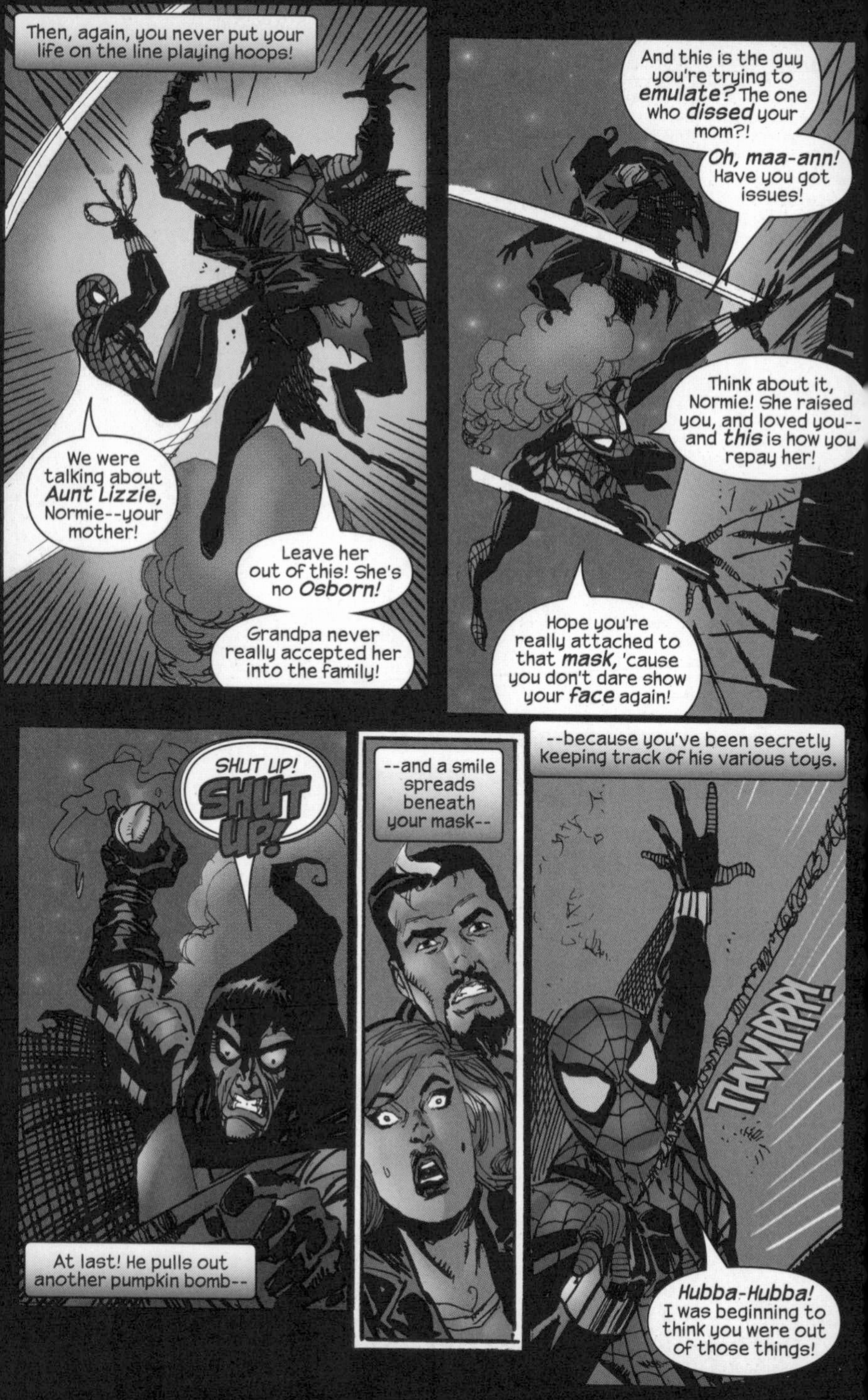
Then, again, you never put your life on the line playing hoops!
We were talking about Aunt Lizzie, Normie--your mother!
Leave her out of this! She's no Osborn!
Grandpa never really accepted her into the family!
And this is the guy you're trying to emulate? The one who dissed your mom?!
Oh, maa-ann! Have you got issues!
Think about it, Normie! She raised you, and loved you-- and this is how you repay her!
Hope you're really attached to that mask, 'cause you don't dare show your face again!
SHUT UP! SHUT UP!
At last! He pulls out another pumpkin bomb--
--and a smile spreads beneath your mask--
--because you've been secretly keeping track of his various toys.
THWIPPP!
Hubba-Hubba! I was beginning to think you were out of those things!

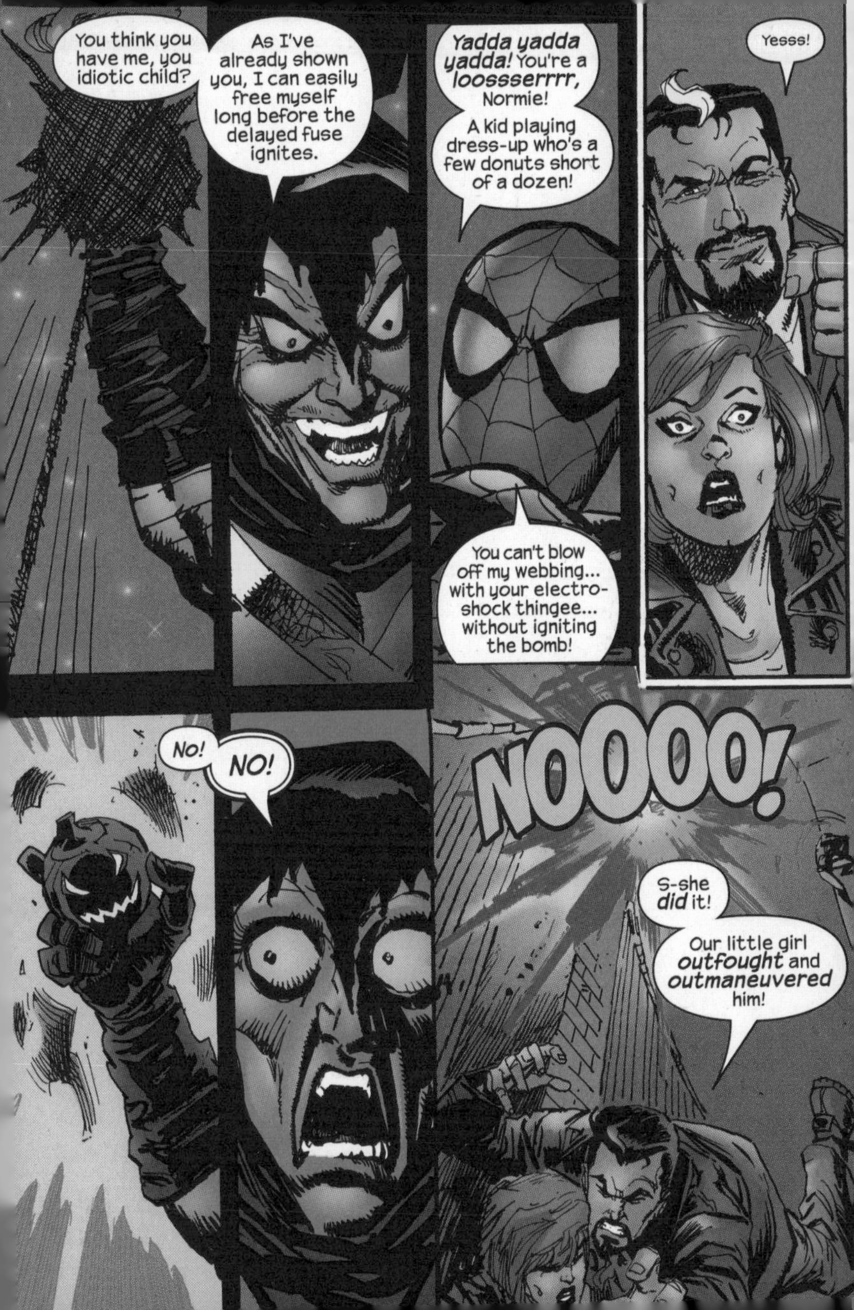
You think you have me, you idiotic child?
As I've already shown you, I can easily free myself long before the delayed fuse ignites.
Yadda yadda yadda! You're a loossserrrr, Normie!
A kid playing dress-up who's a few donuts short of a dozen!
You can't blow off my webbing... with your electro-shock thingee... without igniting the bomb!
Yesss!
No!
NO!
NOOOO!
S-she did it!
Our little girl outfought and outmaneuvered him!

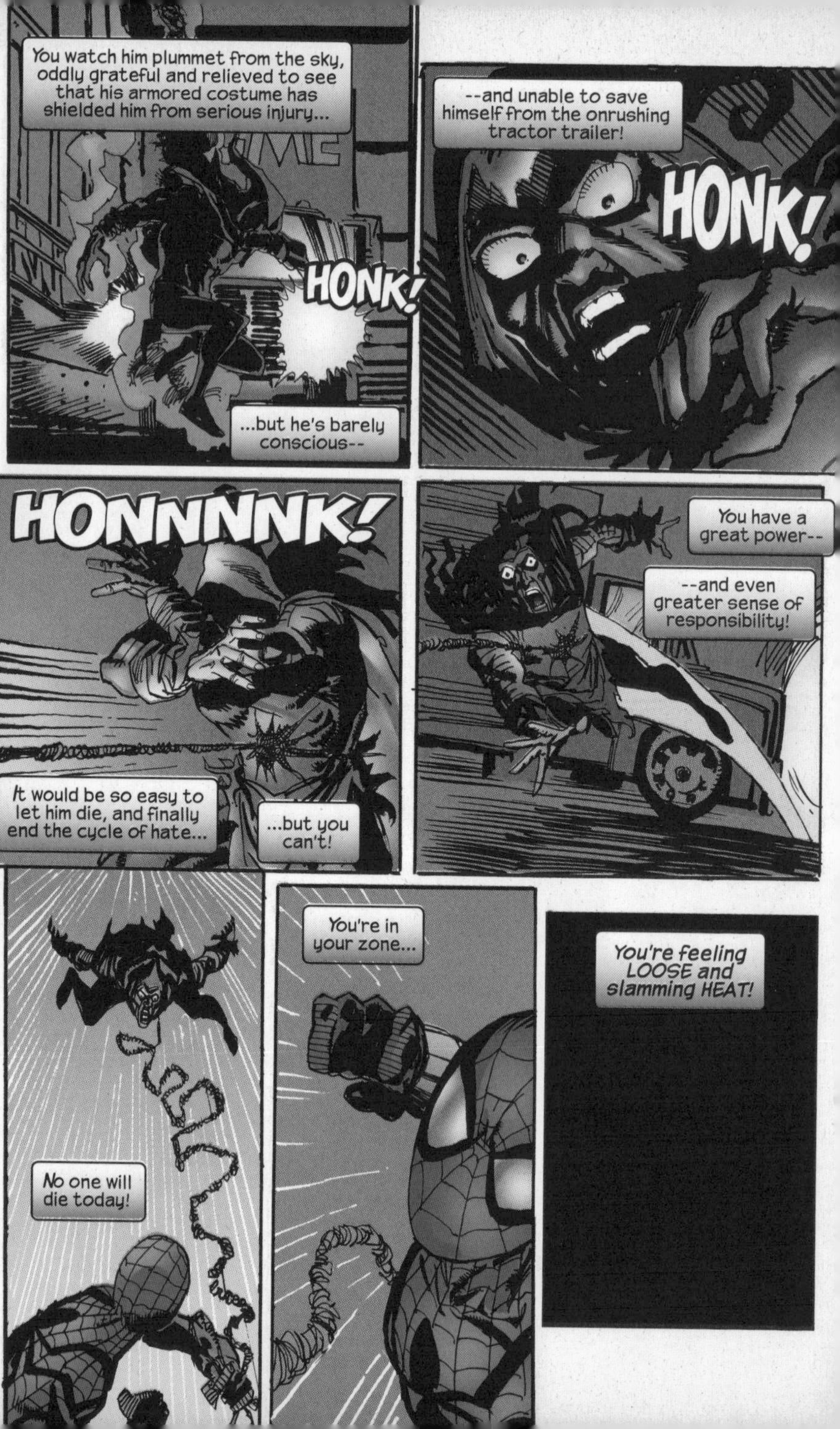
You watch him plummet from the sky, oddly grateful and relieved to see that his armored costume has shielded him from serious injury...
HONK!
...but he's barely conscious--
--and unable to save himself from the onrushing tractor trailer!
HONK!
HONNNNK!
It would be so easy to let him die, and finally end the cycle of hate...
...but you can't!
You have a great power--
--and even greater sense of responsibility!
No one will die today!
You're in your zone...
You're feeling LOOSE and slamming HEAT!

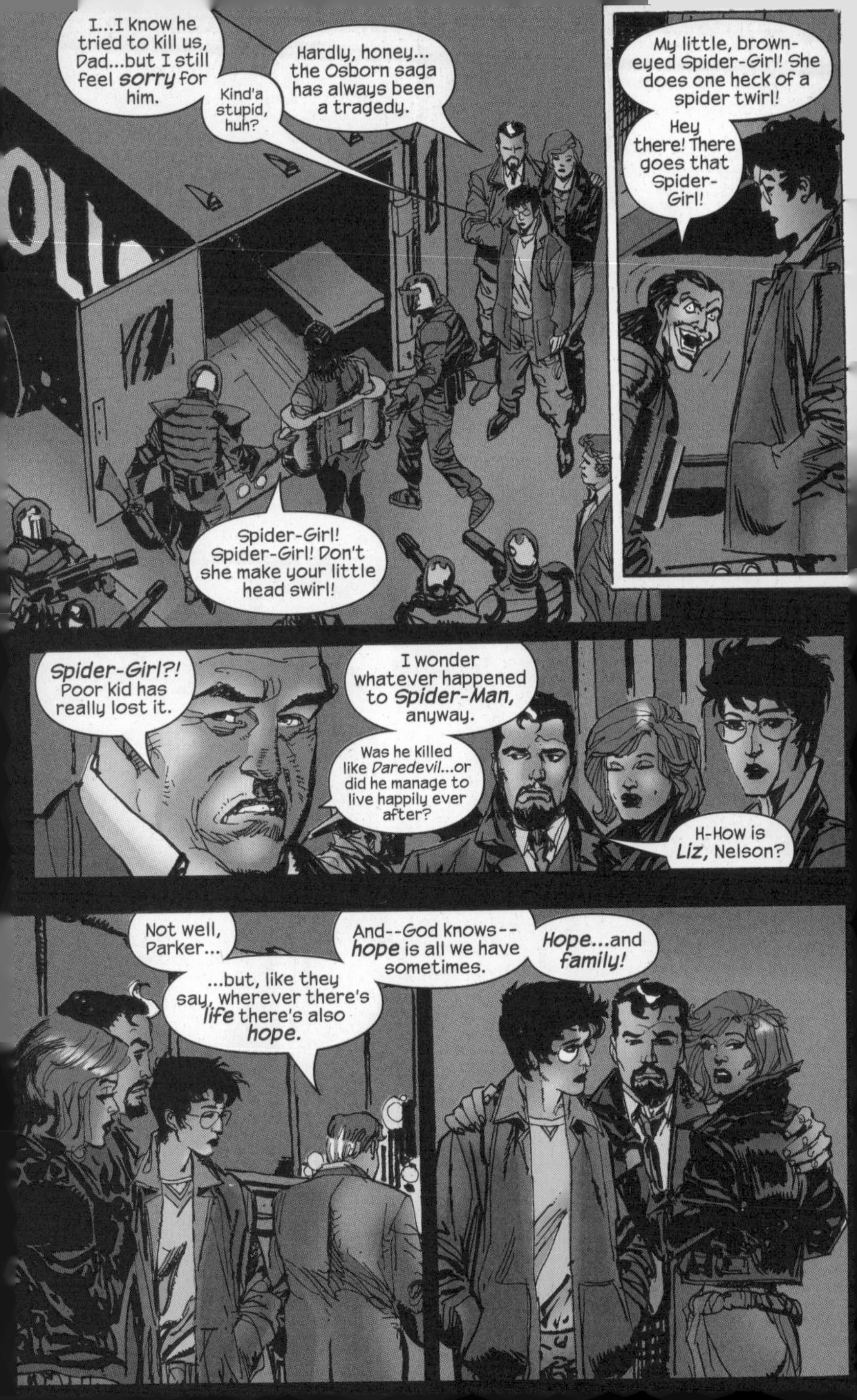

I...I know he tried to kill us, Dad...but I still feel *sorry* for him.
Kind'a stupid, huh?
Hardly, honey... the Osborn saga has always been a tragedy.
Spider-Girl! Spider-Girl! Don't she make your little head swirl!
My little, brown-eyed Spider-Girl! She does one heck of a spider twirl!
Hey there! There goes that Spider-Girl!
Spider-Girl?! Poor kid has really lost it.
I wonder whatever happened to *Spider-Man,* anyway.
Was he killed like *Daredevil*...or did he manage to live happily ever after?
H-How is *Liz,* Nelson?
Not well, Parker...
...but, like they say, wherever there's *life* there's also *hope.*
And--God knows--*hope* is all we have sometimes.
Hope...and *family!*

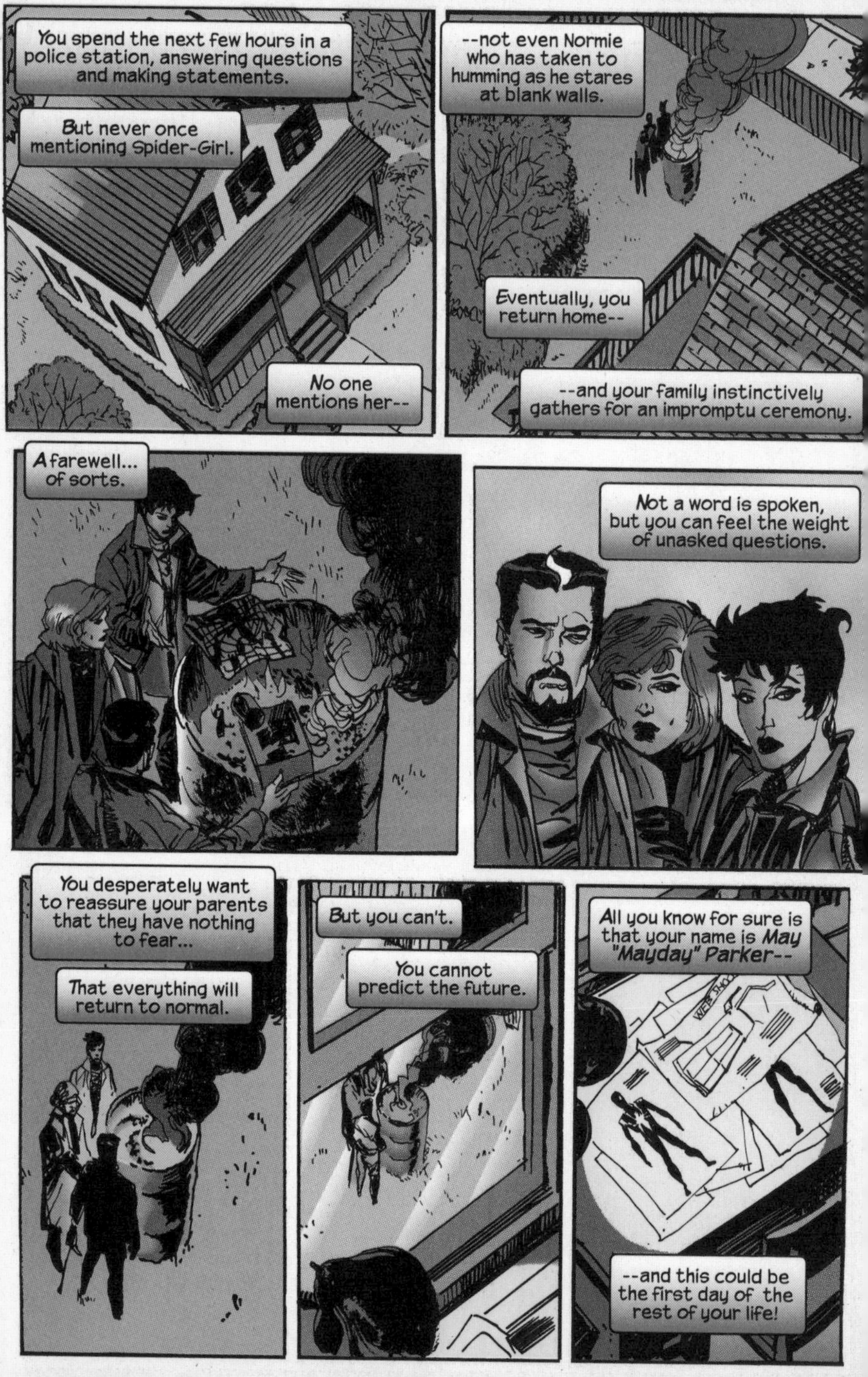
You spend the next few hours in a police station, answering questions and making statements.
But never once mentioning Spider-Girl.
No one mentions her--
--not even Normie who has taken to humming as he stares at blank walls.
Eventually, you return home--
--and your family instinctively gathers for an impromptu ceremony.
A farewell... of sorts.
Not a word is spoken, but you can feel the weight of unasked questions.
You desperately want to reassure your parents that they have nothing to fear...
That everything will return to normal.
But you can't.
You cannot predict the future.
All you know for sure is that your name is *May "Mayday" Parker*--
--and this could be the first day of the rest of your life!

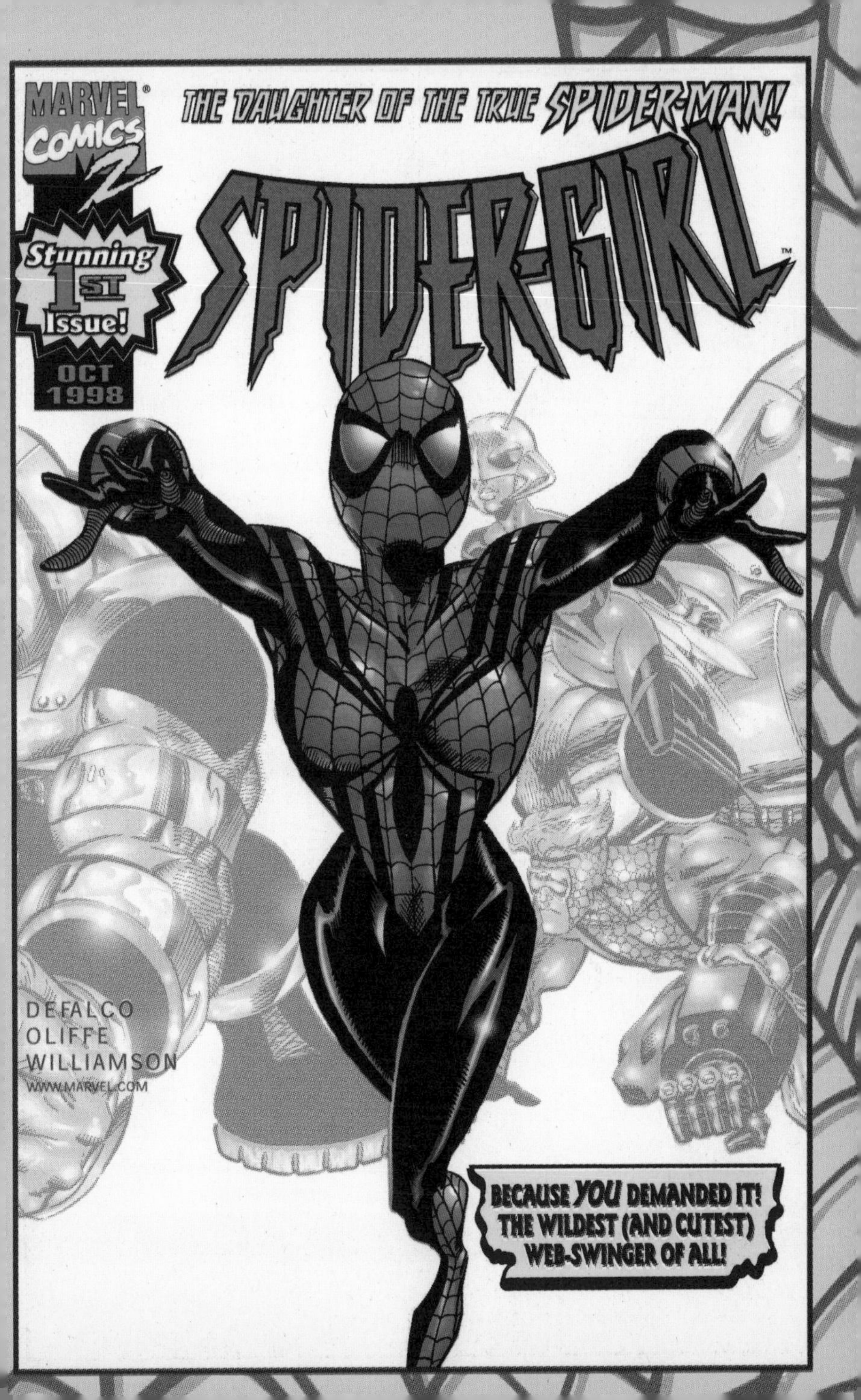
MARVEL COMICS 2
THE DAUGHTER OF THE TRUE SPIDER-MAN!
SPIDER-GIRL
Stunning 1st Issue!
OCT 1998
DEFALCO
OLIFFE
WILLIAMSON
WWW.MARVEL.COM
BECAUSE YOU DEMANDED IT! THE WILDEST (AND CUTEST) WEB-SWINGER OF ALL!

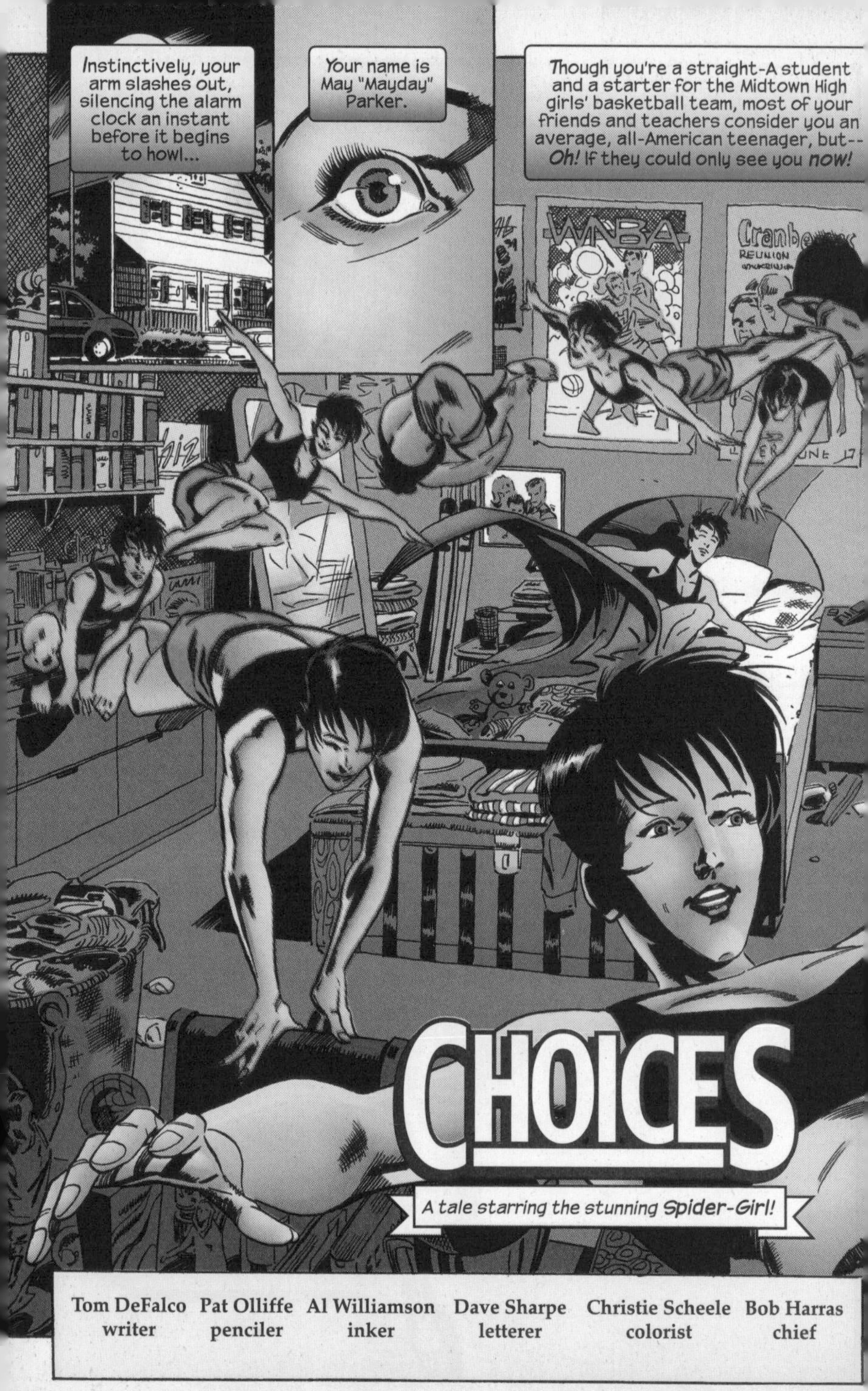
Instinctively, your arm slashes out, silencing the alarm clock an instant before it begins to howl...
Your name is May "Mayday" Parker.
Though you're a straight-A student and a starter for the Midtown High girls' basketball team, most of your friends and teachers consider you an average, all-American teenager, but-- Oh! If they could only see you now!
CHOICES
A tale starring the stunning Spider-Girl!

Tom DeFalco writer · **Pat Olliffe** penciler · **Al Williamson** inker · **Dave Sharpe** letterer · **Christie Scheele** colorist · **Bob Harras** chief

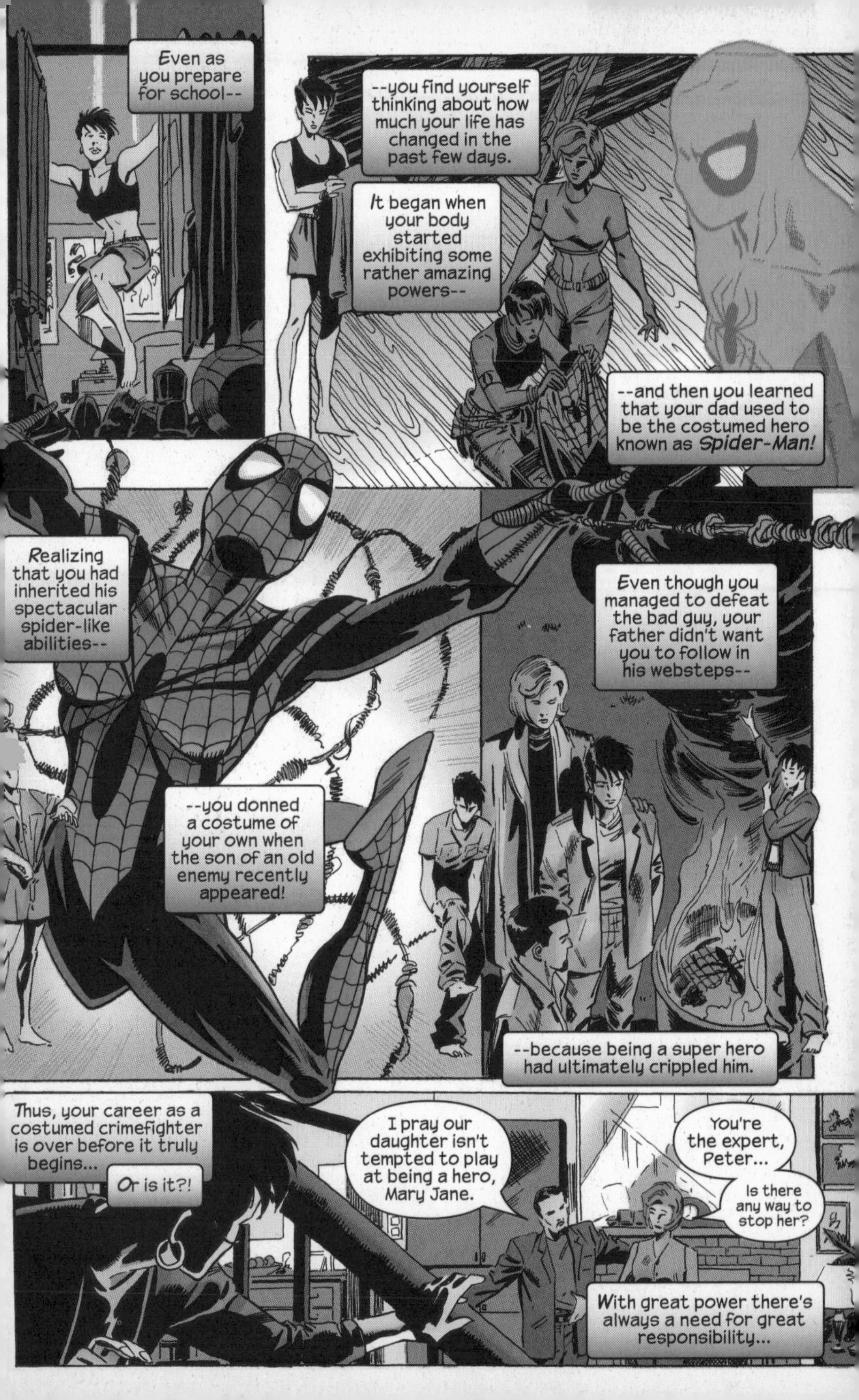
Even as you prepare for school--
--you find yourself thinking about how much your life has changed in the past few days.
It began when your body started exhibiting some rather amazing powers--
--and then you learned that your dad used to be the costumed hero known as Spider-Man!
Realizing that you had inherited his spectacular spider-like abilities--
--you donned a costume of your own when the son of an old enemy recently appeared!
Even though you managed to defeat the bad guy, your father didn't want you to follow in his websteps--
--because being a super hero had ultimately crippled him.
Thus, your career as a costumed crimefighter is over before it truly begins...
Or is it?!
I pray our daughter isn't tempted to play at being a hero, Mary Jane.
You're the expert, Peter...
Is there any way to stop her?
With great power there's always a need for great responsibility...

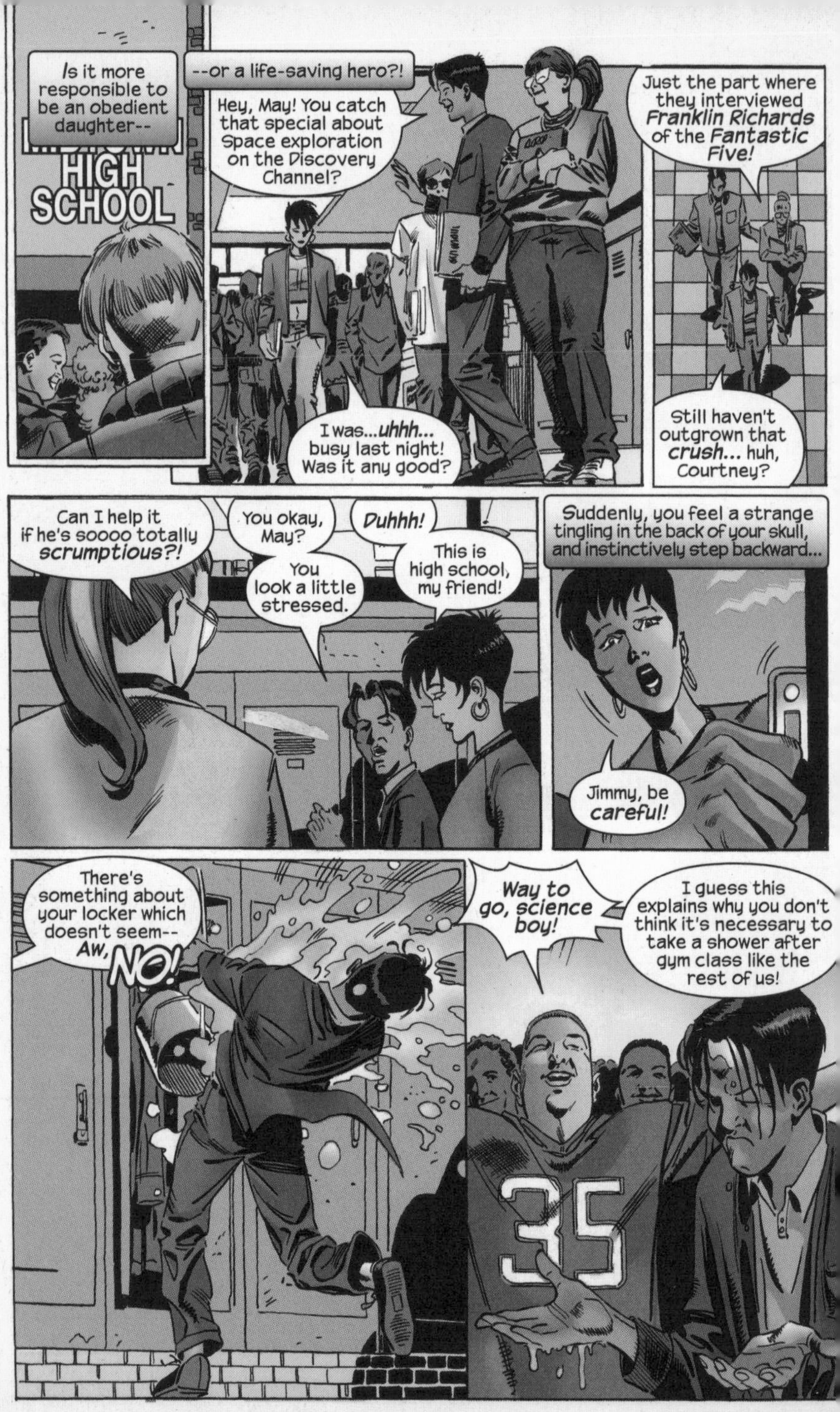

Is it more responsible to be an obedient daughter--
HIGH SCHOOL
--or a life-saving hero?!
Hey, May! You catch that special about Space exploration on the Discovery Channel?
I was...uhhh... busy last night! Was it any good?
Just the part where they interviewed Franklin Richards of the Fantastic Five!
Still haven't outgrown that crush... huh, Courtney?
Can I help it if he's soooo totally scrumptious?!
You okay, May?
You look a little stressed.
Duhhh!
This is high school, my friend!
Suddenly, you feel a strange tingling in the back of your skull, and instinctively step backward...
Jimmy, be careful!
There's something about your locker which doesn't seem-- Aw, NO!
Way to go, science boy!
I guess this explains why you don't think it's necessary to take a shower after gym class like the rest of us!
35

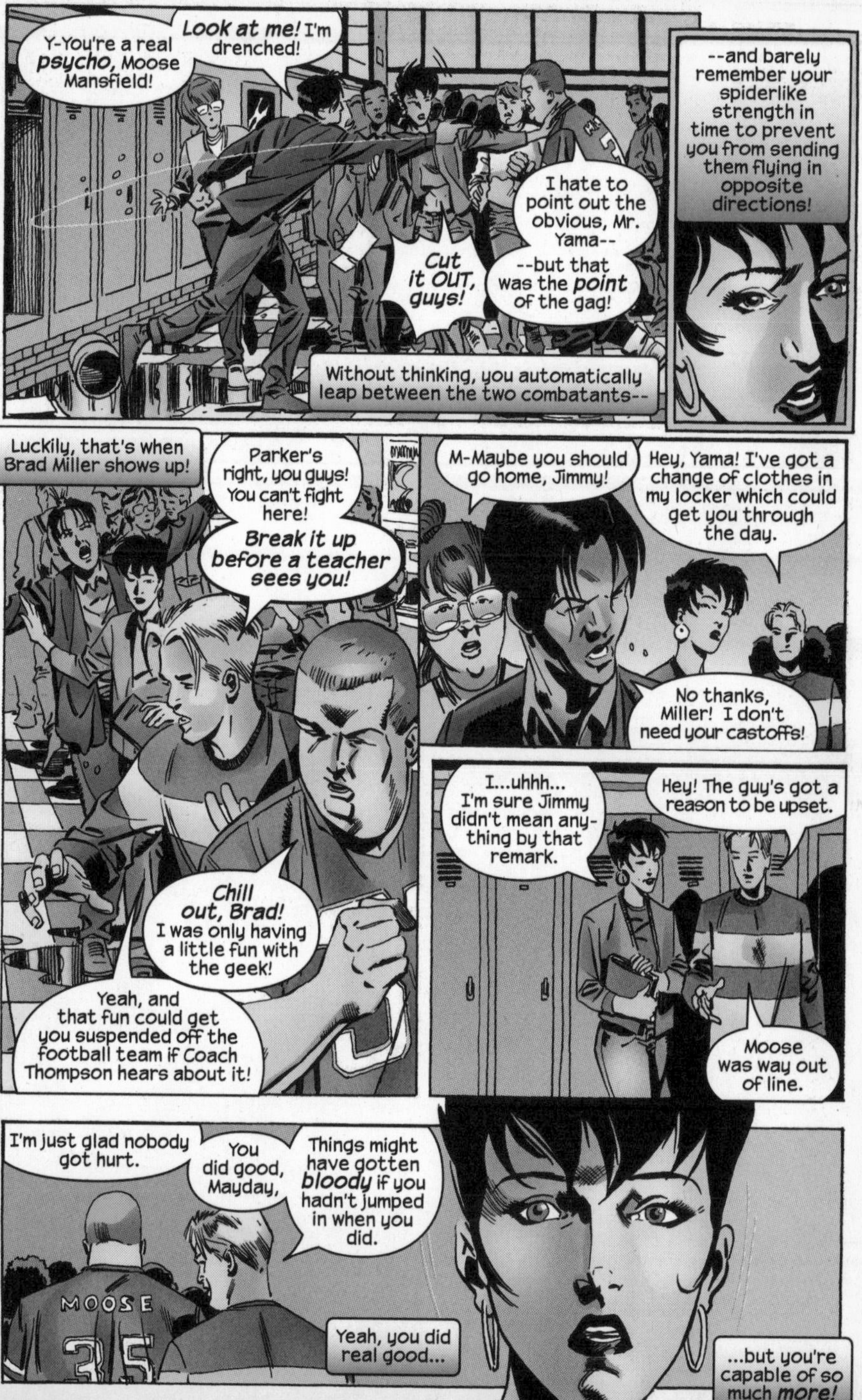
Y-You're a real psycho, Moose Mansfield!
Look at me! I'm drenched!
I hate to point out the obvious, Mr. Yama--
--but that was the point of the gag!
Cut it OUT, guys!
Without thinking, you automatically leap between the two combatants--
--and barely remember your spiderlike strength in time to prevent you from sending them flying in opposite directions!
Luckily, that's when Brad Miller shows up!
Parker's right, you guys! You can't fight here!
Break it up before a teacher sees you!
Chill out, Brad! I was only having a little fun with the geek!
Yeah, and that fun could get you suspended off the football team if Coach Thompson hears about it!
M-Maybe you should go home, Jimmy!
Hey, Yama! I've got a change of clothes in my locker which could get you through the day.
No thanks, Miller! I don't need your castoffs!
I...uhhh... I'm sure Jimmy didn't mean any-thing by that remark.
Hey! The guy's got a reason to be upset.
Moose was way out of line.
I'm just glad nobody got hurt.
You did good, Mayday,
Things might have gotten bloody if you hadn't jumped in when you did.
MOOSE
35
Yeah, you did real good...
...but you're capable of so much more!

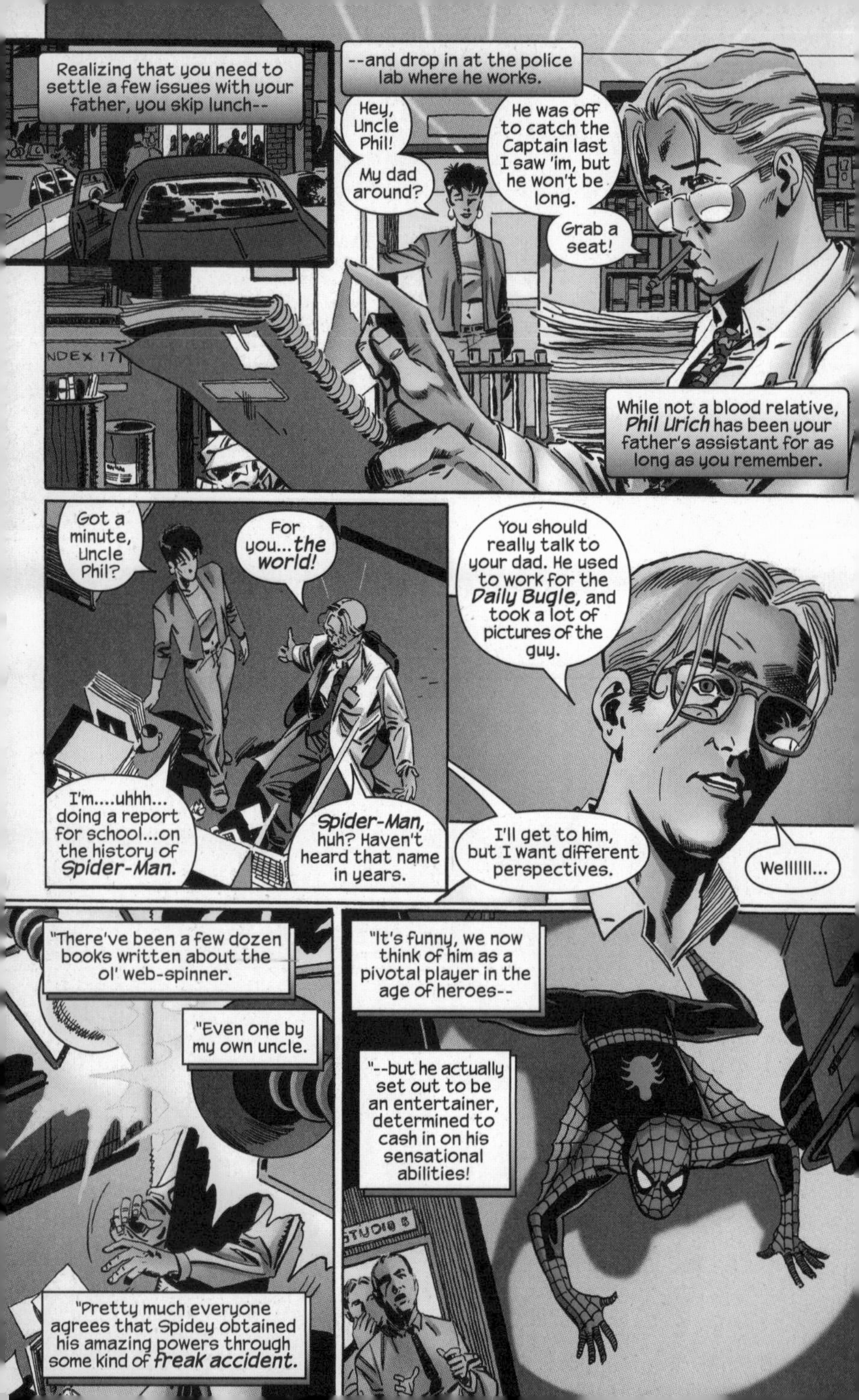

Realizing that you need to settle a few issues with your father, you skip lunch--
--and drop in at the police lab where he works.
Hey, Uncle Phil!
My dad around?
He was off to catch the Captain last I saw 'im, but he won't be long.
Grab a seat!
While not a blood relative, Phil Urich has been your father's assistant for as long as you remember.
NDEX 17
Got a minute, Uncle Phil?
For you...the world!
I'm....uhhh... doing a report for school...on the history of Spider-Man.
Spider-Man, huh? Haven't heard that name in years.
You should really talk to your dad. He used to work for the Daily Bugle, and took a lot of pictures of the guy.
I'll get to him, but I want different perspectives.
Wellllll...
"There've been a few dozen books written about the ol' web-spinner.
"Even one by my own uncle.
"Pretty much everyone agrees that Spidey obtained his amazing powers through some kind of freak accident.
"It's funny, we now think of him as a pivotal player in the age of heroes--
"--but he actually set out to be an entertainer, determined to cash in on his sensational abilities!
STUDIO 8

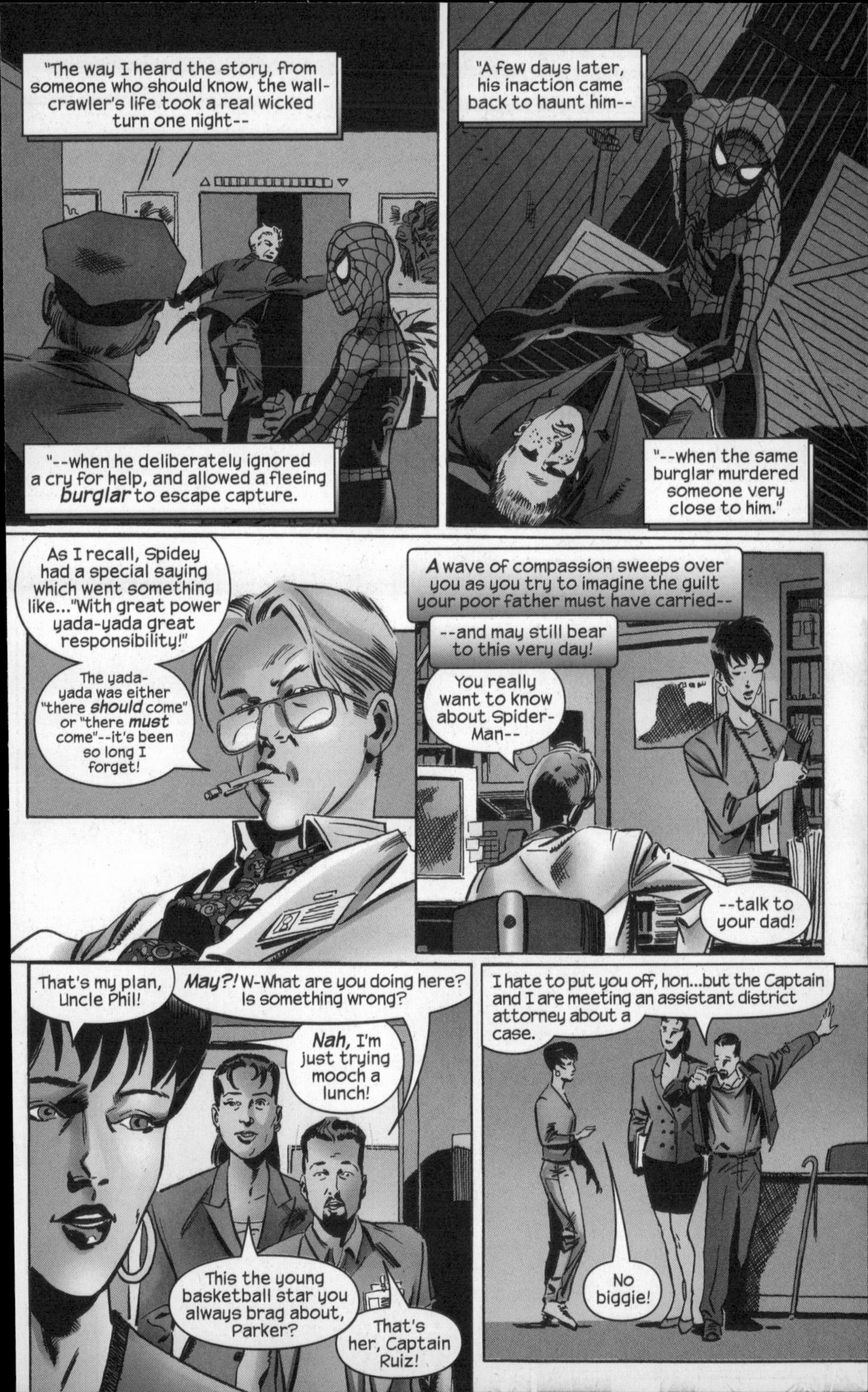
"The way I heard the story, from someone who should know, the wall-crawler's life took a real wicked turn one night--
"--when he deliberately ignored a cry for help, and allowed a fleeing burglar to escape capture.
"A few days later, his inaction came back to haunt him--
"--when the same burglar murdered someone very close to him."
As I recall, Spidey had a special saying which went something like..."With great power yada-yada great responsibility!"
The yada-yada was either "there should come" or "there must come"--it's been so long I forget!
A wave of compassion sweeps over you as you try to imagine the guilt your poor father must have carried--
--and may still bear to this very day!
You really want to know about Spider-Man--
--talk to your dad!
That's my plan, Uncle Phil!
May?! W-What are you doing here? Is something wrong?
Nah, I'm just trying mooch a lunch!
This the young basketball star you always brag about, Parker?
That's her, Captain Ruiz!
I hate to put you off, hon...but the Captain and I are meeting an assistant district attorney about a case.
No biggie!

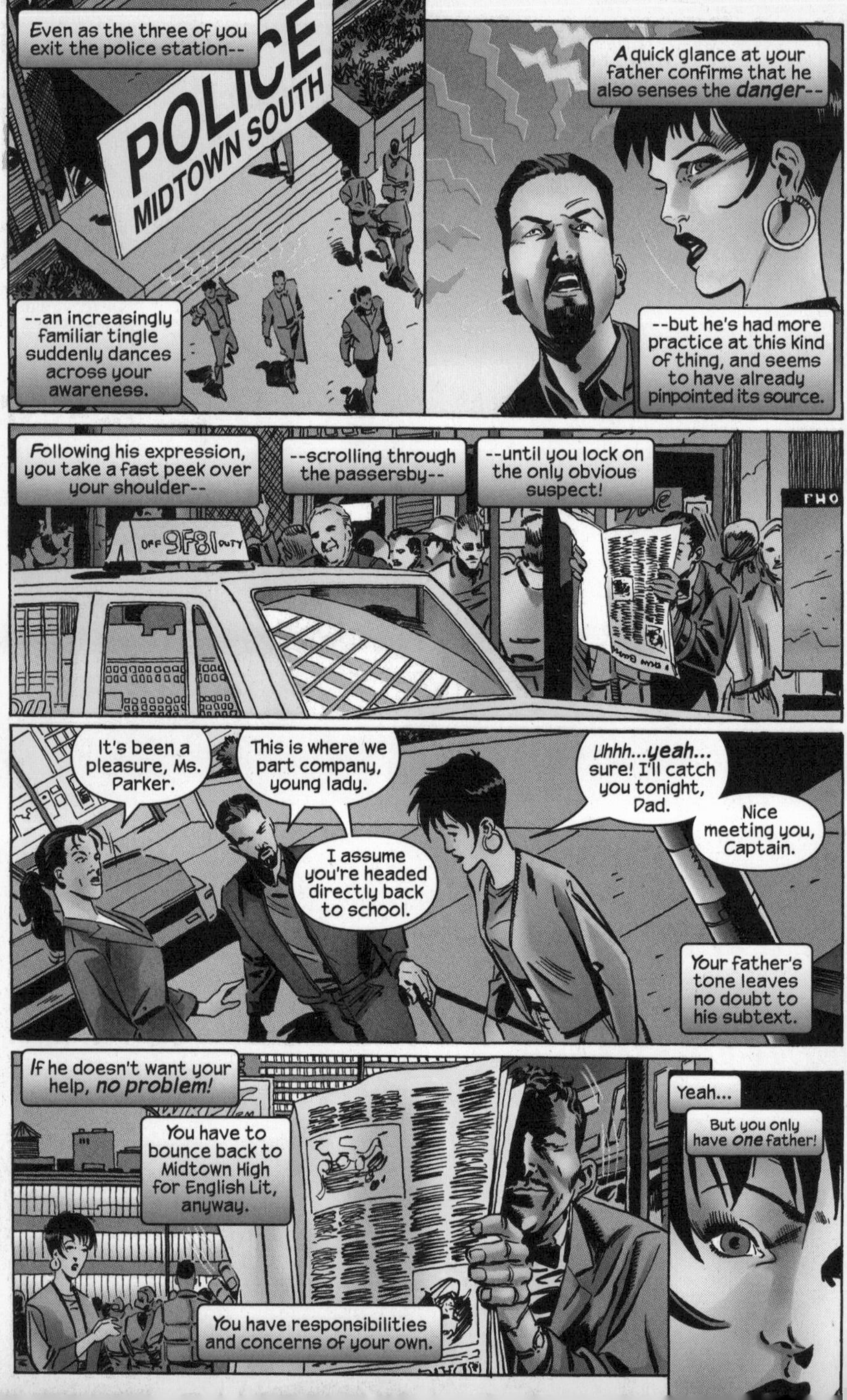
Even as the three of you exit the police station--
POLICE
MIDTOWN SOUTH
--an increasingly familiar tingle suddenly dances across your awareness.
A quick glance at your father confirms that he also senses the *danger*--
--but he's had more practice at this kind of thing, and seems to have already pinpointed its source.
Following his expression, you take a fast peek over your shoulder--
--scrolling through the passersby--
--until you lock on the only obvious suspect!
OFF 9F81 DUTY
It's been a pleasure, Ms. Parker.
This is where we part company, young lady.
I assume you're headed directly back to school.
*Uhhh...***yeah...** sure! I'll catch you tonight, Dad.
Nice meeting you, Captain.
Your father's tone leaves no doubt to his subtext.
If he doesn't want your help, ***no problem!***
You have to bounce back to Midtown High for English Lit, anyway.
You have responsibilities and concerns of your own.
Yeah...
But you only have *one* father!

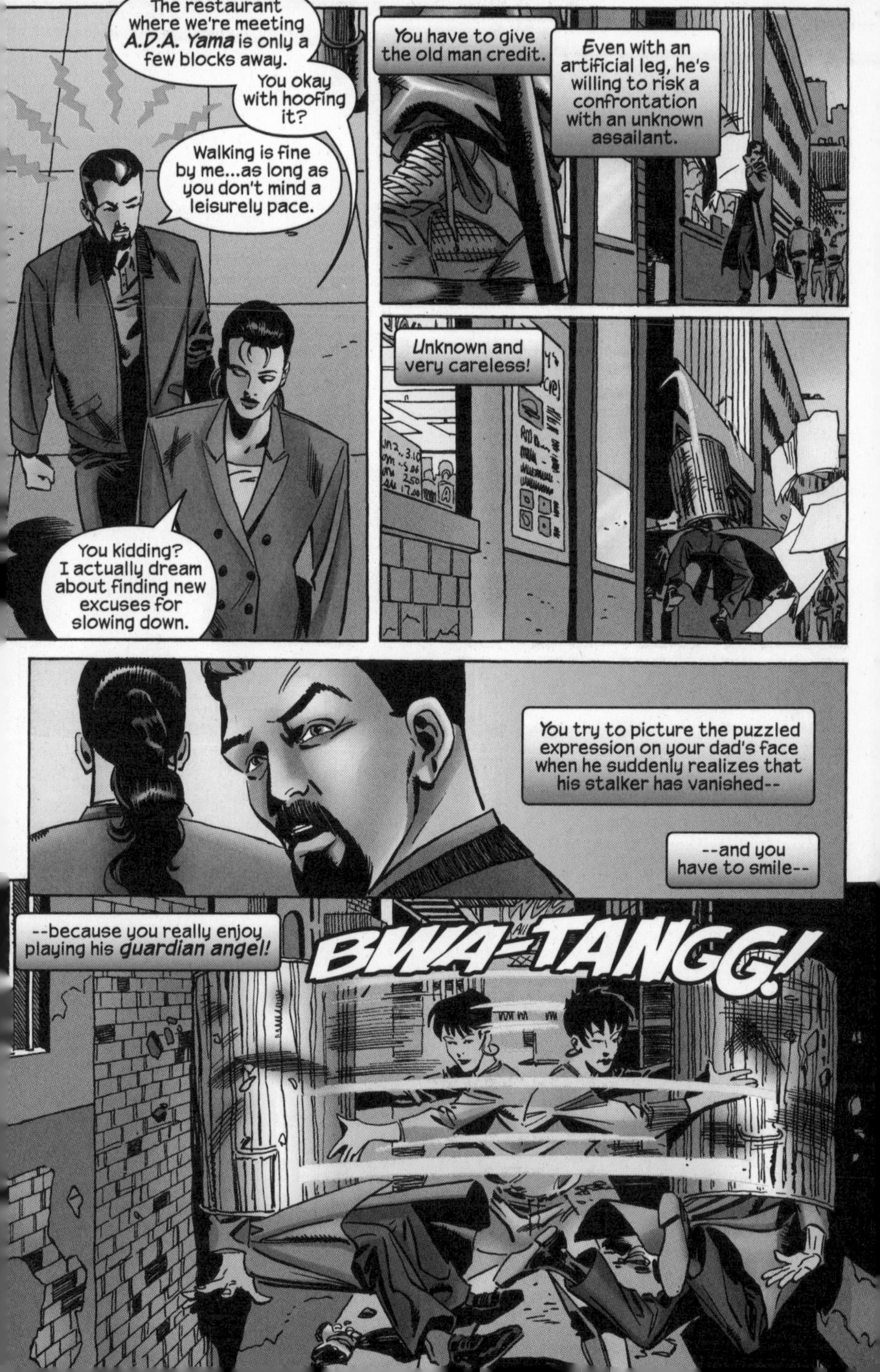
The restaurant where we're meeting A.D.A. Yama is only a few blocks away.
You okay with hoofing it?
Walking is fine by me...as long as you don't mind a leisurely pace.
You kidding? I actually dream about finding new excuses for slowing down.
You have to give the old man credit.
Even with an artificial leg, he's willing to risk a confrontation with an unknown assailant.
Unknown and very careless!
You try to picture the puzzled expression on your dad's face when he suddenly realizes that his stalker has vanished--
--and you have to smile--
--because you really enjoy playing his guardian angel!
BWA-TANGG!

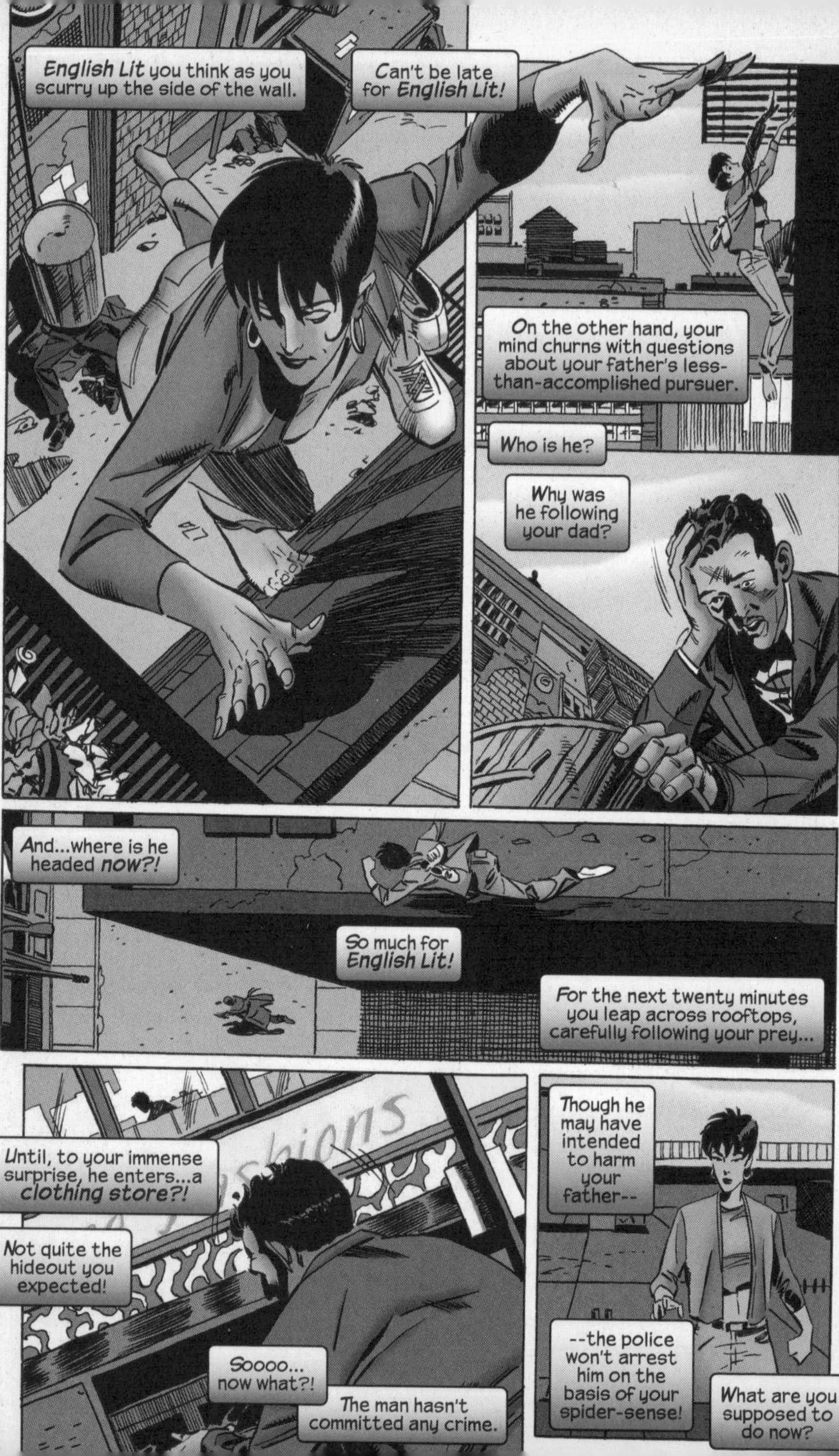

English Lit you think as you scurry up the side of the wall.
Can't be late for English Lit!
On the other hand, your mind churns with questions about your father's less-than-accomplished pursuer.
Who is he?
Why was he following your dad?
And...where is he headed now?!
So much for English Lit!
For the next twenty minutes you leap across rooftops, carefully following your prey...
Until, to your immense surprise, he enters...a clothing store?!
Not quite the hideout you expected!
Soooo... now what?!
The man hasn't committed any crime.
Though he may have intended to harm your father--
--the police won't arrest him on the basis of your spider-sense!
What are you supposed to do now?

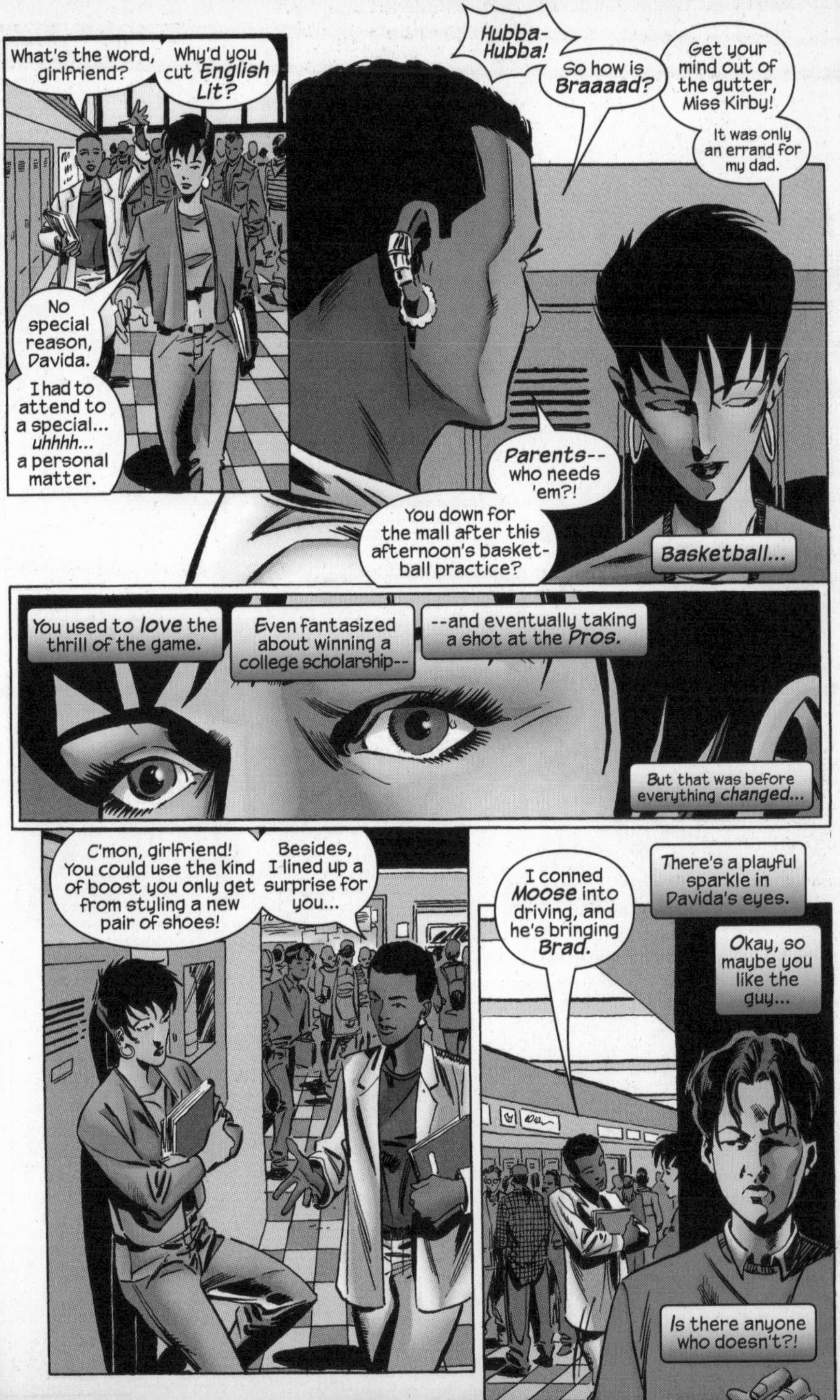
What's the word, girlfriend?
Why'd you cut English Lit?
No special reason, Davida.
I had to attend to a special... uhhhh... a personal matter.
Hubba-Hubba!
So how is Braaaad?
Get your mind out of the gutter, Miss Kirby!
It was only an errand for my dad.
Parents-- who needs 'em?!
You down for the mall after this afternoon's basket-ball practice?
Basketball...
You used to love the thrill of the game.
Even fantasized about winning a college scholarship--
--and eventually taking a shot at the Pros.
But that was before everything changed...
C'mon, girlfriend! You could use the kind of boost you only get from styling a new pair of shoes!
Besides, I lined up a surprise for you...
I conned Moose into driving, and he's bringing Brad.
There's a playful sparkle in Davida's eyes.
Okay, so maybe you like the guy...
Is there anyone who doesn't?!

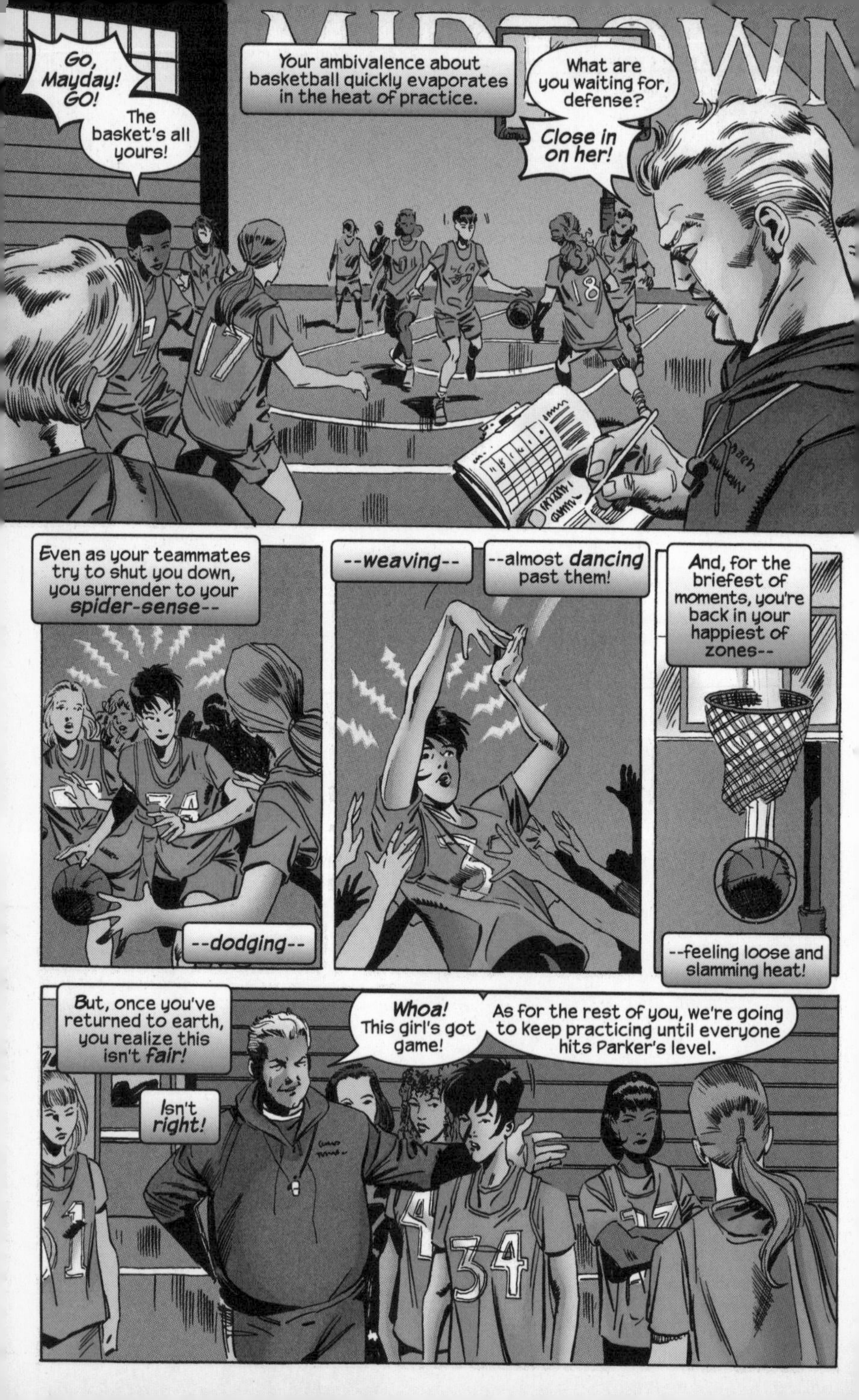

MIDTOWN
Go, Mayday! GO!
The basket's all yours!
Your ambivalence about basketball quickly evaporates in the heat of practice.
What are you waiting for, defense?
Close in on her!
Even as your teammates try to shut you down, you surrender to your spider-sense--
--dodging--
--weaving--
--almost dancing past them!
And, for the briefest of moments, you're back in your happiest of zones--
--feeling loose and slamming heat!
But, once you've returned to earth, you realize this isn't fair!
Isn't right!
Whoa! This girl's got game!
As for the rest of you, we're going to keep practicing until everyone hits Parker's level.

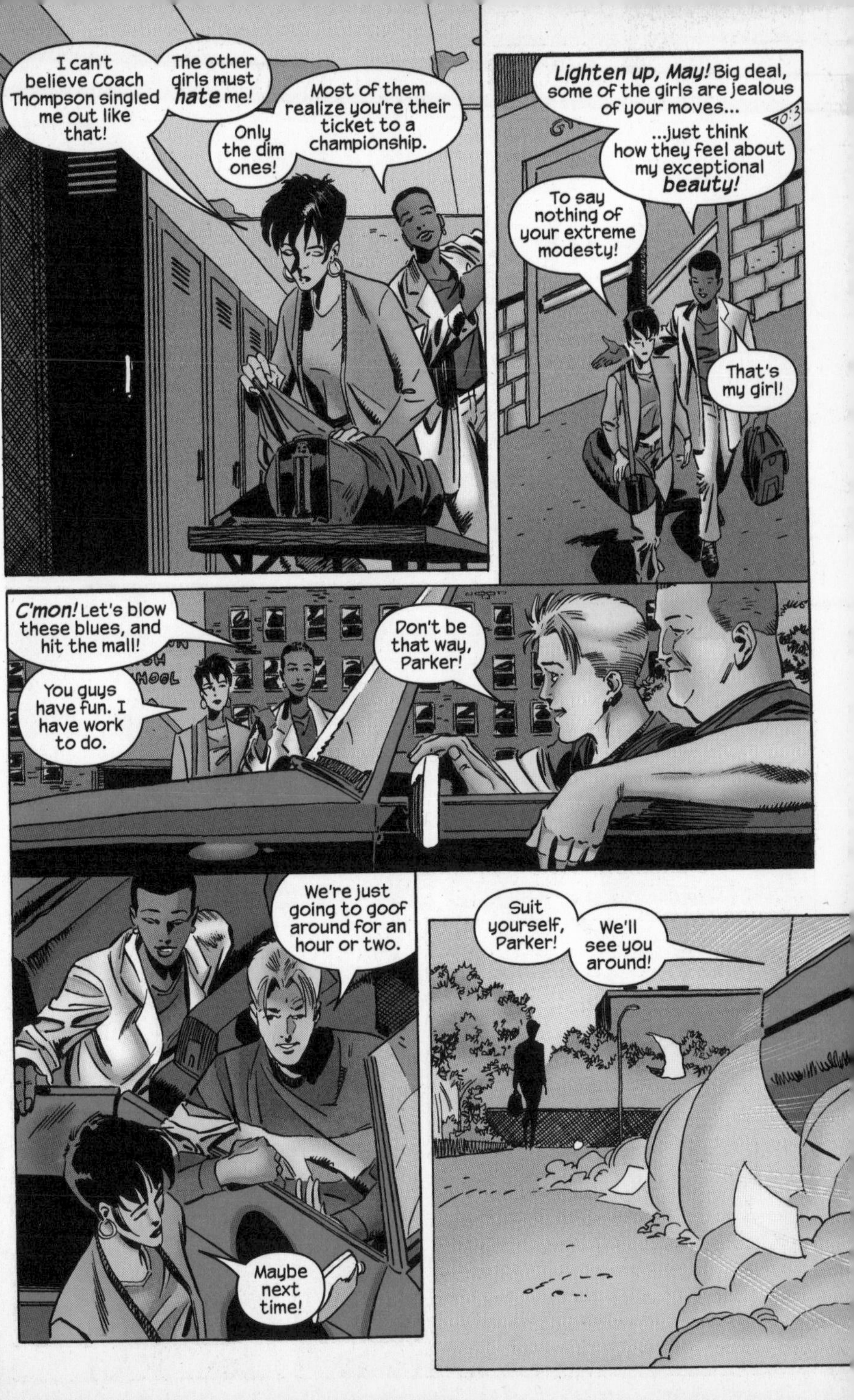

I can't believe Coach Thompson singled me out like that!
The other girls must *hate* me!
Only the dim ones!
Most of them realize you're their ticket to a championship.
Lighten up, May! Big deal, some of the girls are jealous of your moves...
...just think how they feel about my exceptional *beauty!*
To say nothing of your extreme modesty!
That's my girl!
C'mon! Let's blow these blues, and hit the mall!
You guys have fun. I have work to do.
Don't be that way, Parker!
We're just going to goof around for an hour or two.
Maybe next time!
Suit yourself, Parker!
We'll see you around!

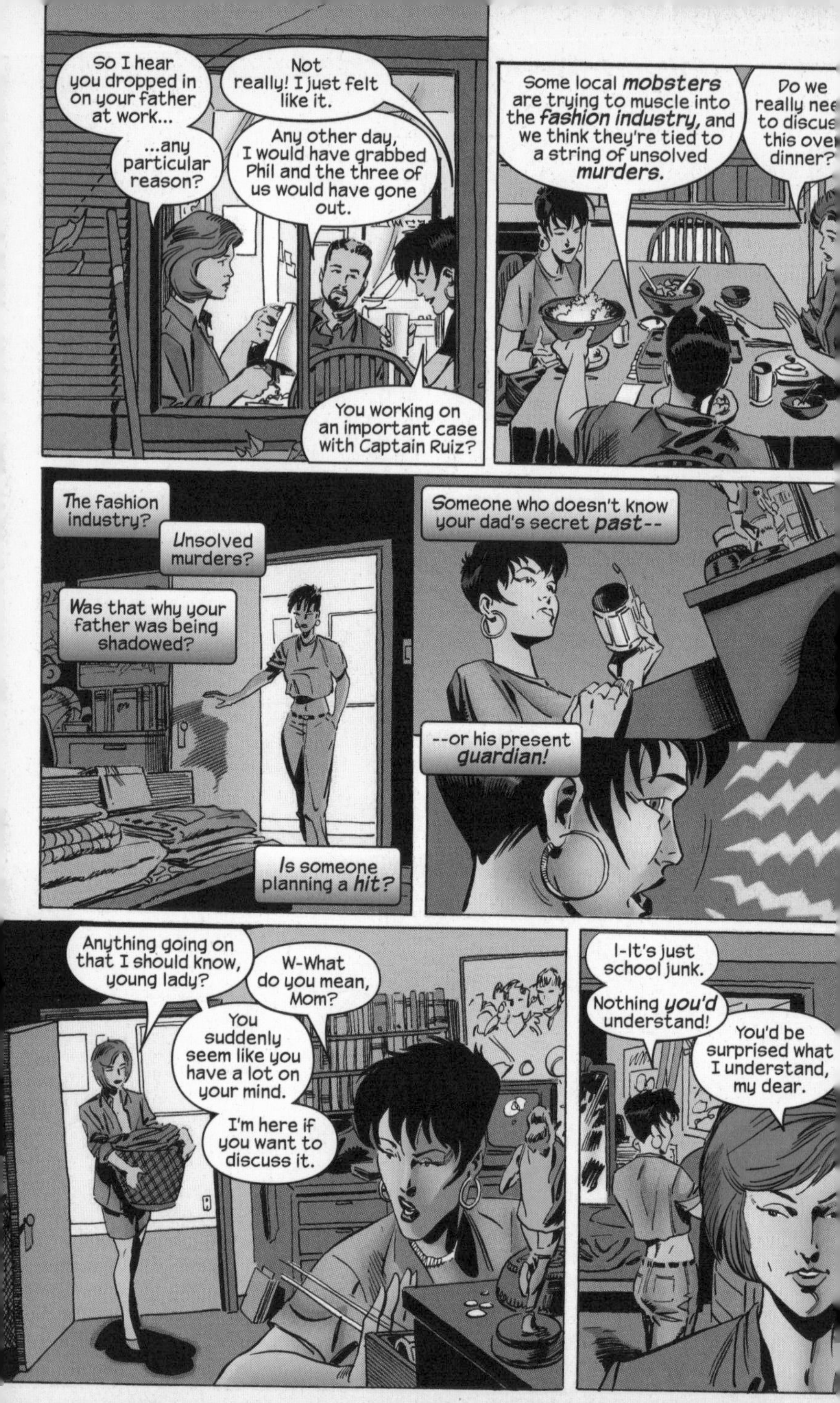

So I hear you dropped in on your father at work...
...any particular reason?
Not really! I just felt like it.
Any other day, I would have grabbed Phil and the three of us would have gone out.
You working on an important case with Captain Ruiz?
Some local mobsters are trying to muscle into the fashion industry, and we think they're tied to a string of unsolved murders.
Do we really nee to discus this ove dinner?
The fashion industry?
Unsolved murders?
Was that why your father was being shadowed?
Is someone planning a hit?
Someone who doesn't know your dad's secret past--
--or his present guardian!
Anything going on that I should know, young lady?
W-What do you mean, Mom?
You suddenly seem like you have a lot on your mind.
I'm here if you want to discuss it.
I-It's just school junk.
Nothing you'd understand!
You'd be surprised what I understand, my dear.

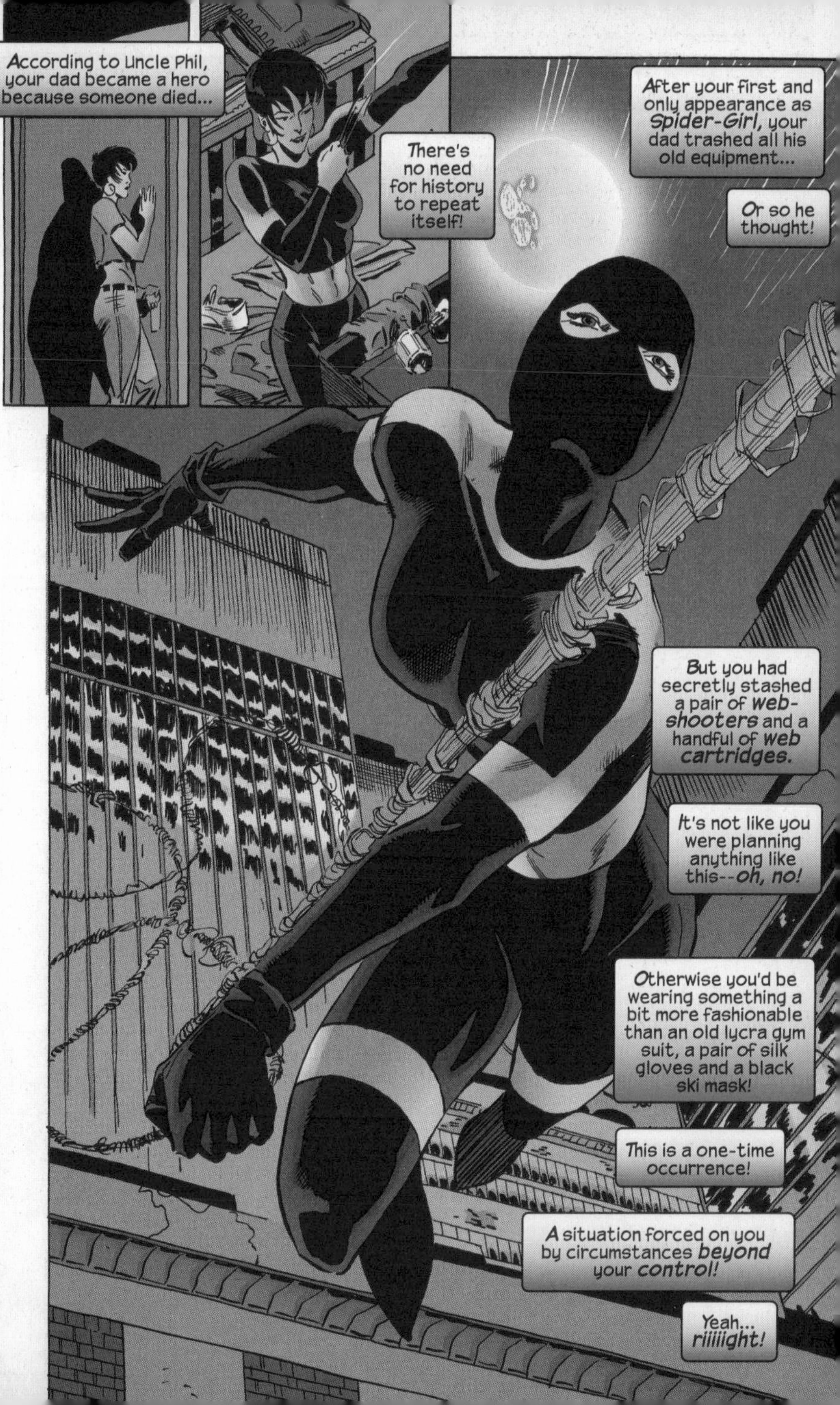
According to Uncle Phil, your dad became a hero because someone died...
There's no need for history to repeat itself!
After your first and only appearance as Spider-Girl, your dad trashed all his old equipment...
Or so he thought!
But you had secretly stashed a pair of web-shooters and a handful of web cartridges.
It's not like you were planning anything like this--oh, no!
Otherwise you'd be wearing something a bit more fashionable than an old lycra gym suit, a pair of silk gloves and a black ski mask!
This is a one-time occurrence!
A situation forced on you by circumstances beyond your control!
Yeah... riiiiight!

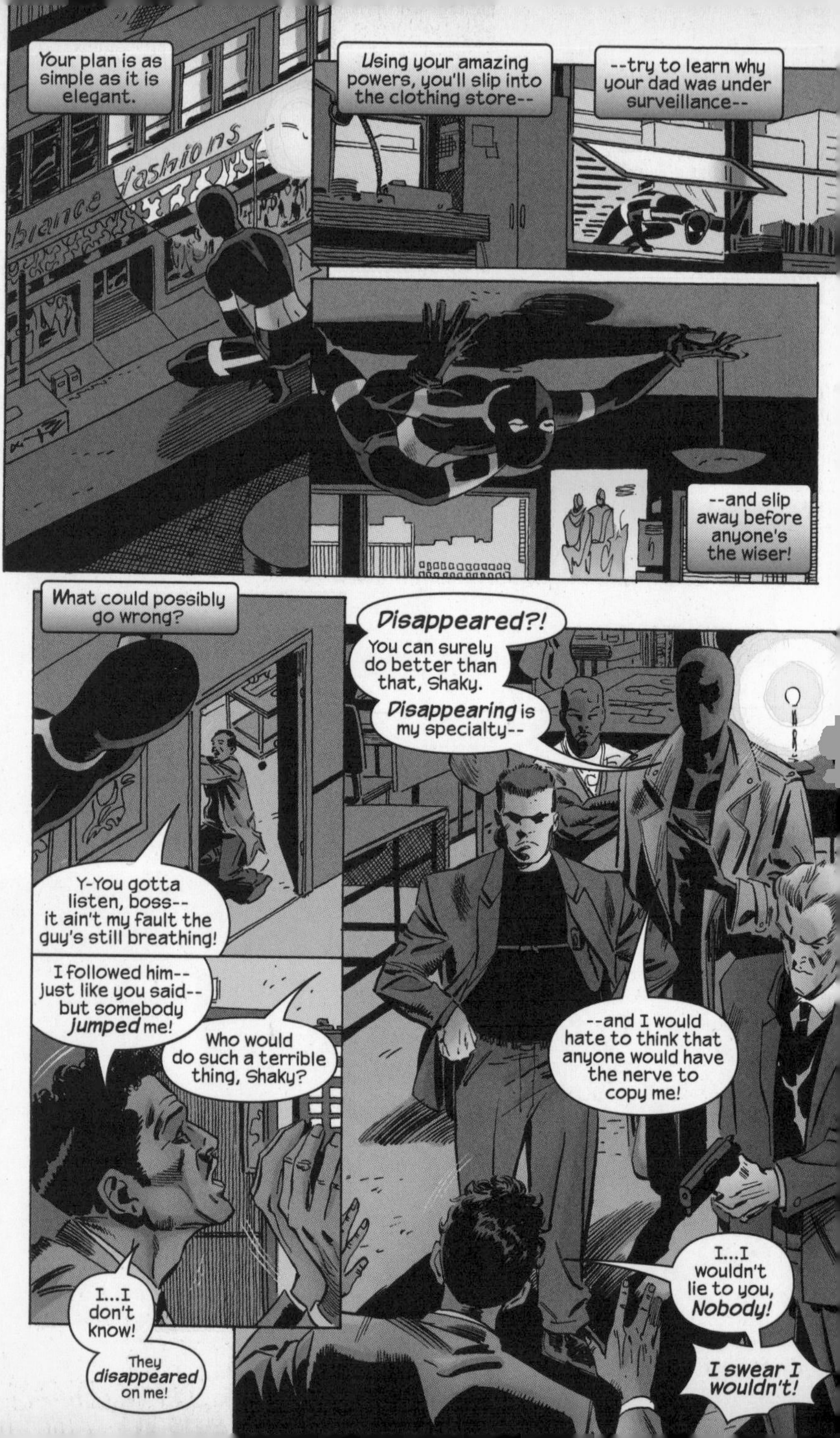
Your plan is as simple as it is elegant.
Using your amazing powers, you'll slip into the clothing store--
--try to learn why your dad was under surveillance--
--and slip away before anyone's the wiser!
What could possibly go wrong?
Y-You gotta listen, boss-- it ain't my fault the guy's still breathing!
Disappeared?! You can surely do better than that, Shaky.
Disappearing is my specialty--
I followed him-- just like you said-- but somebody jumped me!
Who would do such a terrible thing, Shaky?
--and I would hate to think that anyone would have the nerve to copy me!
I...I don't know!
They disappeared on me!
I...I wouldn't lie to you, Nobody!
I swear I wouldn't!

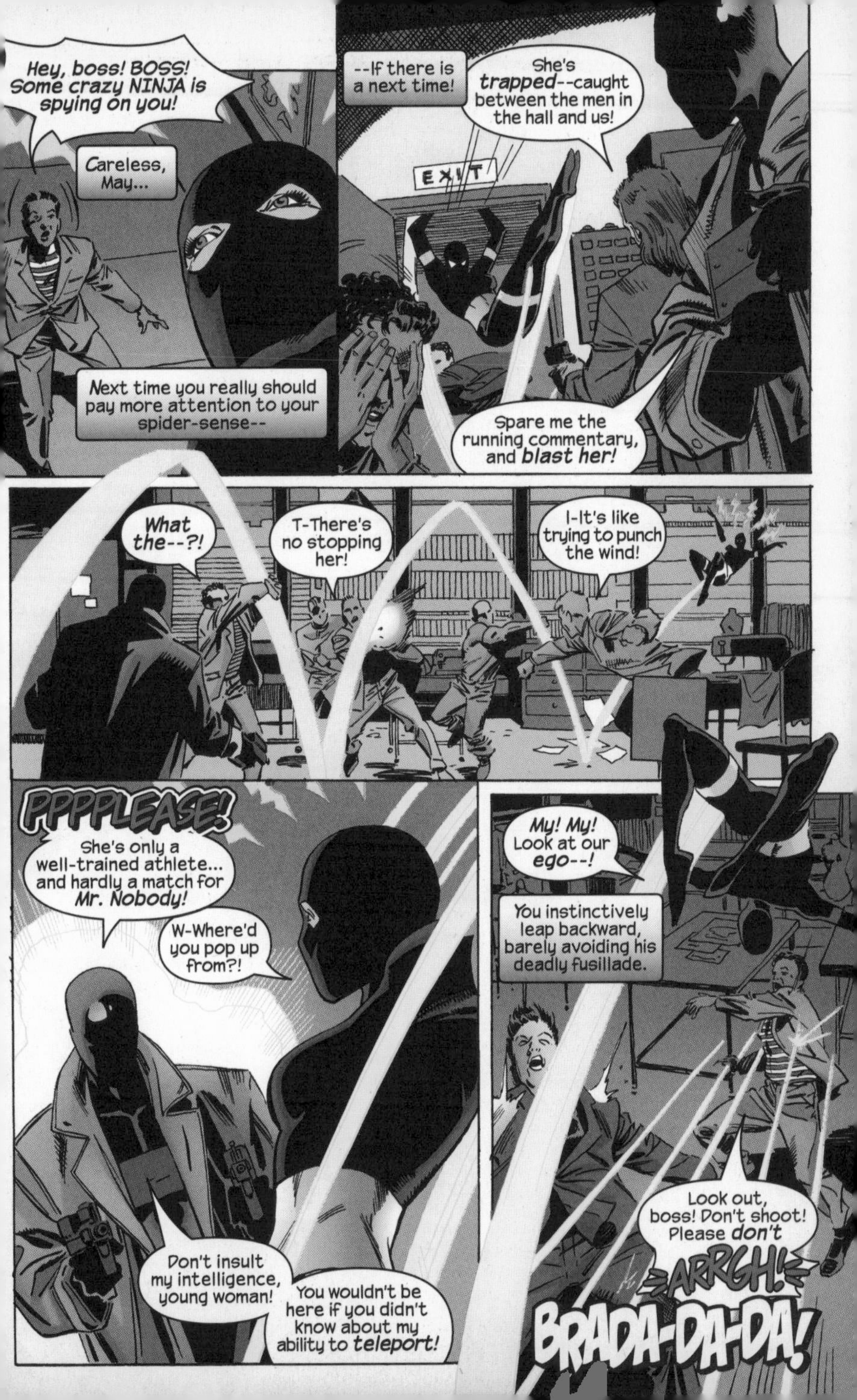
Hey, boss! BOSS! Some crazy NINJA is spying on you!
Careless, May...
Next time you really should pay more attention to your spider-sense--
--If there is a next time!
She's trapped--caught between the men in the hall and us!
EXIT
Spare me the running commentary, and blast her!
What the--?!
T-There's no stopping her!
I-It's like trying to punch the wind!
PPPPLEASE!
She's only a well-trained athlete... and hardly a match for Mr. Nobody!
W-Where'd you pop up from?!
Don't insult my intelligence, young woman!
You wouldn't be here if you didn't know about my ability to teleport!
My! My! Look at our ego--!
You instinctively leap backward, barely avoiding his deadly fusillade.
Look out, boss! Don't shoot! Please don't
ARRGH!
BRADA-DA-DA!

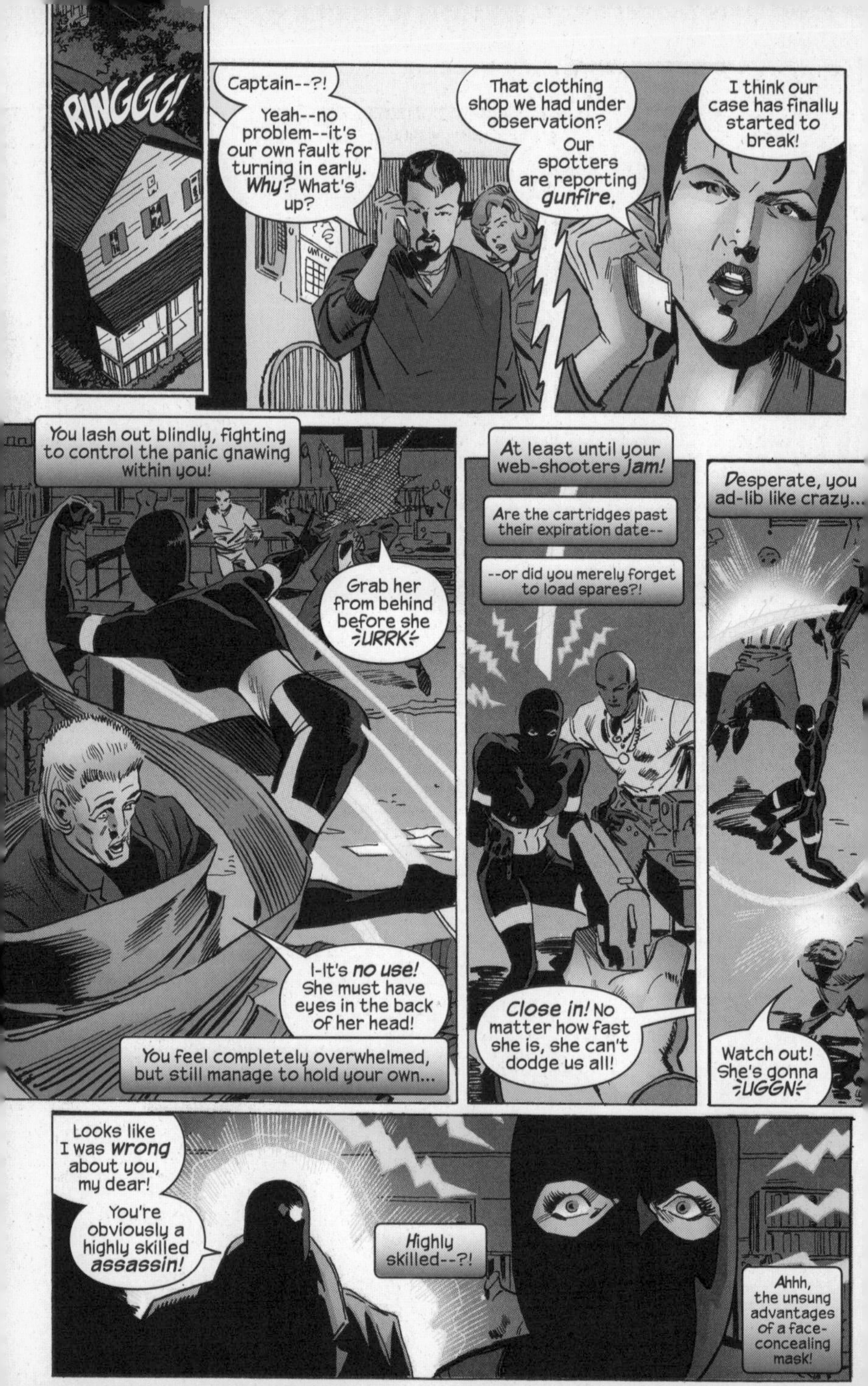

RINGGG!
Captain--?!
Yeah--no problem--it's our own fault for turning in early. *Why?* What's up?
That clothing shop we had under observation?
Our spotters are reporting *gunfire.*
I think our case has finally started to break!
You lash out blindly, fighting to control the panic gnawing within you!
Grab her from behind before she -URRK-
I-It's *no use!* She must have eyes in the back of her head!
You feel completely overwhelmed, but still manage to hold your own...
At least until your web-shooters *jam!*
Are the cartridges past their expiration date--
--or did you merely forget to load spares?!
Close in! No matter how fast she is, she can't dodge us all!
Desperate, you ad-lib like crazy...
Watch out! She's gonna -UGGN-
Looks like I was *wrong* about you, my dear!
You're obviously a highly skilled *assassin!*
Highly skilled--?!
Ahhh, the unsung advantages of a face-concealing mask!

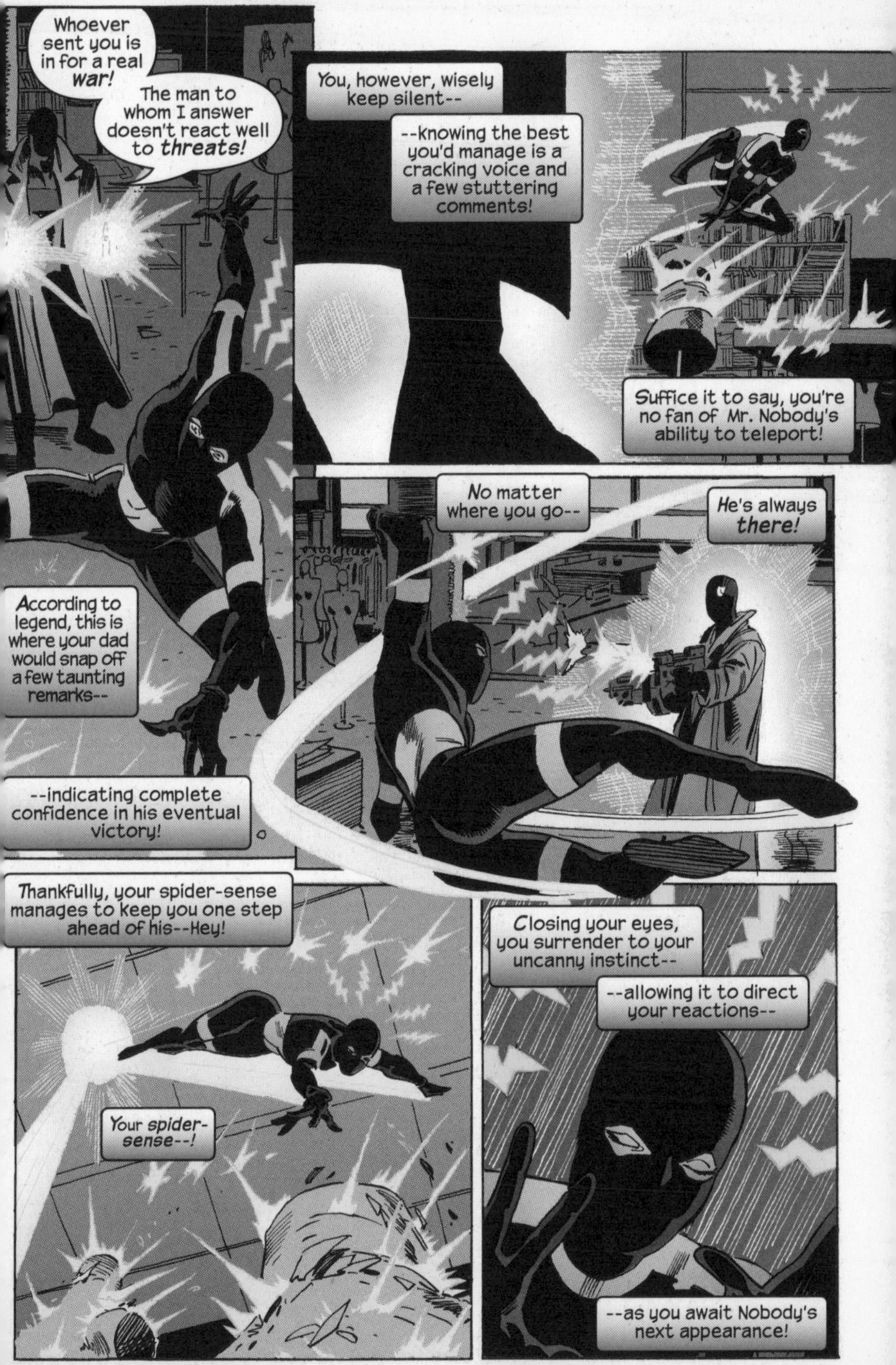
Whoever sent you is in for a real *war!*
The man to whom I answer doesn't react well to *threats!*
You, however, wisely keep silent--
--knowing the best you'd manage is a cracking voice and a few stuttering comments!
Suffice it to say, you're no fan of Mr. Nobody's ability to teleport!
According to legend, this is where your dad would snap off a few taunting remarks--
--indicating complete confidence in his eventual victory!
No matter where you go--
He's always *there!*
Thankfully, your spider-sense manages to keep you one step ahead of his--Hey!
Your spider-sense--!
Closing your eyes, you surrender to your uncanny instinct--
--allowing it to direct your reactions--
--as you await Nobody's next appearance!

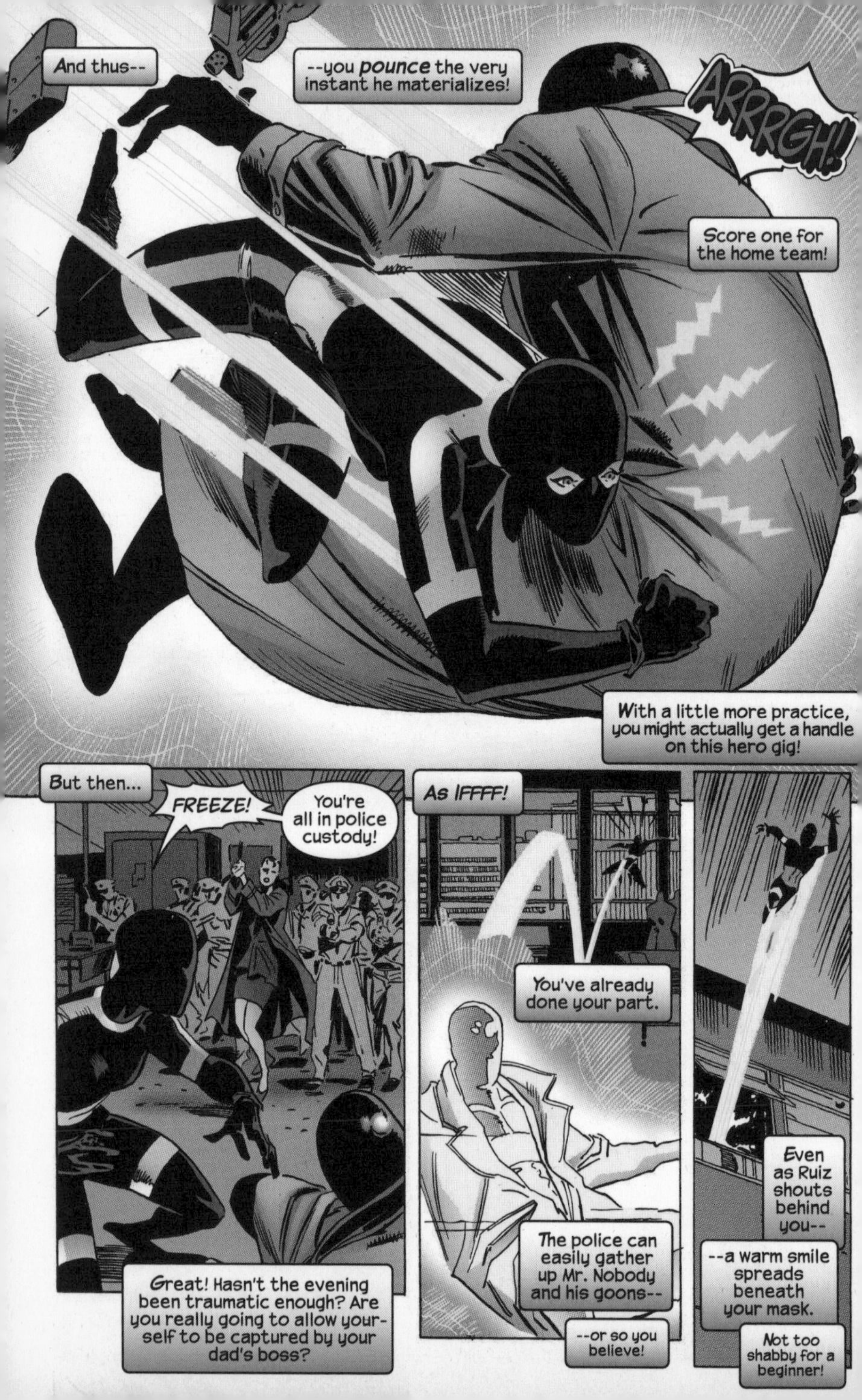
And thus--
--you pounce the very instant he materializes!
ARRRGH!
Score one for the home team!
With a little more practice, you might actually get a handle on this hero gig!
But then...
FREEZE!
You're all in police custody!
Great! Hasn't the evening been traumatic enough? Are you really going to allow your-self to be captured by your dad's boss?
As IFFFF!
You've already done your part.
The police can easily gather up Mr. Nobody and his goons--
--or so you believe!
Even as Ruiz shouts behind you--
--a warm smile spreads beneath your mask.
Not too shabby for a beginner!

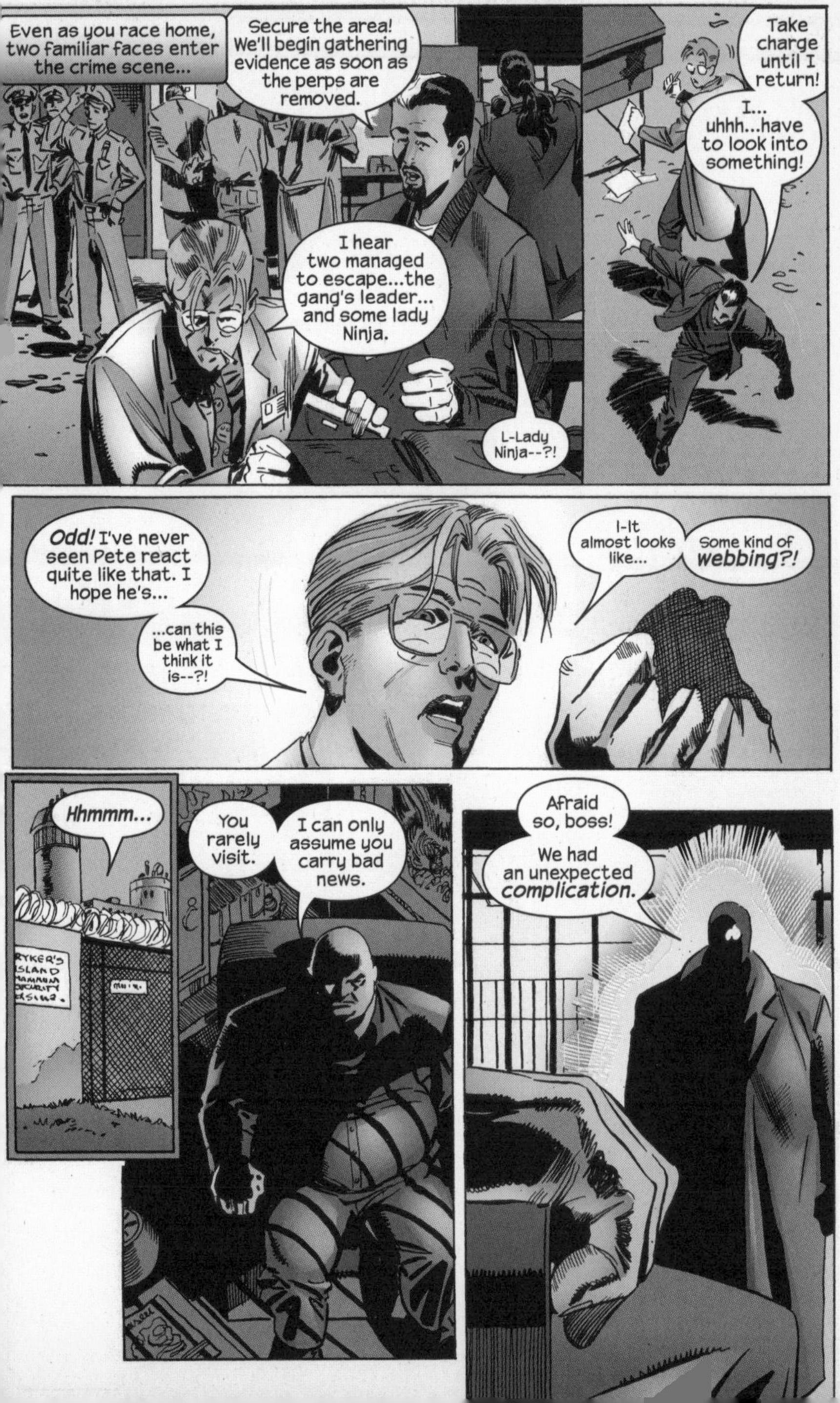
Even as you race home, two familiar faces enter the crime scene...
Secure the area! We'll begin gathering evidence as soon as the perps are removed.
I hear two managed to escape...the gang's leader... and some lady Ninja.
L-Lady Ninja--?!
Take charge until I return!
I... uhhh...have to look into something!
Odd! I've never seen Pete react quite like that. I hope he's...
...can this be what I think it is--?!
I-It almost looks like...
Some kind of webbing?!
Hhmmm...
RYKER'S ISLAND
You rarely visit.
I can only assume you carry bad news.
Afraid so, boss!
We had an unexpected complication.

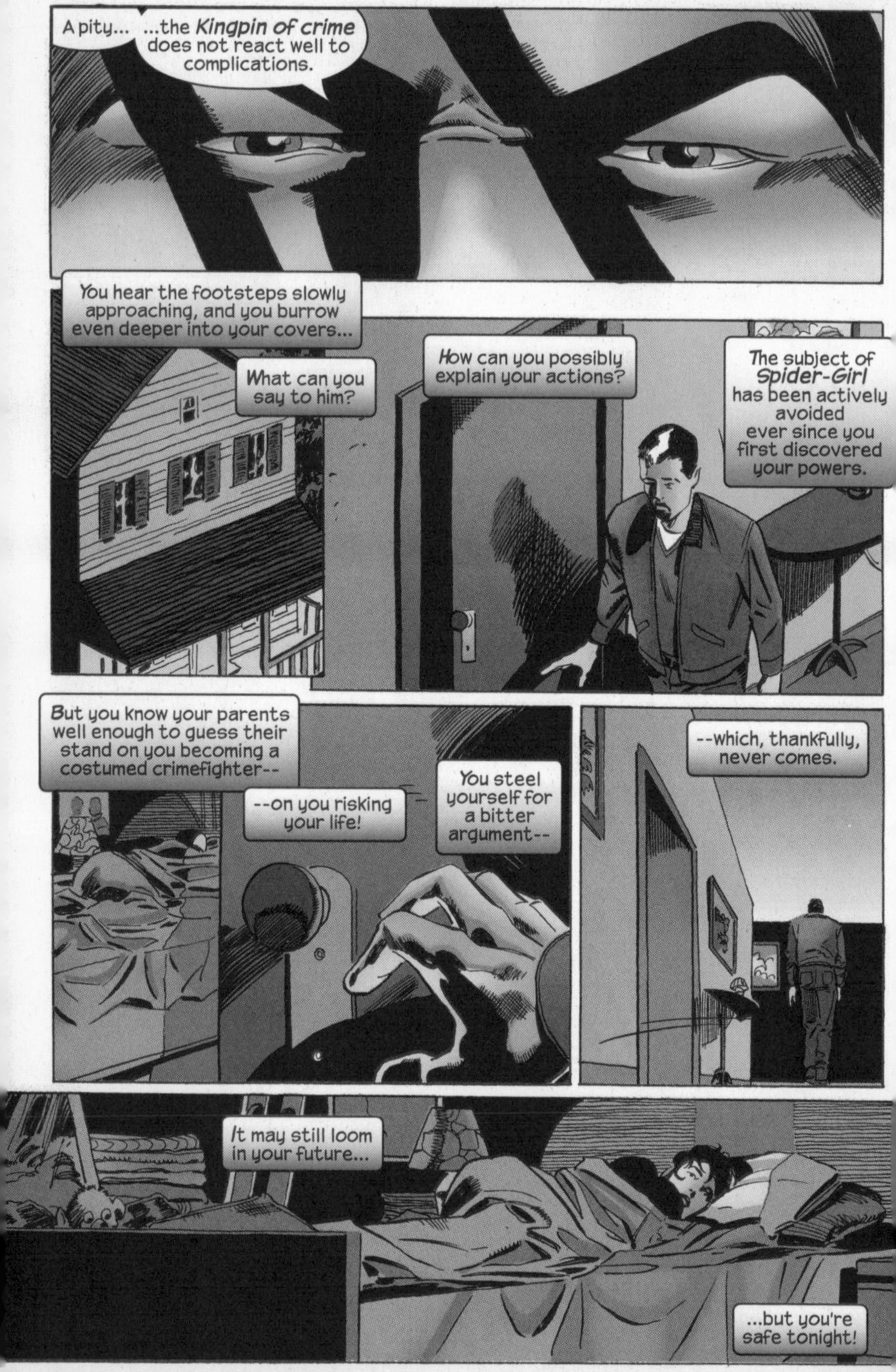
A pity...
...the Kingpin of crime does not react well to complications.
You hear the footsteps slowly approaching, and you burrow even deeper into your covers...
What can you say to him?
How can you possibly explain your actions?
The subject of Spider-Girl has been actively avoided ever since you first discovered your powers.
But you know your parents well enough to guess their stand on you becoming a costumed crimefighter--
--on you risking your life!
You steel yourself for a bitter argument--
--which, thankfully, never comes.
It may still loom in your future...
...but you're safe tonight!

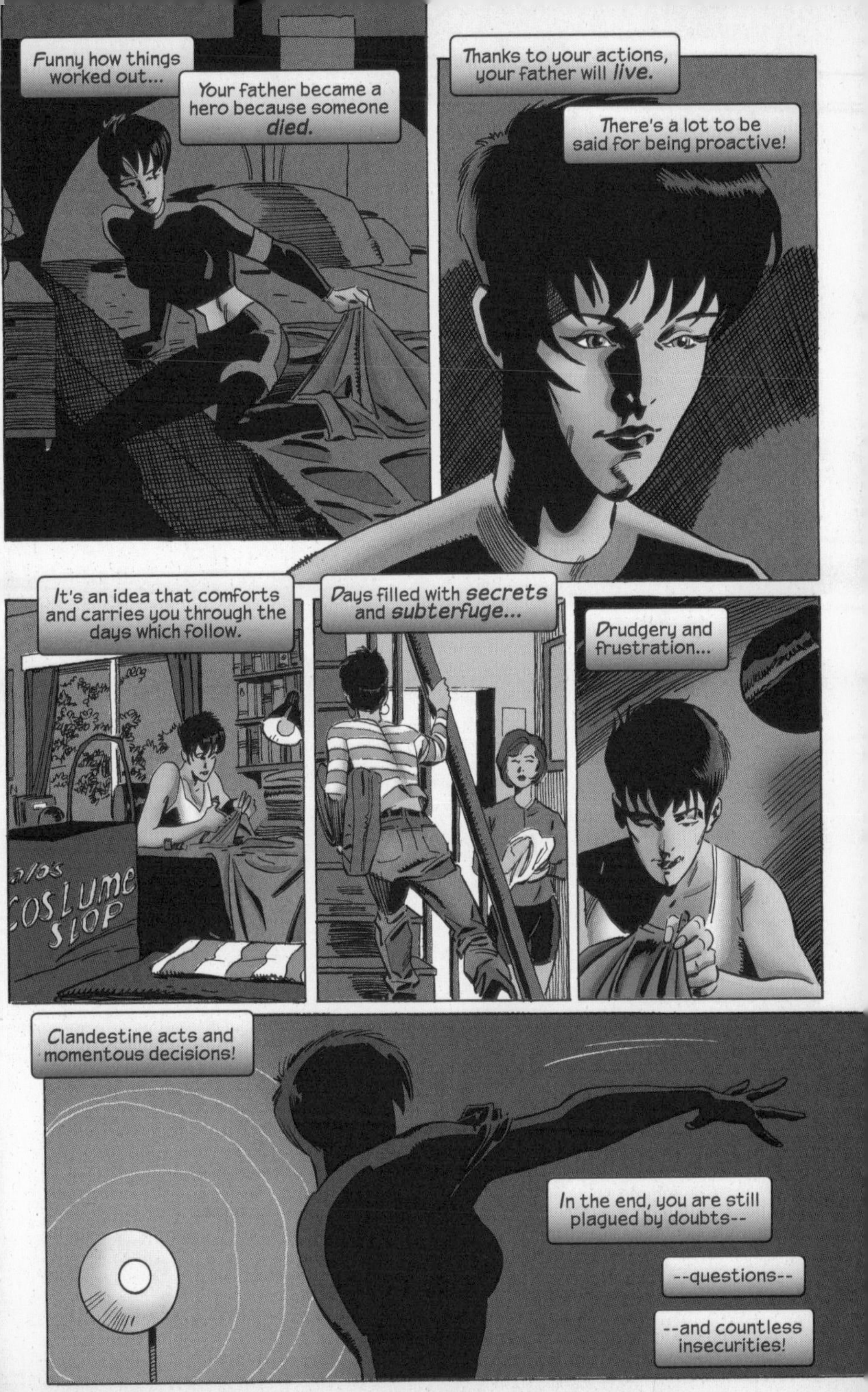
Funny how things worked out...
Your father became a hero because someone *died.*
Thanks to your actions, your father will *live.*
There's a lot to be said for being proactive!
It's an idea that comforts and carries you through the days which follow.
COSTUME SHOP
Days filled with *secrets* and *subterfuge...*
Drudgery and frustration...
Clandestine acts and momentous decisions!
In the end, you are still plagued by doubts--
--questions--
--and countless insecurities!

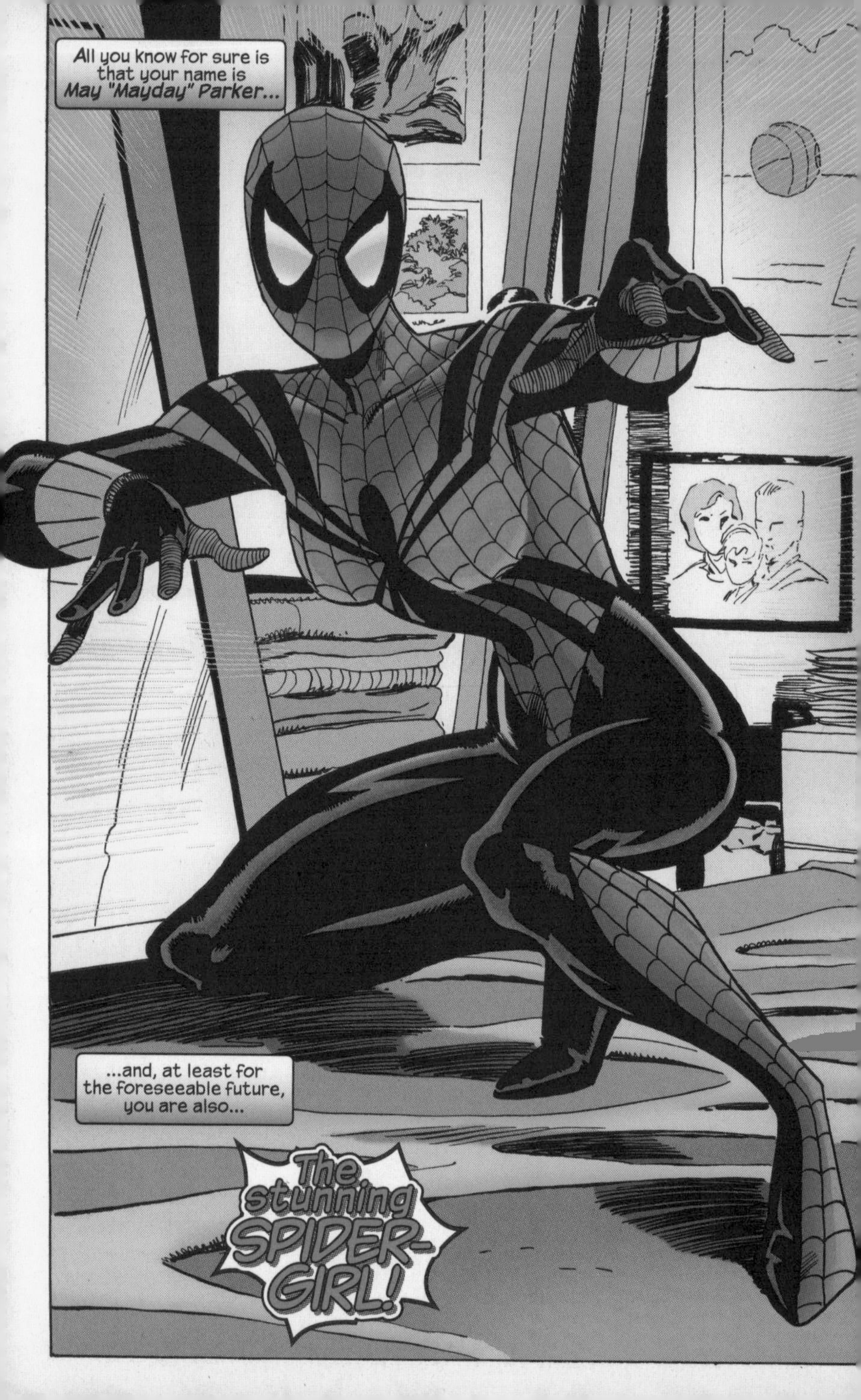
All you know for sure is that your name is May "Mayday" Parker...
...and, at least for the foreseeable future, you are also...
The stunning SPIDER-GIRL!

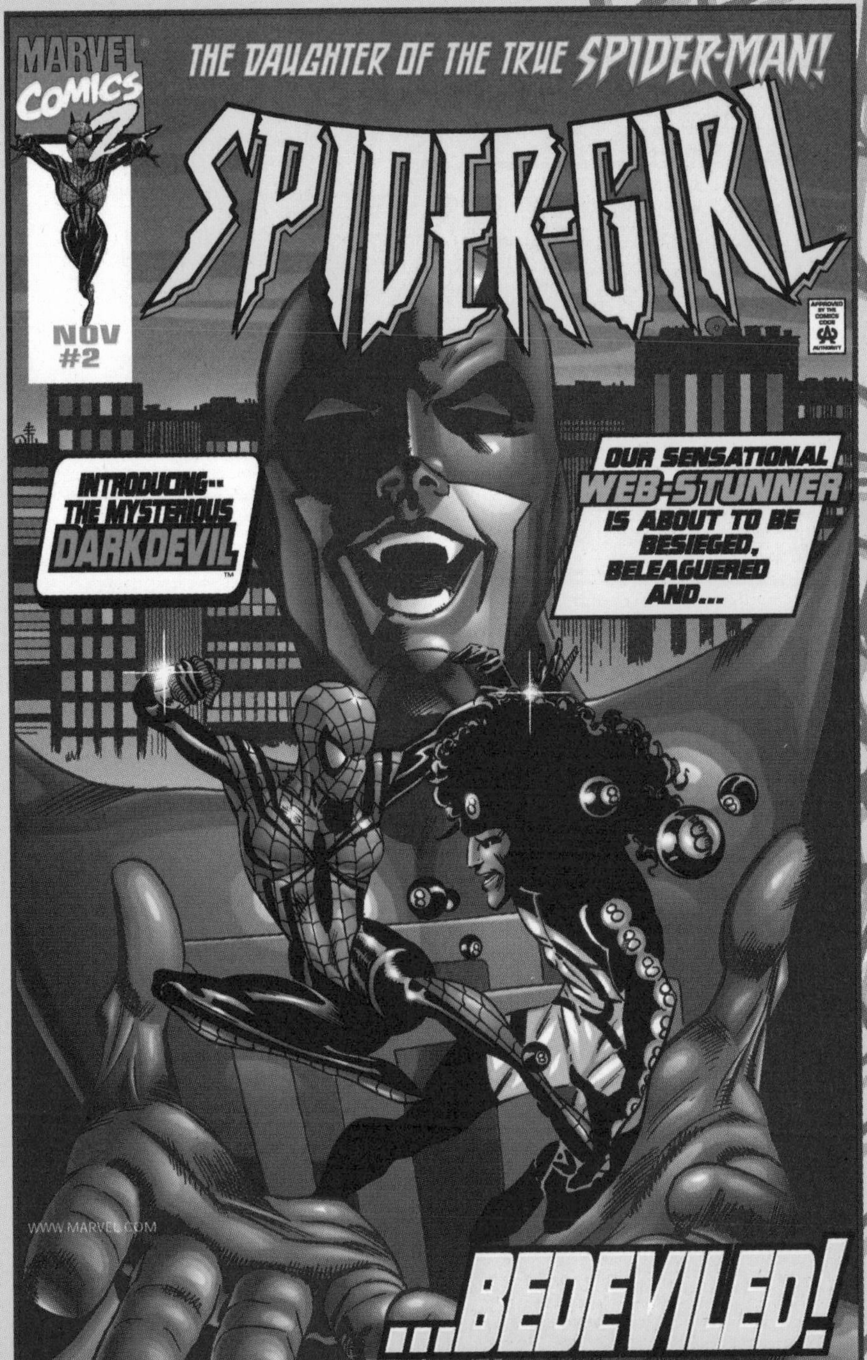
MARVEL COMICS 2
NOV #2
THE DAUGHTER OF THE TRUE SPIDER-MAN!
SPIDER-GIRL
APPROVED BY THE COMICS CODE AUTHORITY
INTRODUCING-- THE MYSTERIOUS DARKDEVIL
OUR SENSATIONAL WEB-STUNNER IS ABOUT TO BE BESIEGED, BELEAGUERED AND...
WWW.MARVEL.COM
...BEDEVILED!
DEFALCO OLLIFFE WILLIAMSON

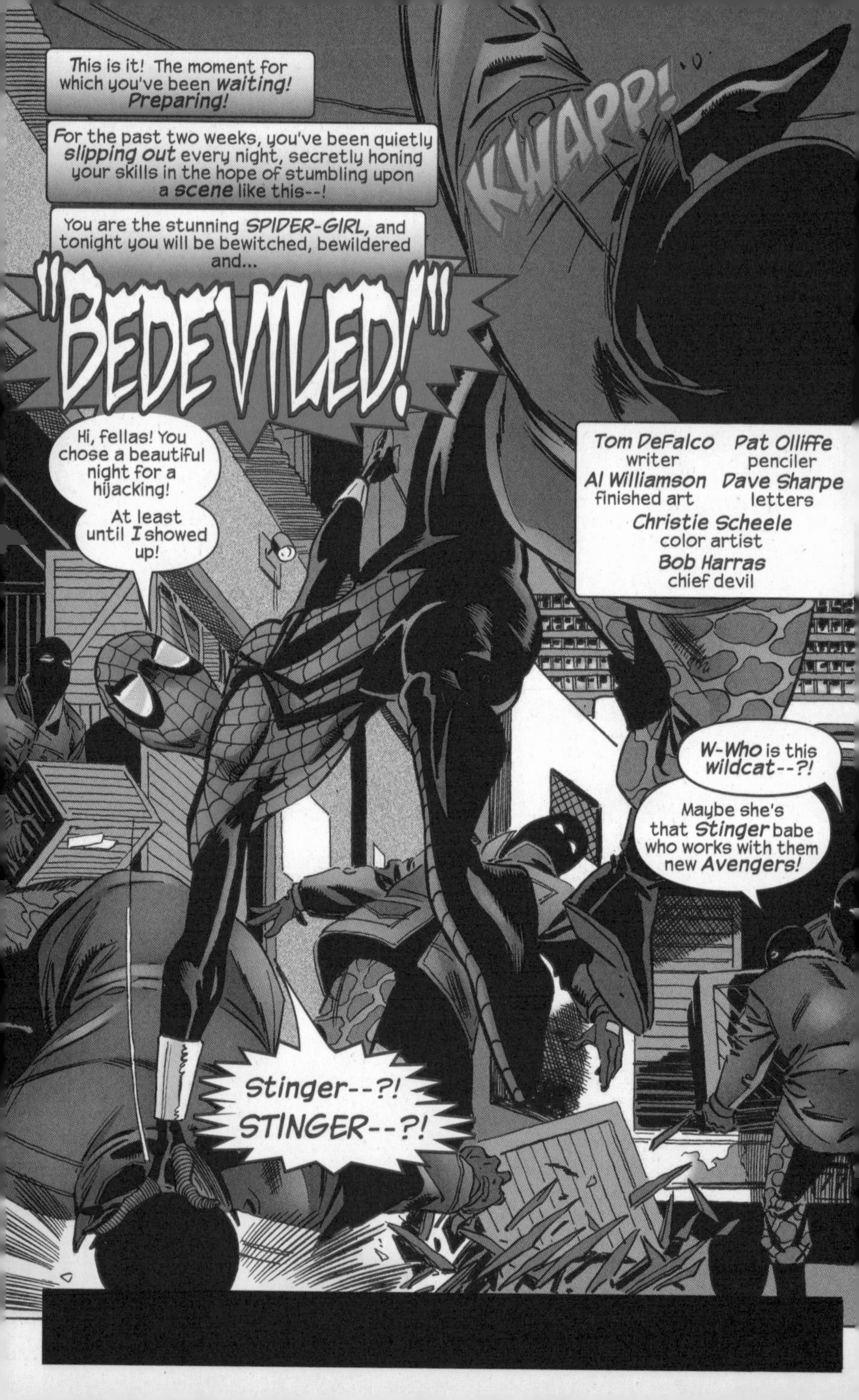
This is it! The moment for which you've been waiting! Preparing!
For the past two weeks, you've been quietly slipping out every night, secretly honing your skills in the hope of stumbling upon a scene like this--!
KWAPP!
You are the stunning SPIDER-GIRL, and tonight you will be bewitched, bewildered and...
"BEDEVILED!"
Hi, fellas! You chose a beautiful night for a hijacking!
At least until I showed up!
Tom DeFalco writer
Pat Olliffe penciler
Al Williamson finished art
Dave Sharpe letters
Christie Scheele color artist
Bob Harras chief devil
W-Who is this wildcat--?!
Maybe she's that Stinger babe who works with them new Avengers!
Stinger--?! STINGER--?!

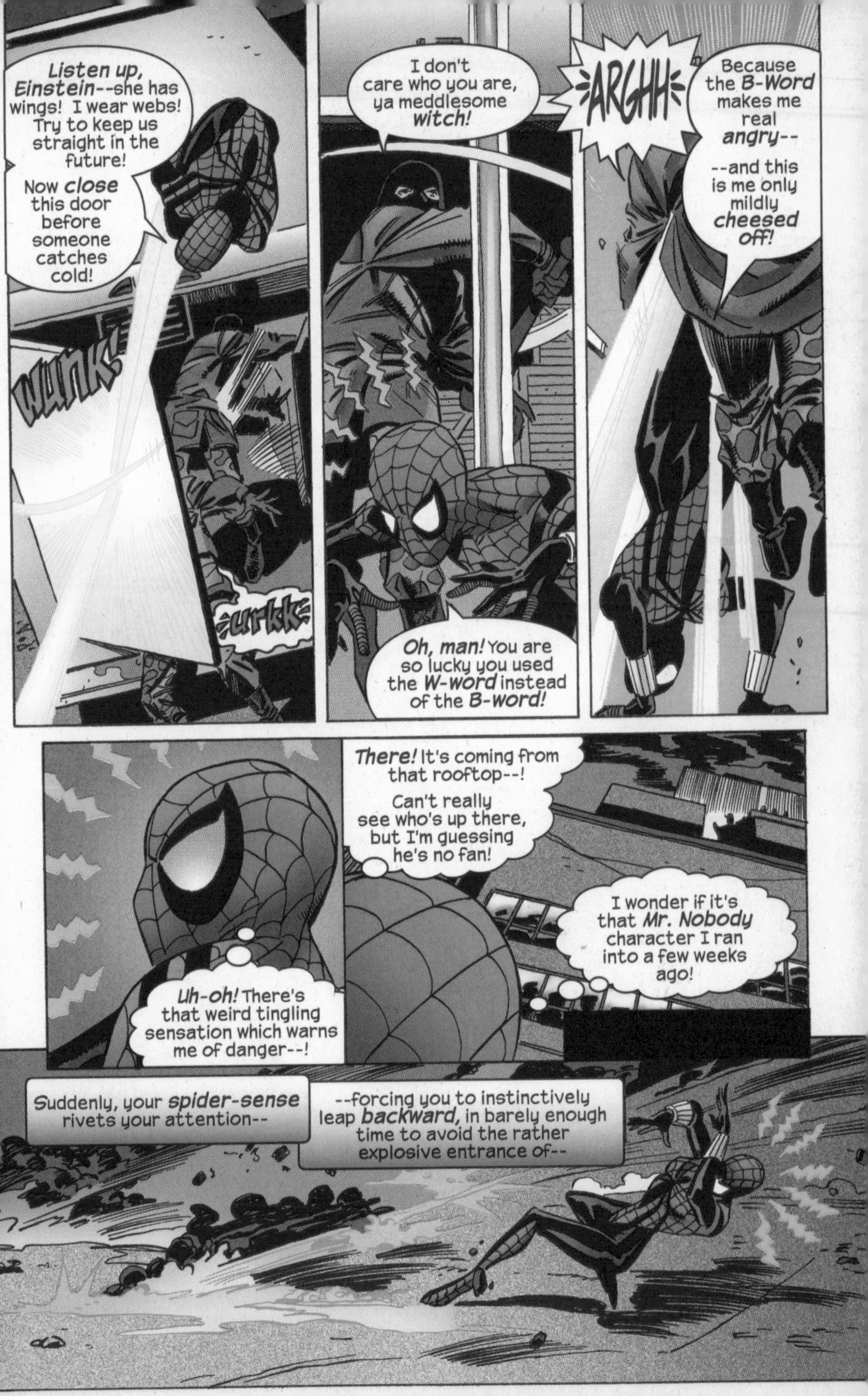
Listen up, Einstein--she has wings! I wear webs! Try to keep us straight in the future!
Now close this door before someone catches cold!
WUNK!
urkk
I don't care who you are, ya meddlesome witch!
Oh, man! You are so lucky you used the W-word instead of the B-word!
ARGHH
Because the B-Word makes me real angry--
--and this is me only mildly cheesed off!
Uh-oh! There's that weird tingling sensation which warns me of danger--!
There! It's coming from that rooftop--!
Can't really see who's up there, but I'm guessing he's no fan!
I wonder if it's that Mr. Nobody character I ran into a few weeks ago!
Suddenly, your spider-sense rivets your attention--
--forcing you to instinctively leap backward, in barely enough time to avoid the rather explosive entrance of--

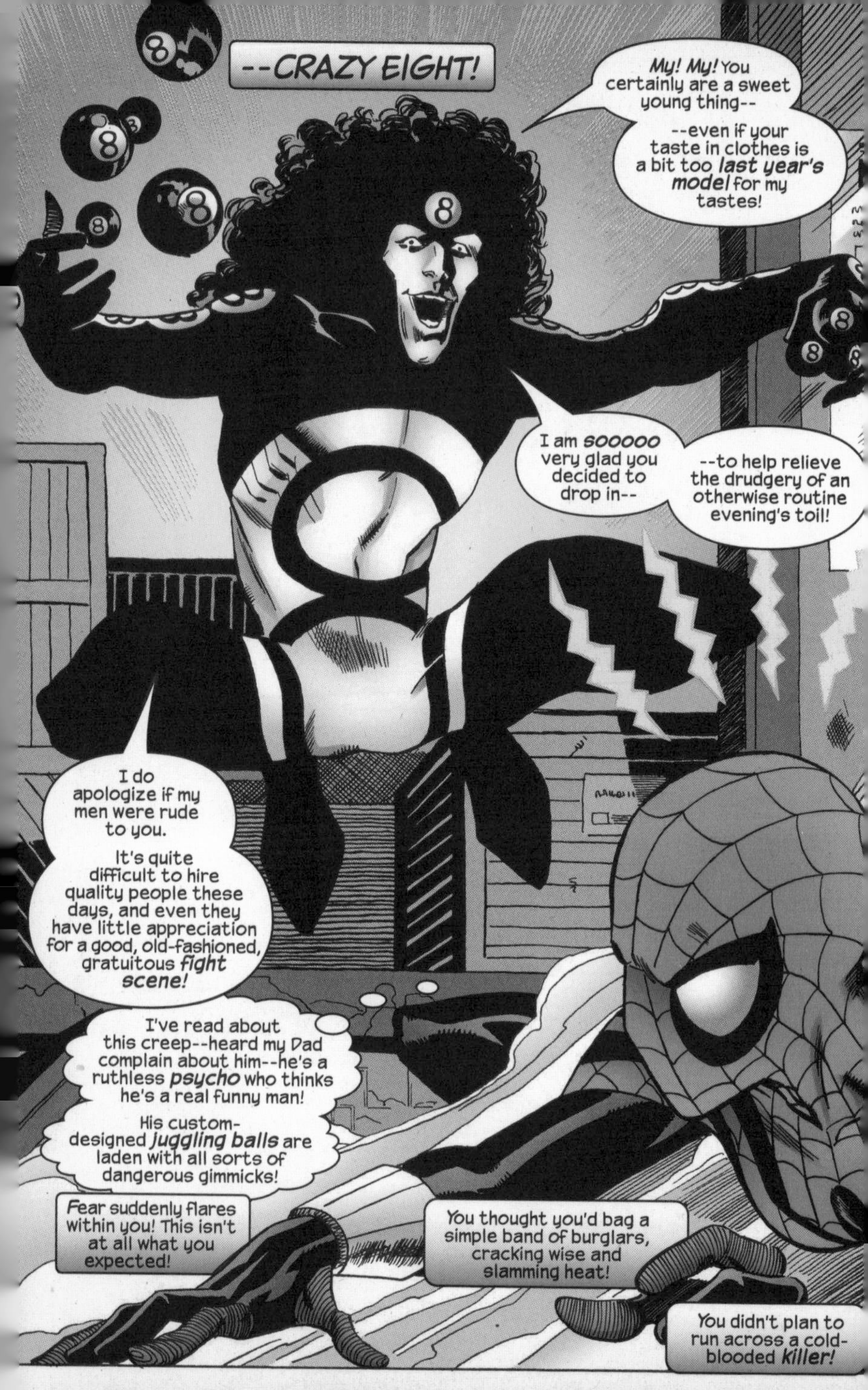
--CRAZY EIGHT!
My! My! You certainly are a sweet young thing--
--even if your taste in clothes is a bit too last year's model for my tastes!
I am SOOOOO very glad you decided to drop in--
--to help relieve the drudgery of an otherwise routine evening's toil!
I do apologize if my men were rude to you.
It's quite difficult to hire quality people these days, and even they have little appreciation for a good, old-fashioned, gratuitous fight scene!
I've read about this creep--heard my Dad complain about him--he's a ruthless psycho who thinks he's a real funny man!
His custom-designed juggling balls are laden with all sorts of dangerous gimmicks!
Fear suddenly flares within you! This isn't at all what you expected!
You thought you'd bag a simple band of burglars, cracking wise and slamming heat!
You didn't plan to run across a cold-blooded killer!

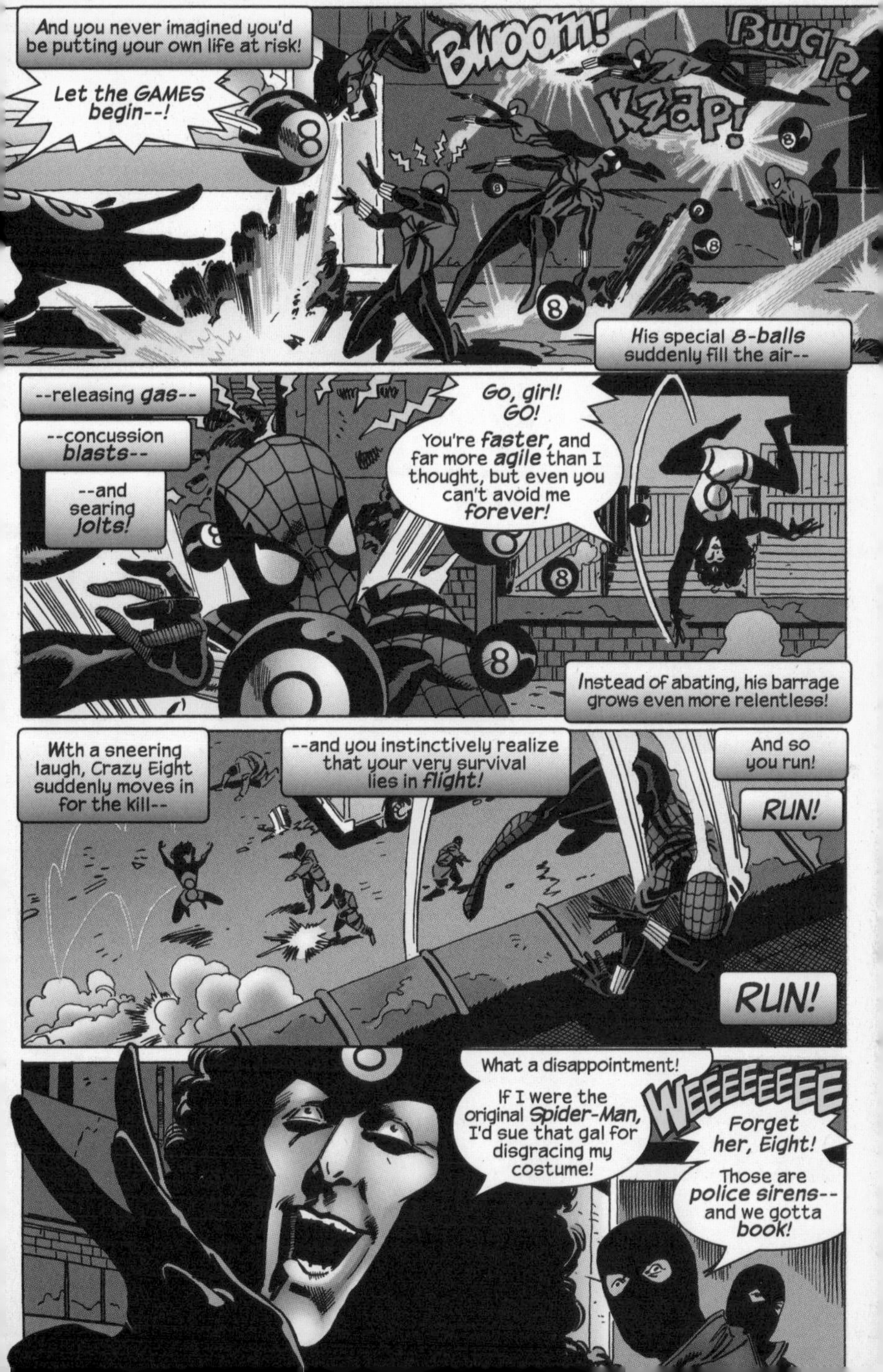

And you never imagined you'd be putting your own life at risk!
Let the GAMES begin--!
BHOOM!
BWAP!
KZAP!
His special 8-balls suddenly fill the air--
--releasing gas--
--concussion blasts--
--and searing jolts!
Go, girl! GO!
You're faster, and far more agile than I thought, but even you can't avoid me forever!
Instead of abating, his barrage grows even more relentless!
With a sneering laugh, Crazy Eight suddenly moves in for the kill--
--and you instinctively realize that your very survival lies in flight!
And so you run!
RUN!
RUN!
What a disappointment!
If I were the original Spider-Man, I'd sue that gal for disgracing my costume!
WEEEEEEEE
Forget her, Eight!
Those are police sirens-- and we gotta book!

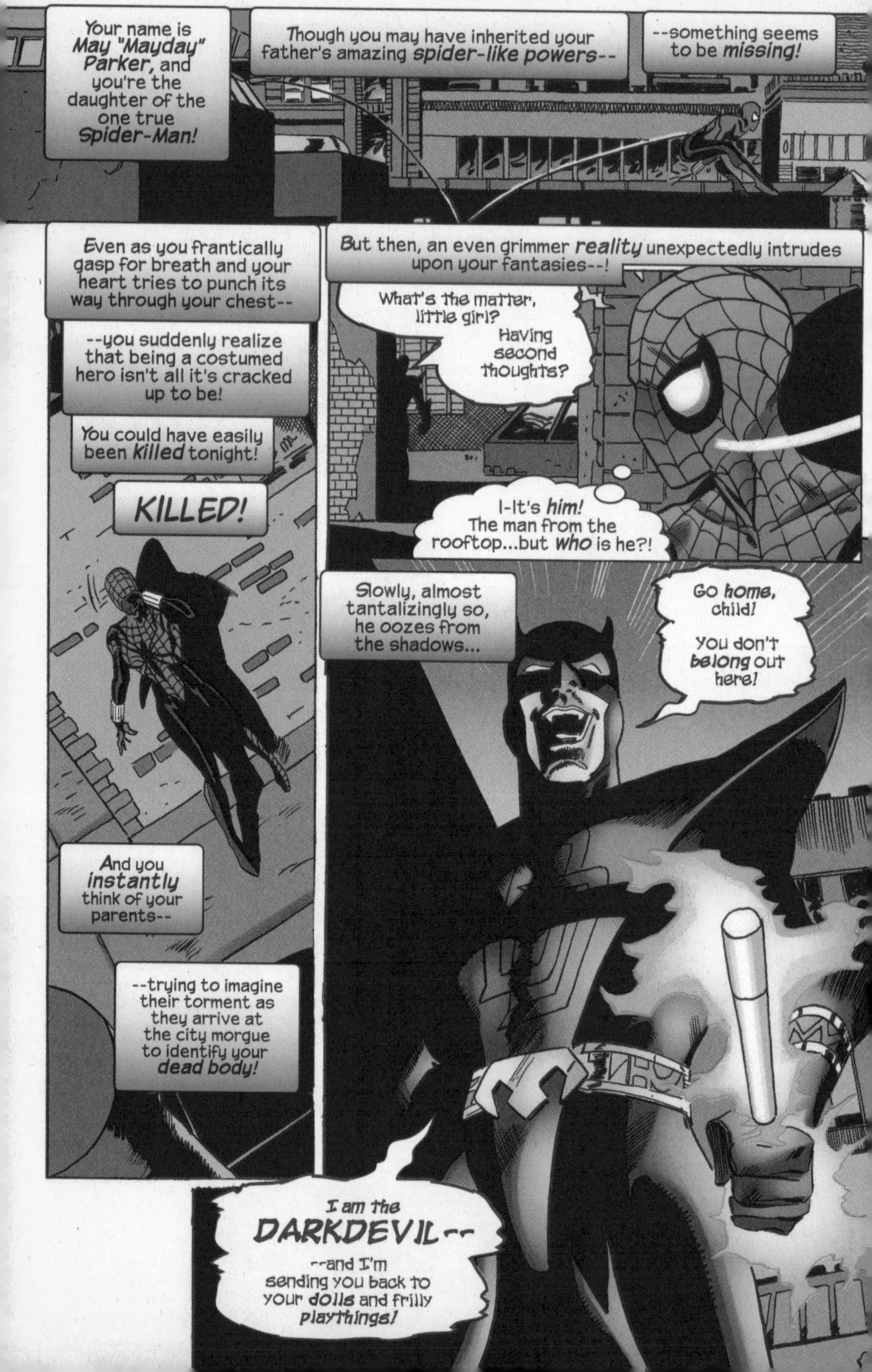

Your name is May "Mayday" Parker, and you're the daughter of the one true Spider-Man!
Though you may have inherited your father's amazing spider-like powers--
--something seems to be missing!
Even as you frantically gasp for breath and your heart tries to punch its way through your chest--
--you suddenly realize that being a costumed hero isn't all it's cracked up to be!
You could have easily been killed tonight!
KILLED!
And you instantly think of your parents--
--trying to imagine their torment as they arrive at the city morgue to identify your dead body!
But then, an even grimmer reality unexpectedly intrudes upon your fantasies--!
What's the matter, little girl?
Having second thoughts?
I-It's him! The man from the rooftop...but who is he?!
Slowly, almost tantalizingly so, he oozes from the shadows...
Go home, child!
You don't belong out here!
I am the DARKDEVIL--
--and I'm sending you back to your dolls and frilly playthings!

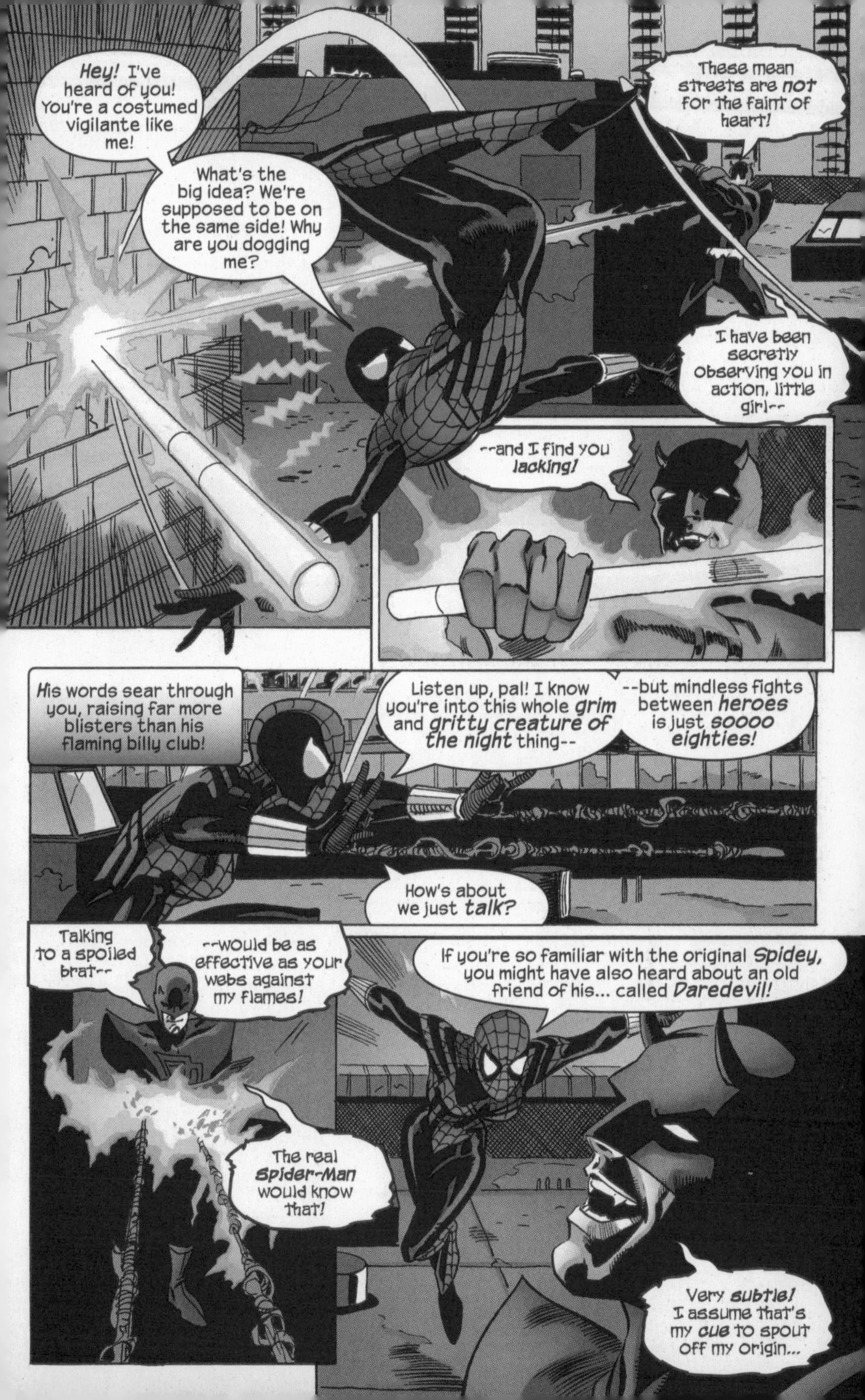
Hey! I've heard of you! You're a costumed vigilante like me!
These mean streets are not for the faint of heart!
What's the big idea? We're supposed to be on the same side! Why are you dogging me?
I have been secretly observing you in action, little girl--
--and I find you lacking!
His words sear through you, raising far more blisters than his flaming billy club!
Listen up, pal! I know you're into this whole grim and gritty creature of the night thing--
--but mindless fights between heroes is just soooo eighties!
How's about we just talk?
Talking to a spoiled brat--
--would be as effective as your webs against my flames!
If you're so familiar with the original Spidey, you might have also heard about an old friend of his... called Daredevil!
The real Spider-Man would know that!
Very subtle! I assume that's my cue to spout off my origin...

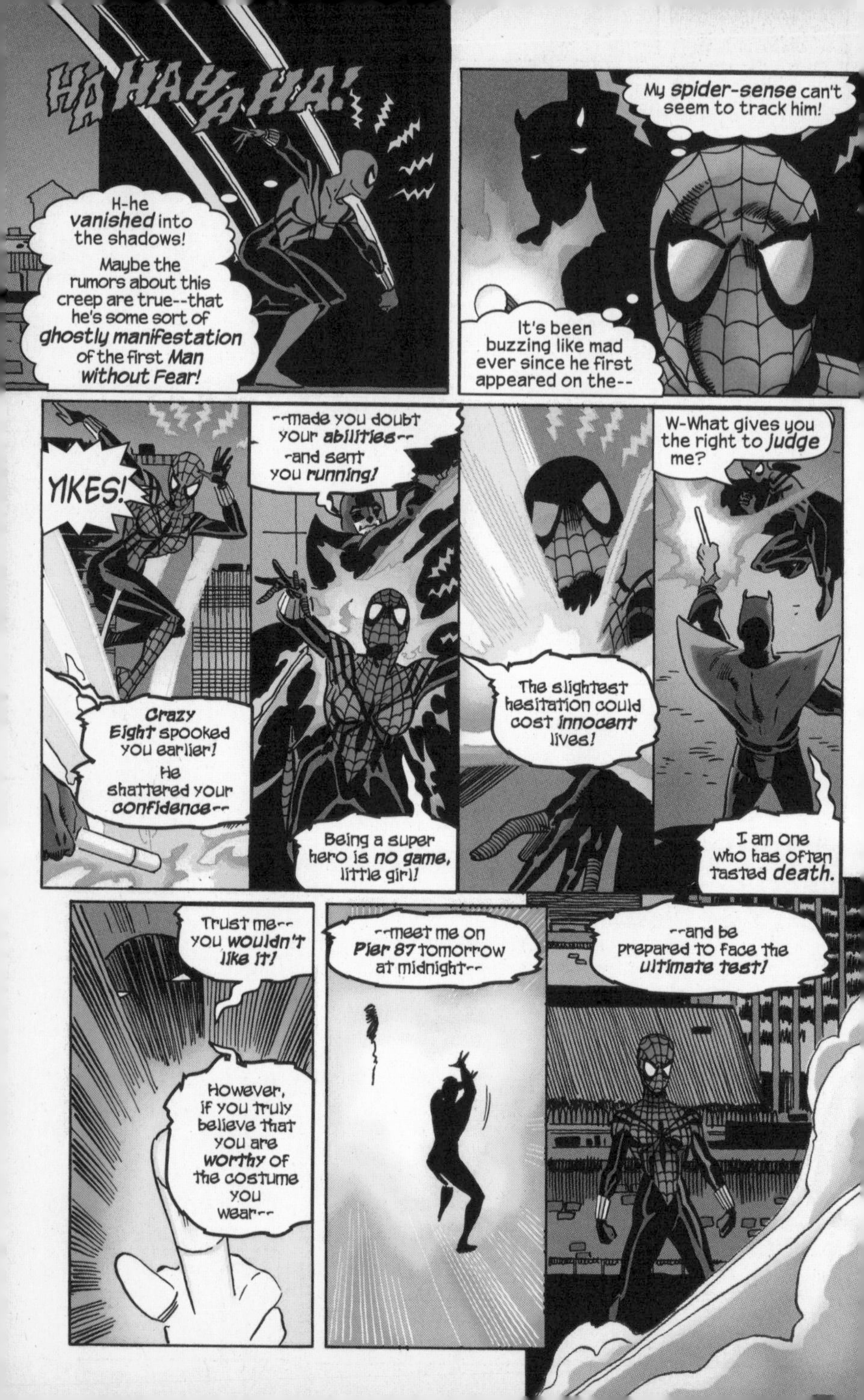
HA HA HA HA HA!
H-he vanished into the shadows!
Maybe the rumors about this creep are true--that he's some sort of ghostly manifestation of the first Man without Fear!
My spider-sense can't seem to track him!
It's been buzzing like mad ever since he first appeared on the--
YIKES!
Crazy Eight spooked you earlier!
He shattered your confidence--
--made you doubt your abilities--
--and sent you running!
Being a super hero is no game, little girl!
The slightest hesitation could cost innocent lives!
W-What gives you the right to judge me?
I am one who has often tasted death.
Trust me--you wouldn't like it!
However, if you truly believe that you are worthy of the costume you wear--
--meet me on Pier 87 tomorrow at midnight--
--and be prepared to face the ultimate test!

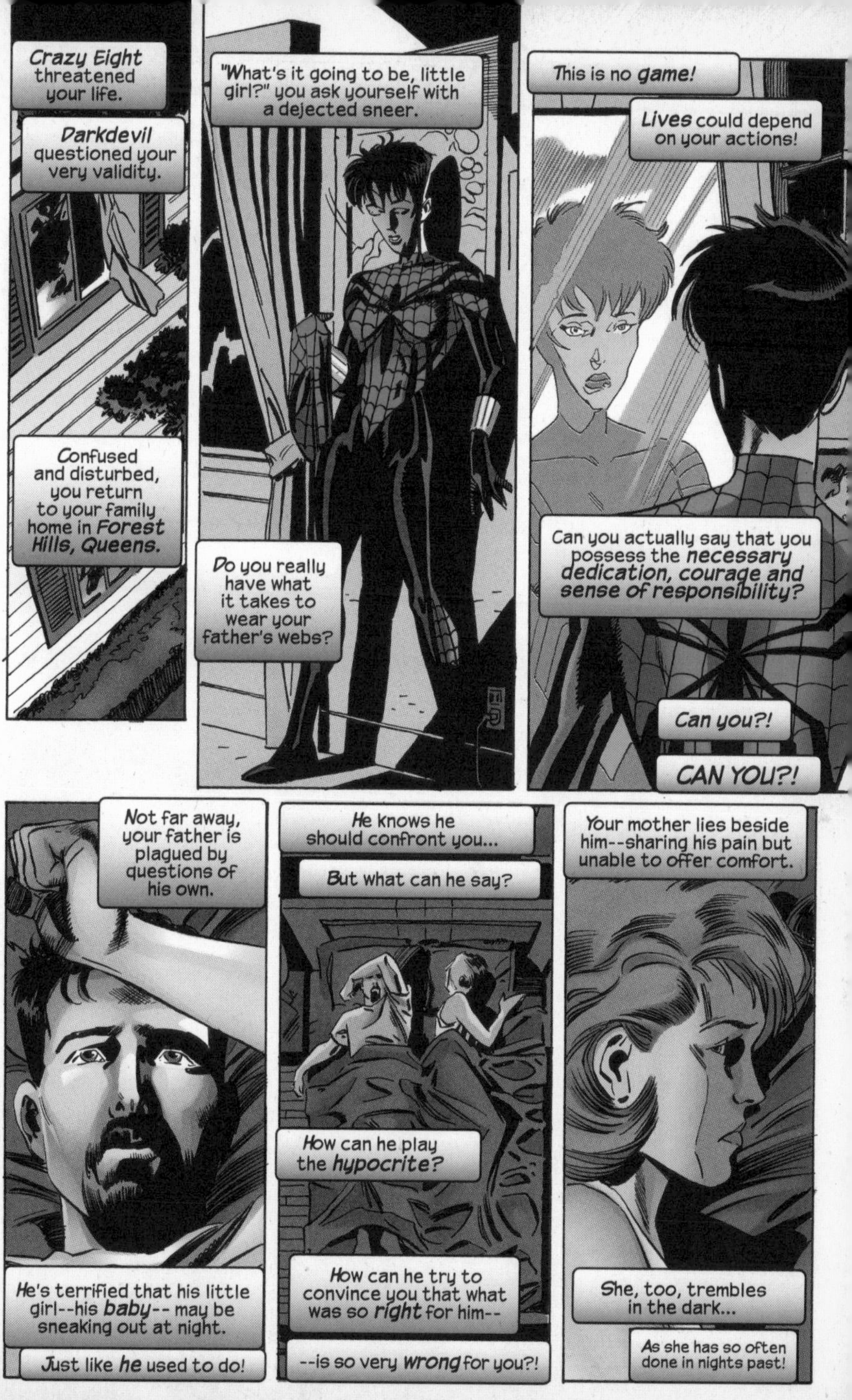
Crazy Eight threatened your life.
Darkdevil questioned your very validity.
Confused and disturbed, you return to your family home in Forest Hills, Queens.
"What's it going to be, little girl?" you ask yourself with a dejected sneer.
Do you really have what it takes to wear your father's webs?
This is no game!
Lives could depend on your actions!
Can you actually say that you possess the necessary dedication, courage and sense of responsibility?
Can you?!
CAN YOU?!
Not far away, your father is plagued by questions of his own.
He's terrified that his little girl--his baby-- may be sneaking out at night.
Just like he used to do!
He knows he should confront you...
But what can he say?
How can he play the hypocrite?
How can he try to convince you that what was so right for him--
--is so very wrong for you?!
Your mother lies beside him--sharing his pain but unable to offer comfort.
She, too, trembles in the dark...
As she has so often done in nights past!

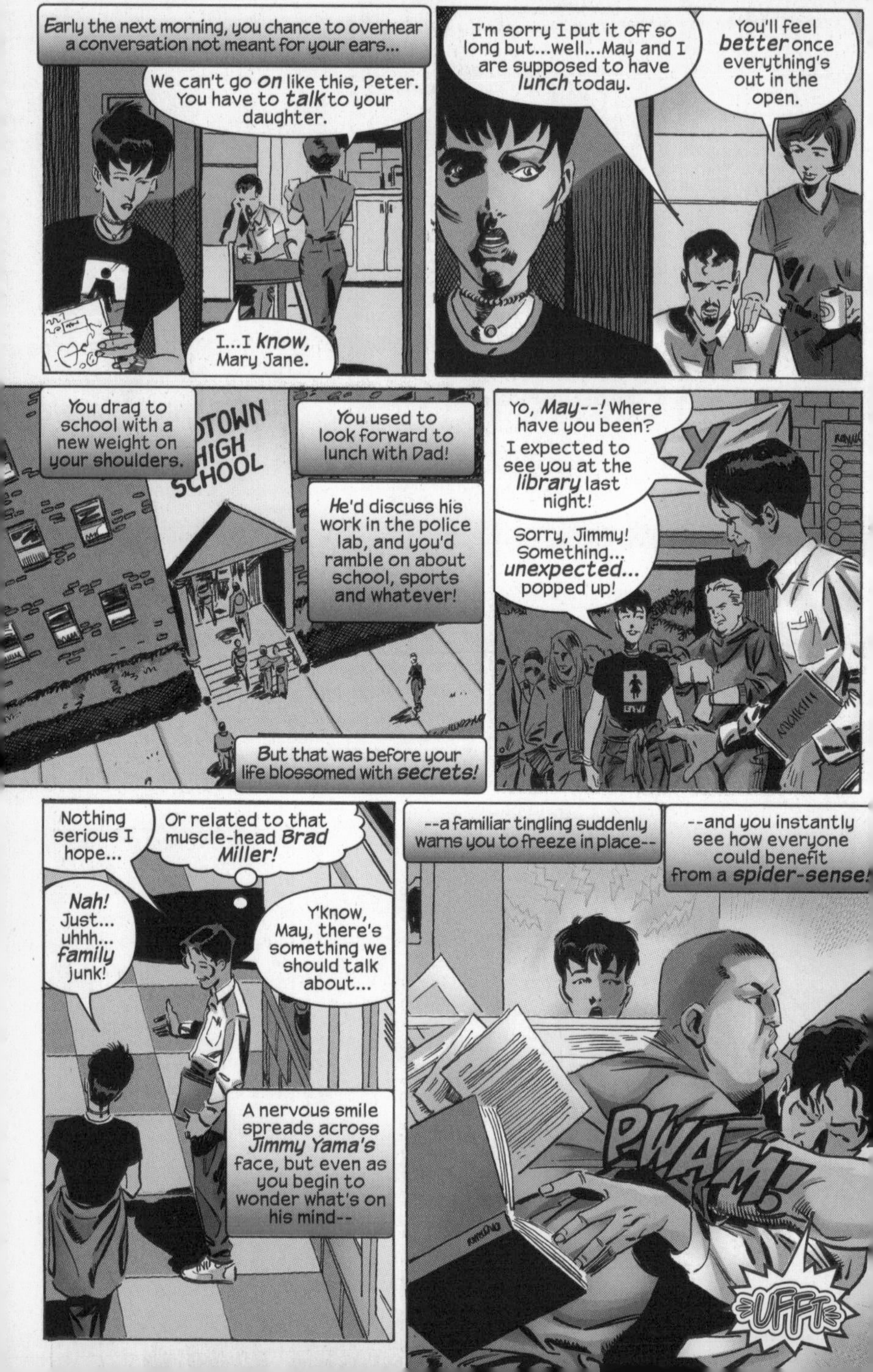

Early the next morning, you chance to overhear a conversation not meant for your ears...
We can't go on like this, Peter. You have to talk to your daughter.
I...I know, Mary Jane.
I'm sorry I put it off so long but...well...May and I are supposed to have lunch today.
You'll feel better once everything's out in the open.
You drag to school with a new weight on your shoulders.
DTOWN HIGH SCHOOL
You used to look forward to lunch with Dad!
He'd discuss his work in the police lab, and you'd ramble on about school, sports and whatever!
But that was before your life blossomed with secrets!
Yo, May--! Where have you been? I expected to see you at the library last night!
Sorry, Jimmy! Something... unexpected... popped up!
Nothing serious I hope...
Or related to that muscle-head Brad Miller!
Nah! Just... uhhh... family junk!
Y'know, May, there's something we should talk about...
A nervous smile spreads across Jimmy Yama's face, but even as you begin to wonder what's on his mind--
--a familiar tingling suddenly warns you to freeze in place--
--and you instantly see how everyone could benefit from a spider-sense!
PWAM!
UFFT

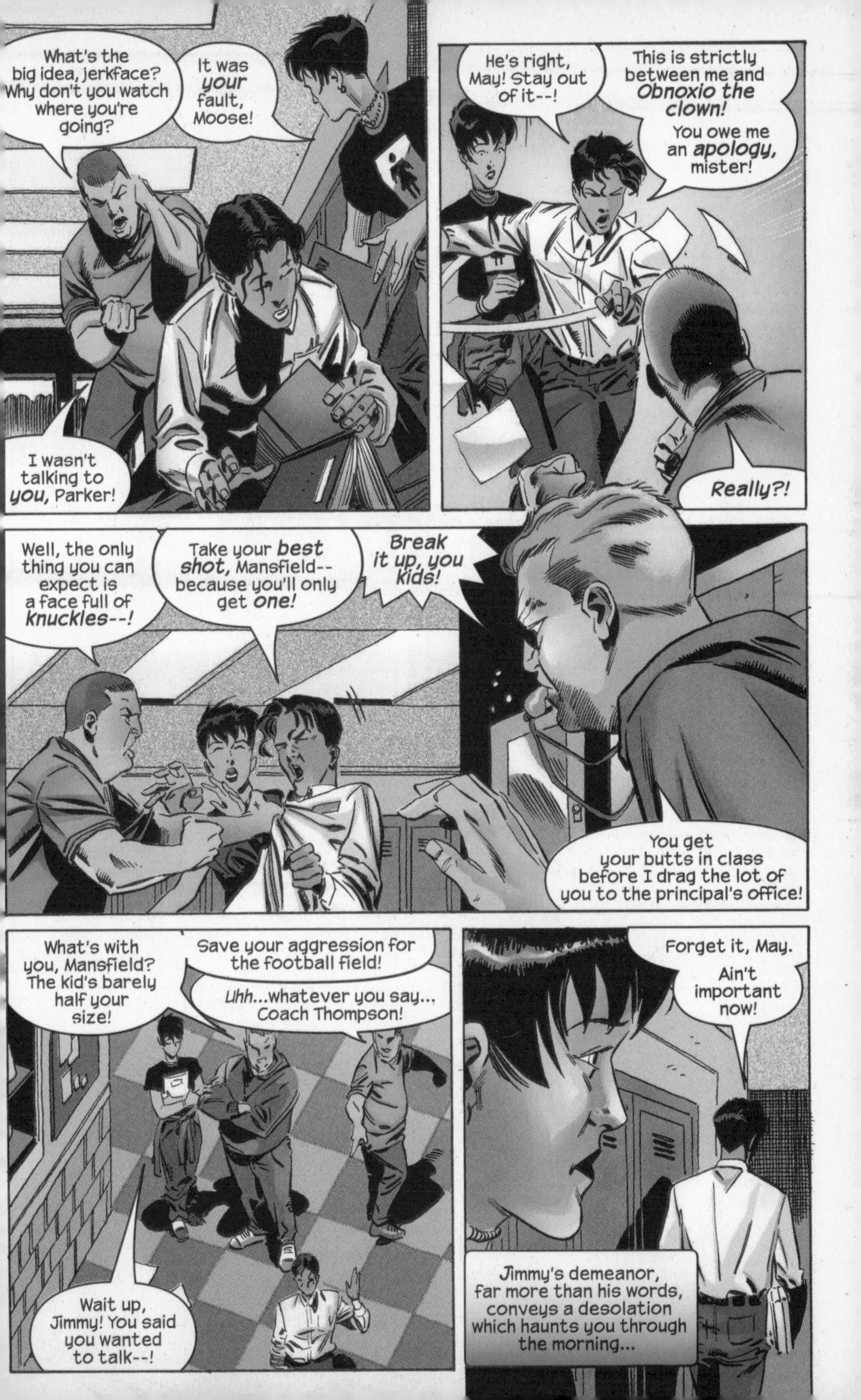
What's the big idea, jerkface? Why don't you watch where you're going?
It was your fault, Moose!
I wasn't talking to you, Parker!
He's right, May! Stay out of it--!
This is strictly between me and Obnoxio the clown!
You owe me an apology, mister!
Really?!
Well, the only thing you can expect is a face full of knuckles--!
Take your best shot, Mansfield-- because you'll only get one!
Break it up, you kids!
You get your butts in class before I drag the lot of you to the principal's office!
What's with you, Mansfield? The kid's barely half your size!
Save your aggression for the football field!
Uhh...whatever you say... Coach Thompson!
Wait up, Jimmy! You said you wanted to talk--!
Forget it, May.
Ain't important now!
Jimmy's demeanor, far more than his words, conveys a desolation which haunts you through the morning...

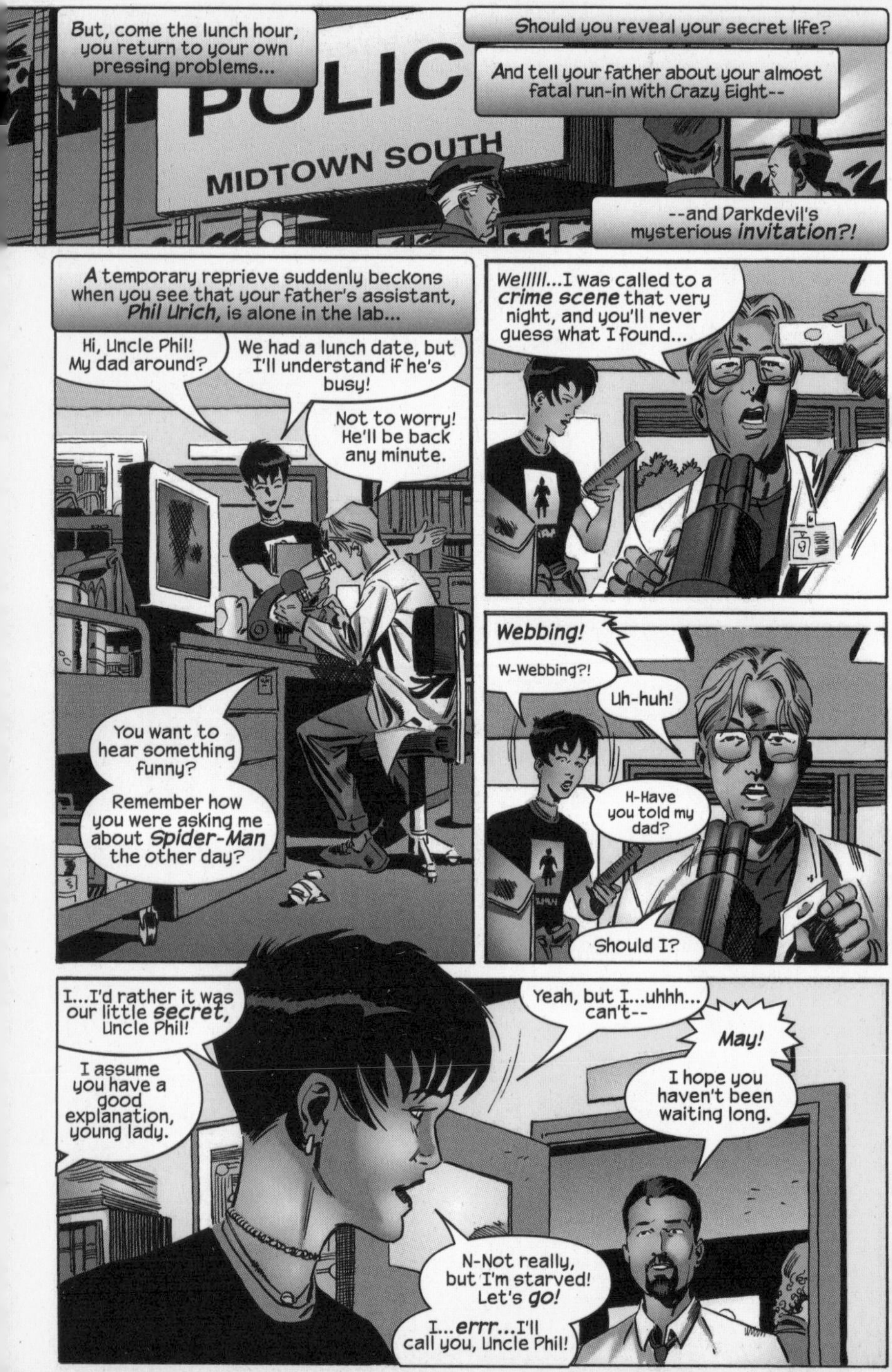

But, come the lunch hour, you return to your own pressing problems...
POLIC
MIDTOWN SOUTH
Should you reveal your secret life?
And tell your father about your almost fatal run-in with Crazy Eight--
--and Darkdevil's mysterious invitation?!
A temporary reprieve suddenly beckons when you see that your father's assistant, Phil Urich, is alone in the lab...
Hi, Uncle Phil! My dad around?
We had a lunch date, but I'll understand if he's busy!
Not to worry! He'll be back any minute.
You want to hear something funny?
Remember how you were asking me about Spider-Man the other day?
Wellllll...I was called to a crime scene that very night, and you'll never guess what I found...
Webbing!
W-Webbing?!
Uh-huh!
H-Have you told my dad?
Should I?
I...I'd rather it was our little secret, Uncle Phil!
Yeah, but I...uhhh... can't--
May!
I hope you haven't been waiting long.
I assume you have a good explanation, young lady.
N-Not really, but I'm starved! Let's go!
I...errr...I'll call you, Uncle Phil!

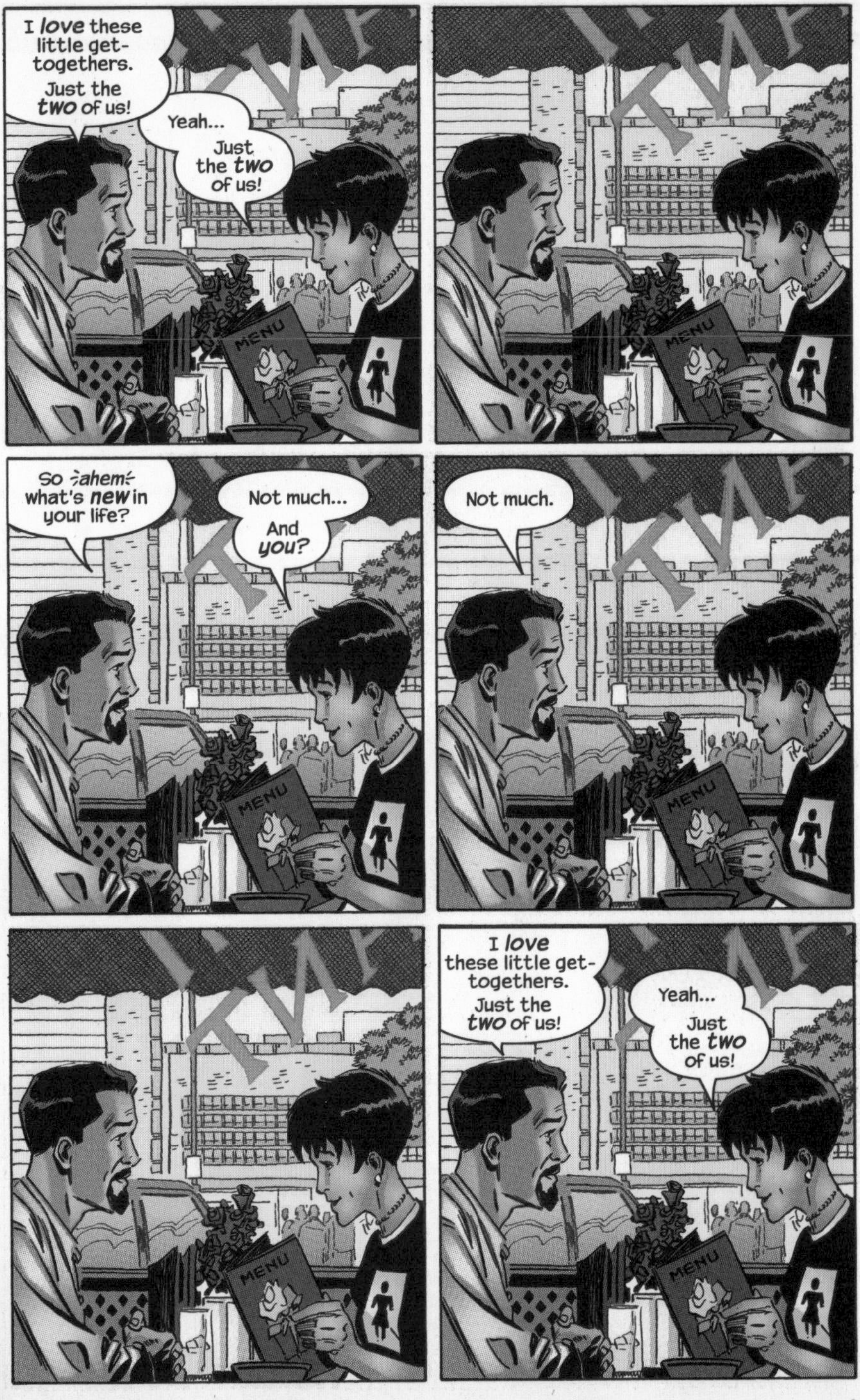

I love these little get-togethers. Just the two of us!
Yeah... Just the two of us!
So -ahem- what's new in your life?
Not much... And you?
Not much.
I love these little get-togethers. Just the two of us!
Yeah... Just the two of us!

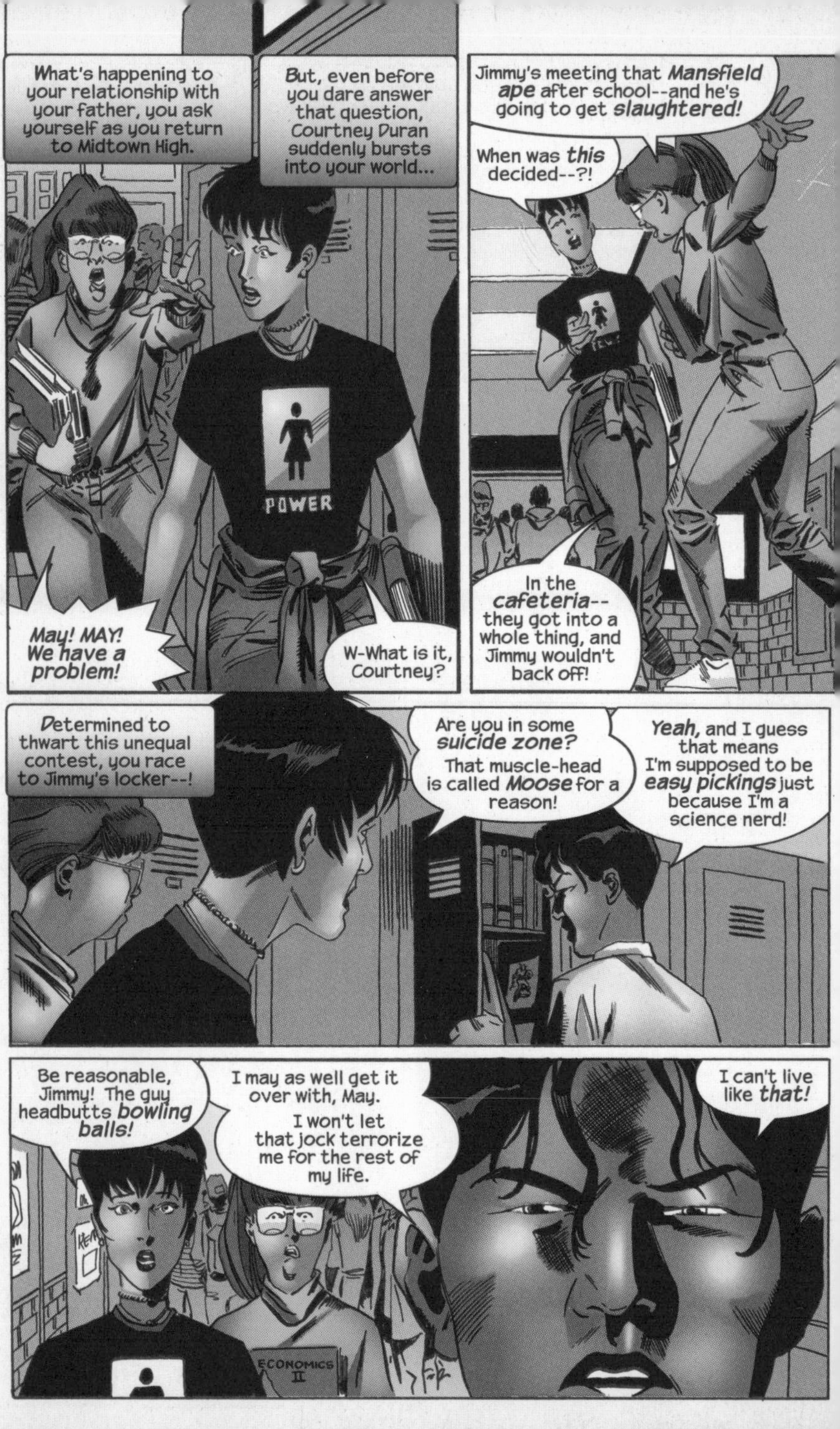

What's happening to your relationship with your father, you ask yourself as you return to Midtown High.
But, even before you dare answer that question, Courtney Duran suddenly bursts into your world...
May! MAY! We have a problem!
W-What is it, Courtney?
Jimmy's meeting that Mansfield ape after school--and he's going to get slaughtered!
When was this decided--?!
In the cafeteria--they got into a whole thing, and Jimmy wouldn't back off!
POWER
Determined to thwart this unequal contest, you race to Jimmy's locker--!
Are you in some suicide zone? That muscle-head is called Moose for a reason!
Yeah, and I guess that means I'm supposed to be easy pickings just because I'm a science nerd!
Be reasonable, Jimmy! The guy headbutts bowling balls!
I may as well get it over with, May.
I won't let that jock terrorize me for the rest of my life.
I can't live like that!
ECONOMICS II

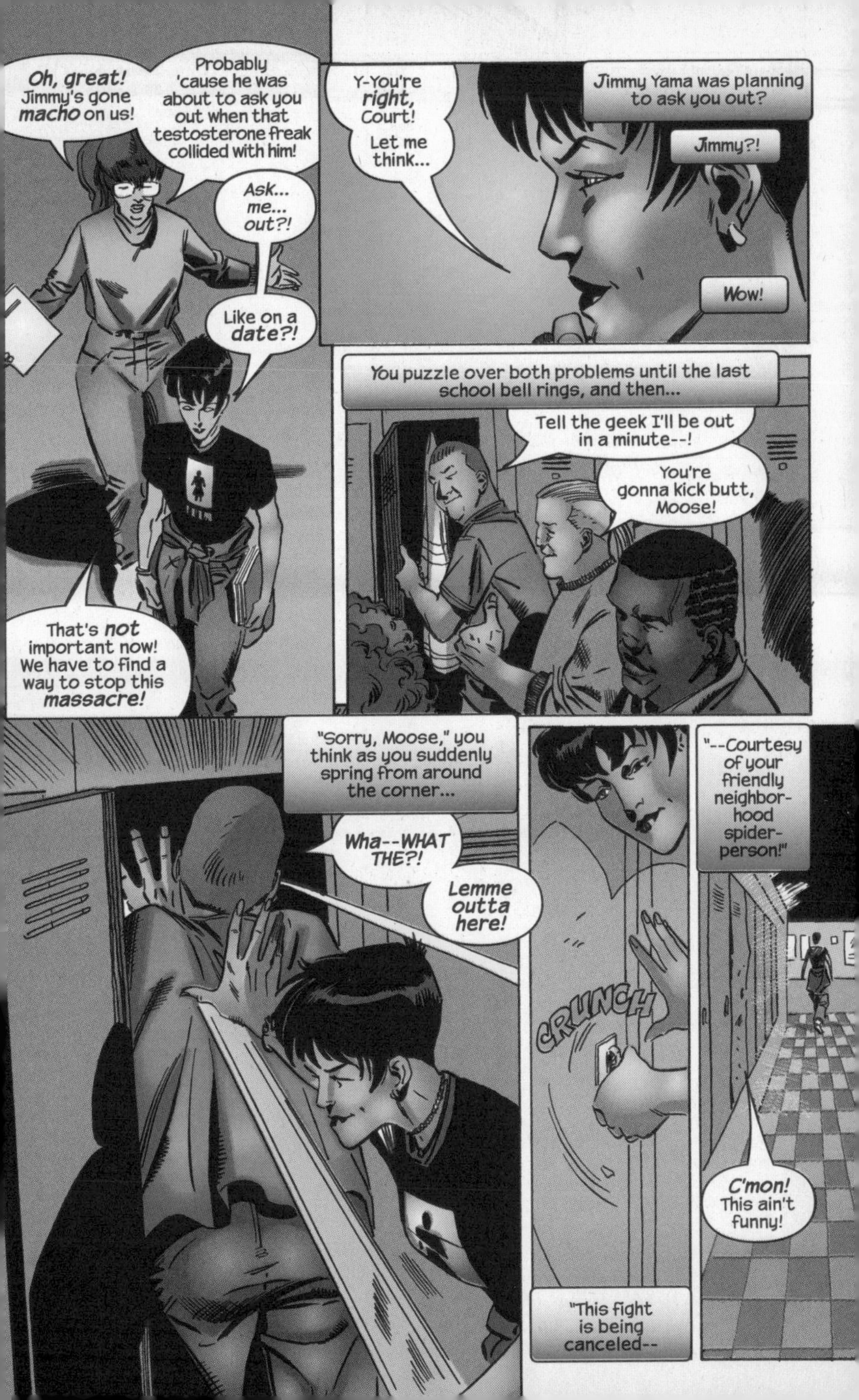
Oh, great! Jimmy's gone macho on us!
Probably 'cause he was about to ask you out when that testosterone freak collided with him!
Ask... me... out?!
Like on a date?!
That's not important now! We have to find a way to stop this massacre!
Y-You're right, Court!
Let me think...
Jimmy Yama was planning to ask you out?
Jimmy?!
Wow!
You puzzle over both problems until the last school bell rings, and then...
Tell the geek I'll be out in a minute--!
You're gonna kick butt, Moose!
"Sorry, Moose," you think as you suddenly spring from around the corner...
Wha--WHAT THE?!
Lemme outta here!
CRUNCH
"This fight is being canceled--
"--Courtesy of your friendly neighbor-hood spider-person!"
C'mon! This ain't funny!

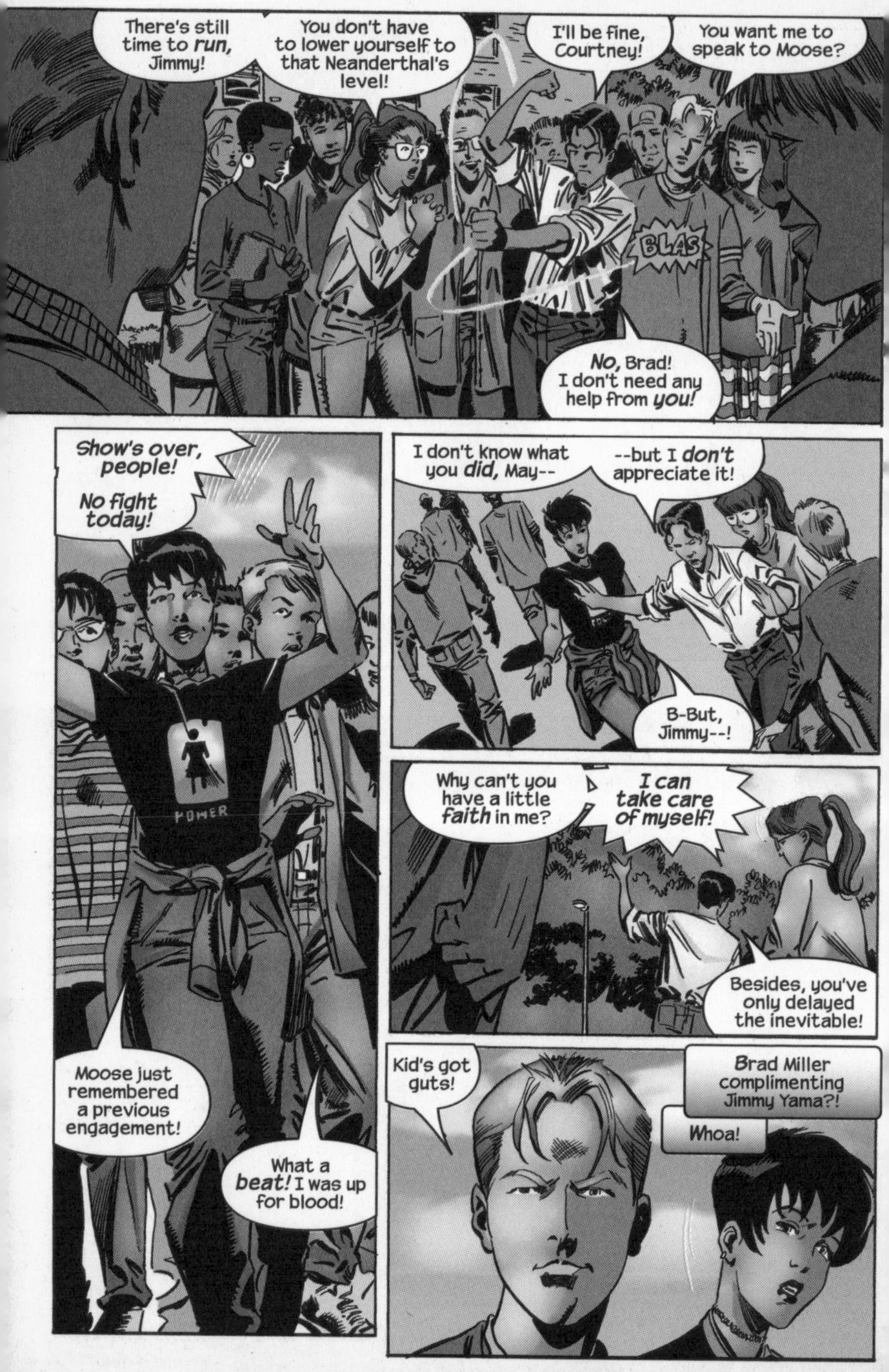
There's still time to *run,* Jimmy!
You don't have to lower yourself to that Neanderthal's level!
I'll be fine, Courtney!
You want me to speak to Moose?
No, Brad! I don't need any help from *you!*
BLAS
Show's over, people!
No fight today!
POWER
Moose just remembered a previous engagement!
What a *beat!* I was up for blood!
I don't know what you *did,* May--
--but I *don't* appreciate it!
B-But, Jimmy--!
Why can't you have a little *faith* in me?
I can take care of myself!
Besides, you've only delayed the inevitable!
Kid's got guts!
Brad Miller complimenting Jimmy Yama?!
Whoa!

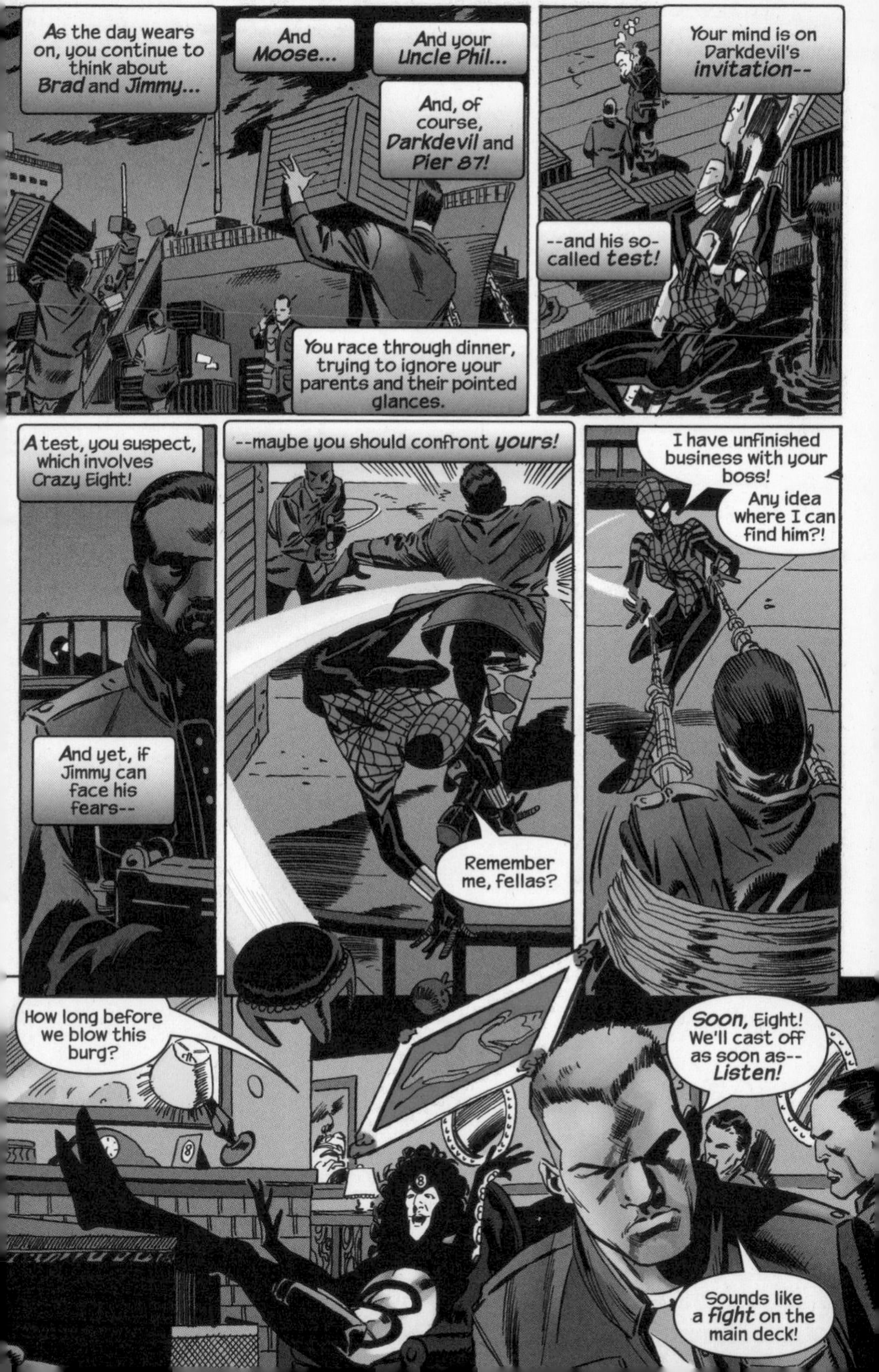

As the day wears on, you continue to think about Brad and Jimmy...
And Moose...
And your Uncle Phil...
And, of course, Darkdevil and Pier 87!
You race through dinner, trying to ignore your parents and their pointed glances.
Your mind is on Darkdevil's invitation--
--and his so-called test!
A test, you suspect, which involves Crazy Eight!
And yet, if Jimmy can face his fears--
--maybe you should confront yours!
Remember me, fellas?
I have unfinished business with your boss!
Any idea where I can find him?!
How long before we blow this burg?
Soon, Eight! We'll cast off as soon as-- Listen!
Sounds like a fight on the main deck!

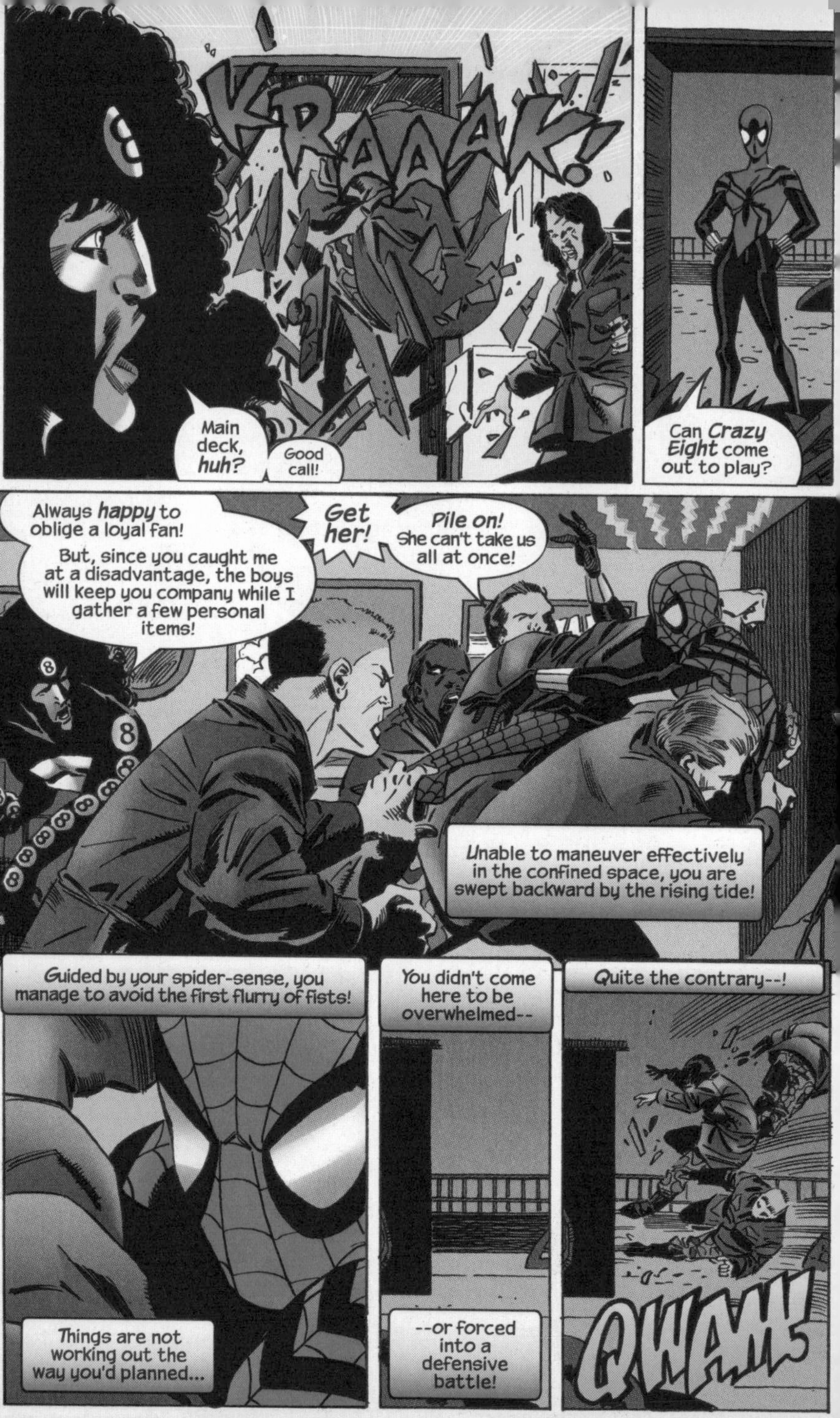
KRAAAK!
Main deck, huh?
Good call!
Can Crazy Eight come out to play?
Always happy to oblige a loyal fan!
But, since you caught me at a disadvantage, the boys will keep you company while I gather a few personal items!
Get her!
Pile on! She can't take us all at once!
Unable to maneuver effectively in the confined space, you are swept backward by the rising tide!
Guided by your spider-sense, you manage to avoid the first flurry of fists!
Things are not working out the way you'd planned...
You didn't come here to be overwhelmed--
--or forced into a defensive battle!
Quite the contrary--!
QWAH!

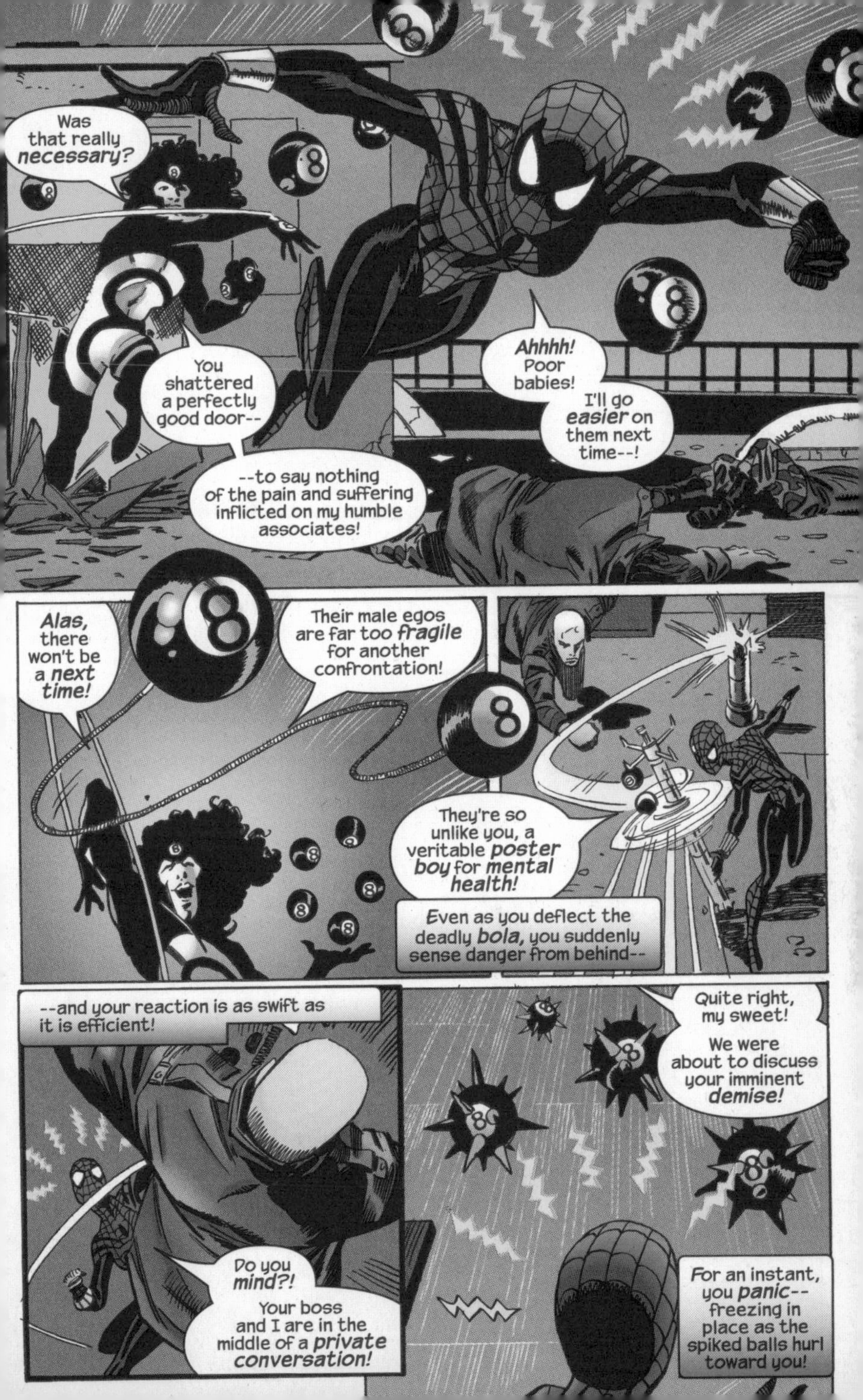

Was that really *necessary?*
You shattered a perfectly good door--
--to say nothing of the pain and suffering inflicted on my humble associates!
Ahhhh! Poor babies!
I'll go *easier* on them next time--!
Alas, there won't be a *next time!*
Their male egos are far too *fragile* for another confrontation!
They're so unlike you, a veritable *poster boy* for *mental health!*
Even as you deflect the deadly *bola,* you suddenly sense danger from behind--
--and your reaction is as swift as it is efficient!
Do you *mind?!*
Your boss and I are in the middle of a *private conversation!*
Quite right, my sweet!
We were about to discuss your imminent *demise!*
For an instant, you *panic--* freezing in place as the spiked balls hurl toward you!

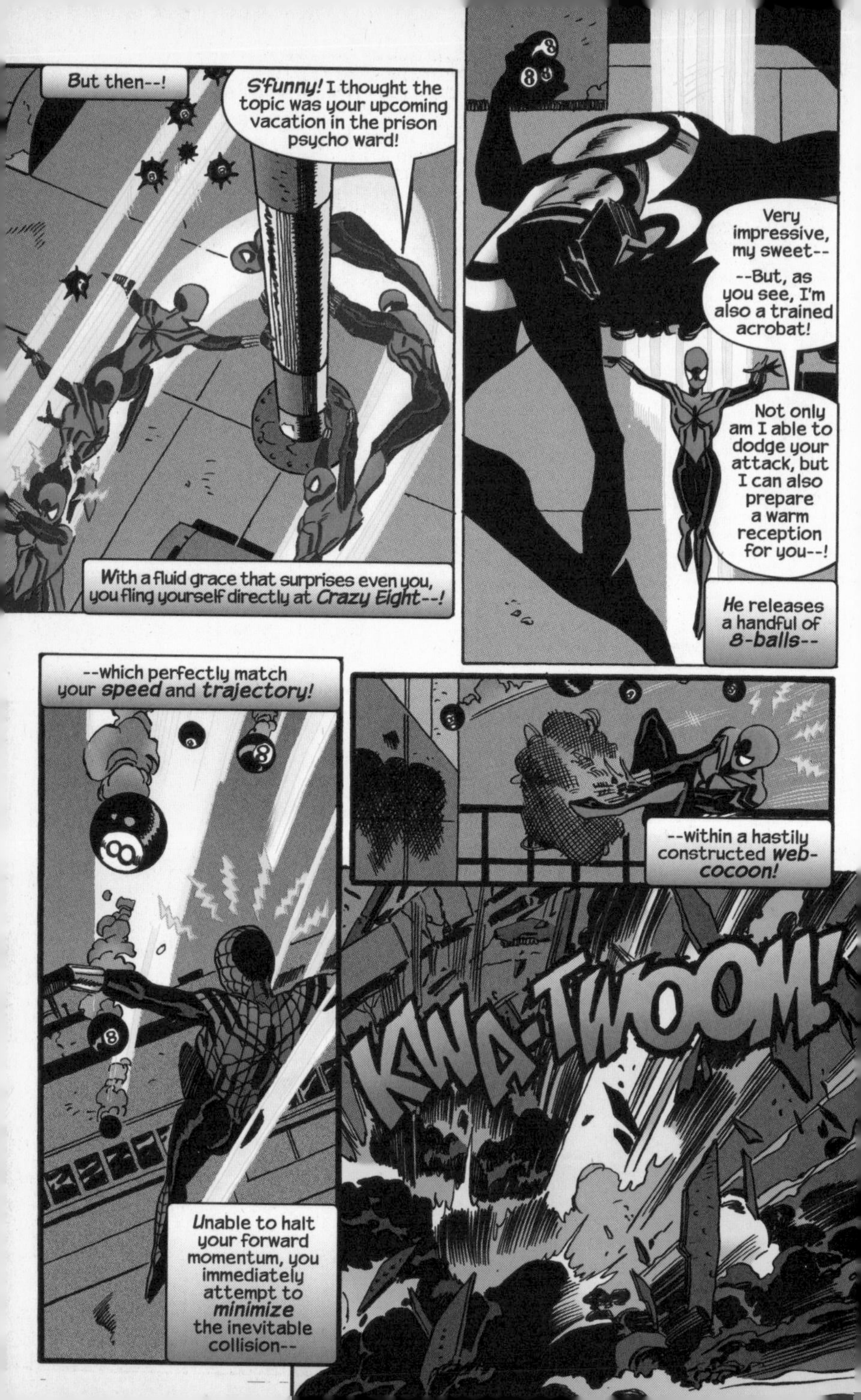
But then--!
S'funny! I thought the topic was your upcoming vacation in the prison psycho ward!
With a fluid grace that surprises even you, you fling yourself directly at Crazy Eight--!
Very impressive, my sweet--
--But, as you see, I'm also a trained acrobat!
Not only am I able to dodge your attack, but I can also prepare a warm reception for you--!
He releases a handful of 8-balls--
--which perfectly match your speed and trajectory!
Unable to halt your forward momentum, you immediately attempt to minimize the inevitable collision--
--within a hastily constructed web-cocoon!
KWA-THOOM!

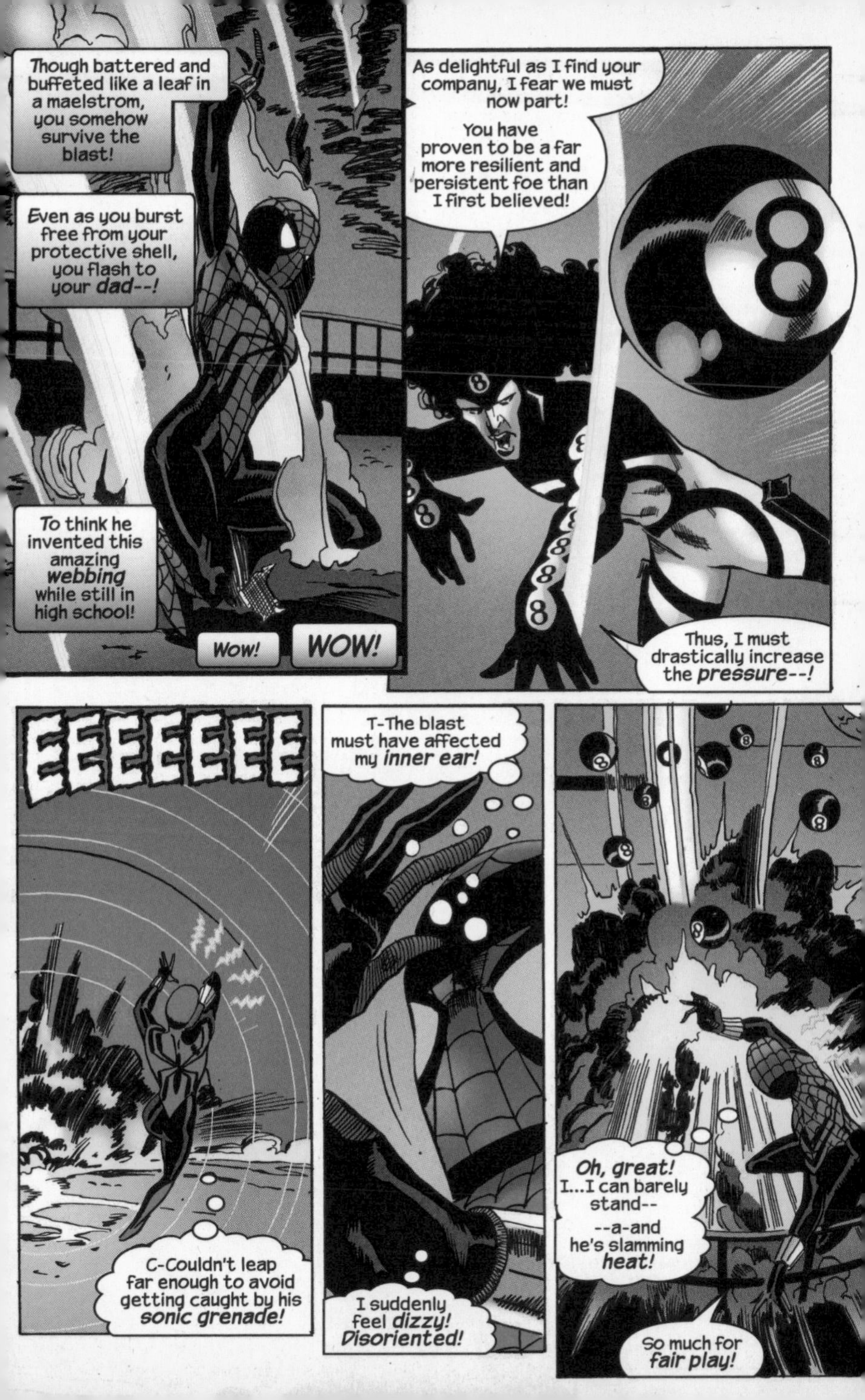

Though battered and buffeted like a leaf in a maelstrom, you somehow survive the blast!
Even as you burst free from your protective shell, you flash to your *dad*--!
To think he invented this amazing *webbing* while still in high school!
Wow!
WOW!
As delightful as I find your company, I fear we must now part!
You have proven to be a far more resilient and persistent foe than I first believed!
Thus, I must drastically increase the *pressure*--!
EEEEEEE
C-Couldn't leap far enough to avoid getting caught by his *sonic grenade!*
T-The blast must have affected my *inner ear!*
I suddenly feel *dizzy! Disoriented!*
Oh, great! I...I can barely stand--
--a-and he's slamming *heat!*
So much for *fair play!*

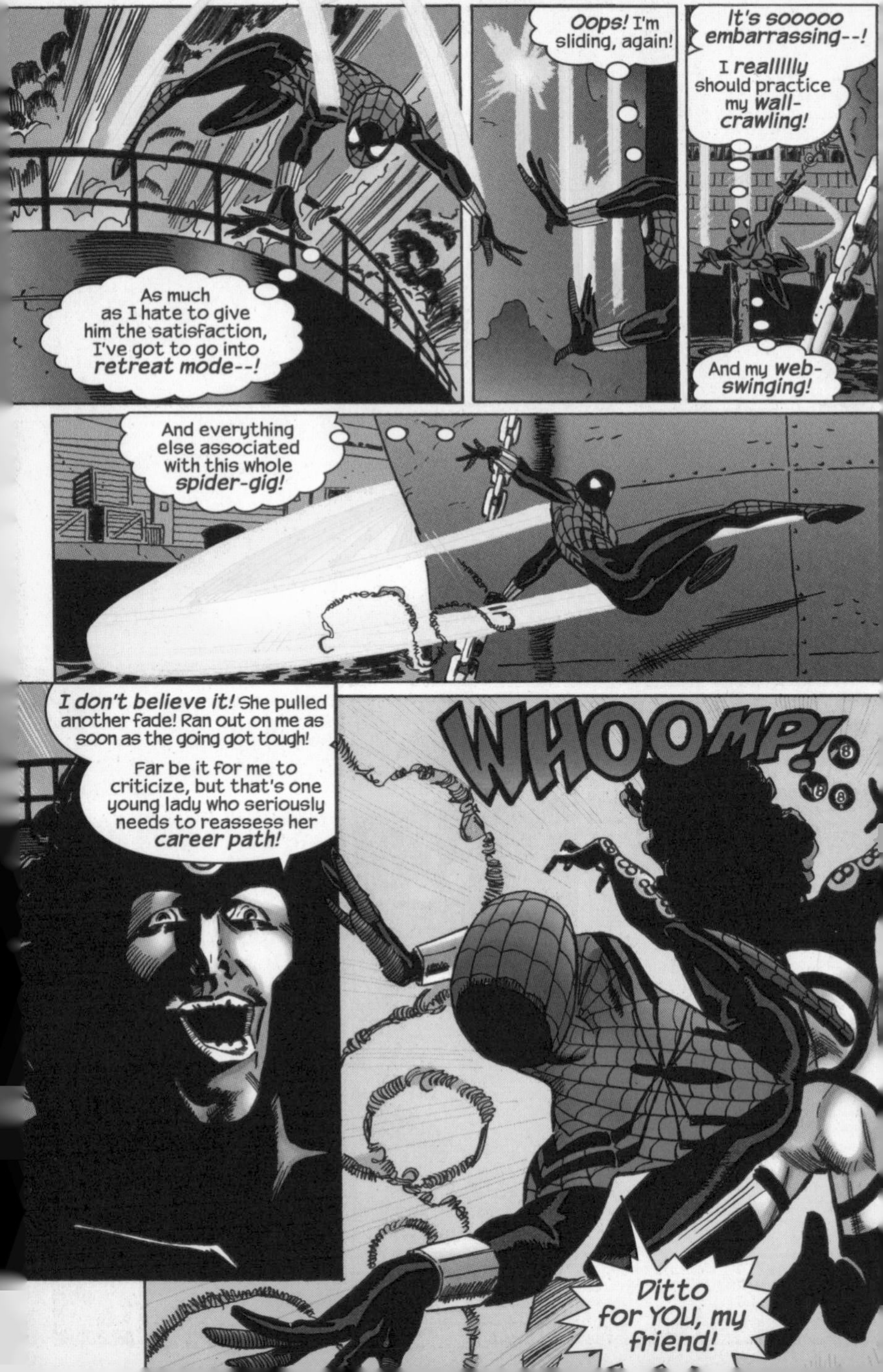

As much as I hate to give him the satisfaction, I've got to go into retreat mode--!
Oops! I'm sliding, again!
It's sooooo embarrassing--!
I reallllly should practice my wall-crawling!
And my web-swinging!
And everything else associated with this whole spider-gig!
I don't believe it! She pulled another fade! Ran out on me as soon as the going got tough!
Far be it for me to criticize, but that's one young lady who seriously needs to reassess her career path!
WHOOMP!
Ditto for YOU, my friend!

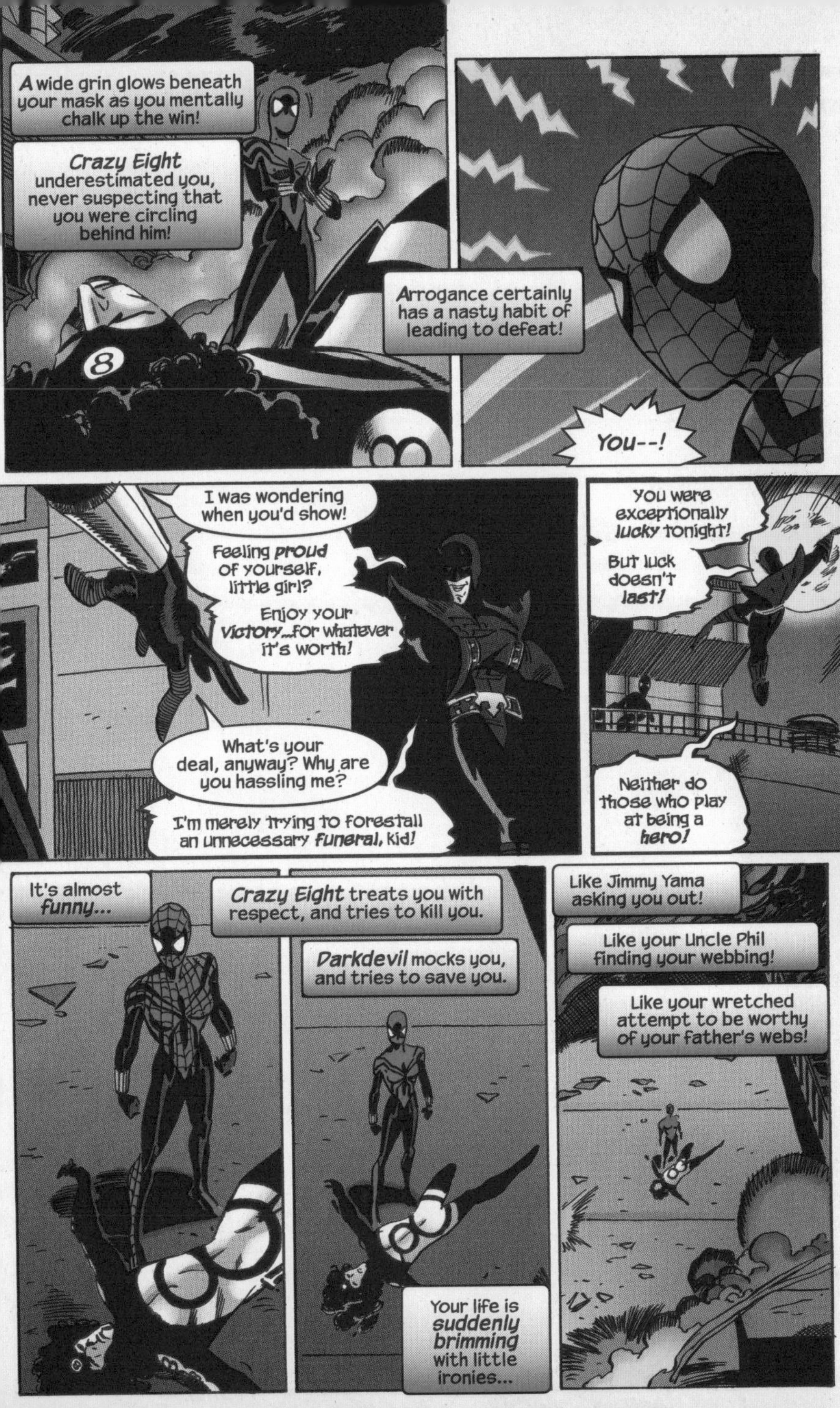

A wide grin glows beneath your mask as you mentally chalk up the win!
Crazy Eight underestimated you, never suspecting that you were circling behind him!
Arrogance certainly has a nasty habit of leading to defeat!
You--!
I was wondering when you'd show!
Feeling *proud* of yourself, little girl?
Enjoy your *victory*...for whatever it's worth!
What's your deal, anyway? Why are you hassling me?
I'm merely trying to forestall an unnecessary *funeral*, kid!
You were exceptionally *lucky* tonight!
But luck doesn't *last!*
Neither do those who play at being a *hero!*
It's almost *funny...*
Crazy Eight treats you with respect, and tries to kill you.
Darkdevil mocks you, and tries to save you.
Like Jimmy Yama asking you out!
Like your Uncle Phil finding your webbing!
Like your wretched attempt to be worthy of your father's webs!
Your life is *suddenly brimming* with little ironies...

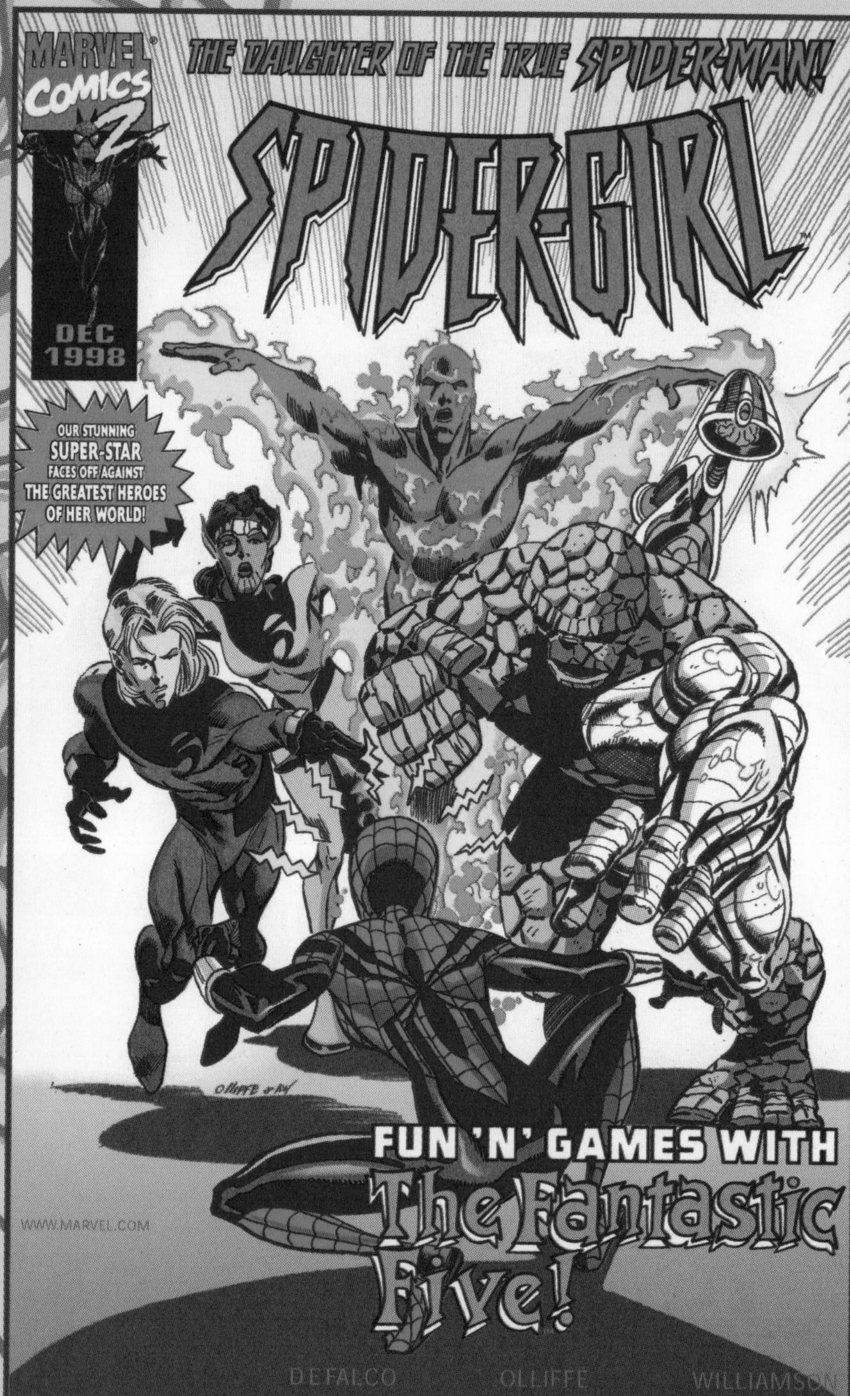
MARVEL COMICS 2
THE DAUGHTER OF THE TRUE SPIDER-MAN!
SPIDER-GIRL
DEC 1998
OUR STUNNING SUPER-STAR FACES OFF AGAINST THE GREATEST HEROES OF HER WORLD!
FUN 'N' GAMES WITH The Fantastic Five!
WWW.MARVEL.COM
DEFALCO
OLLIFFE
WILLIAMSON

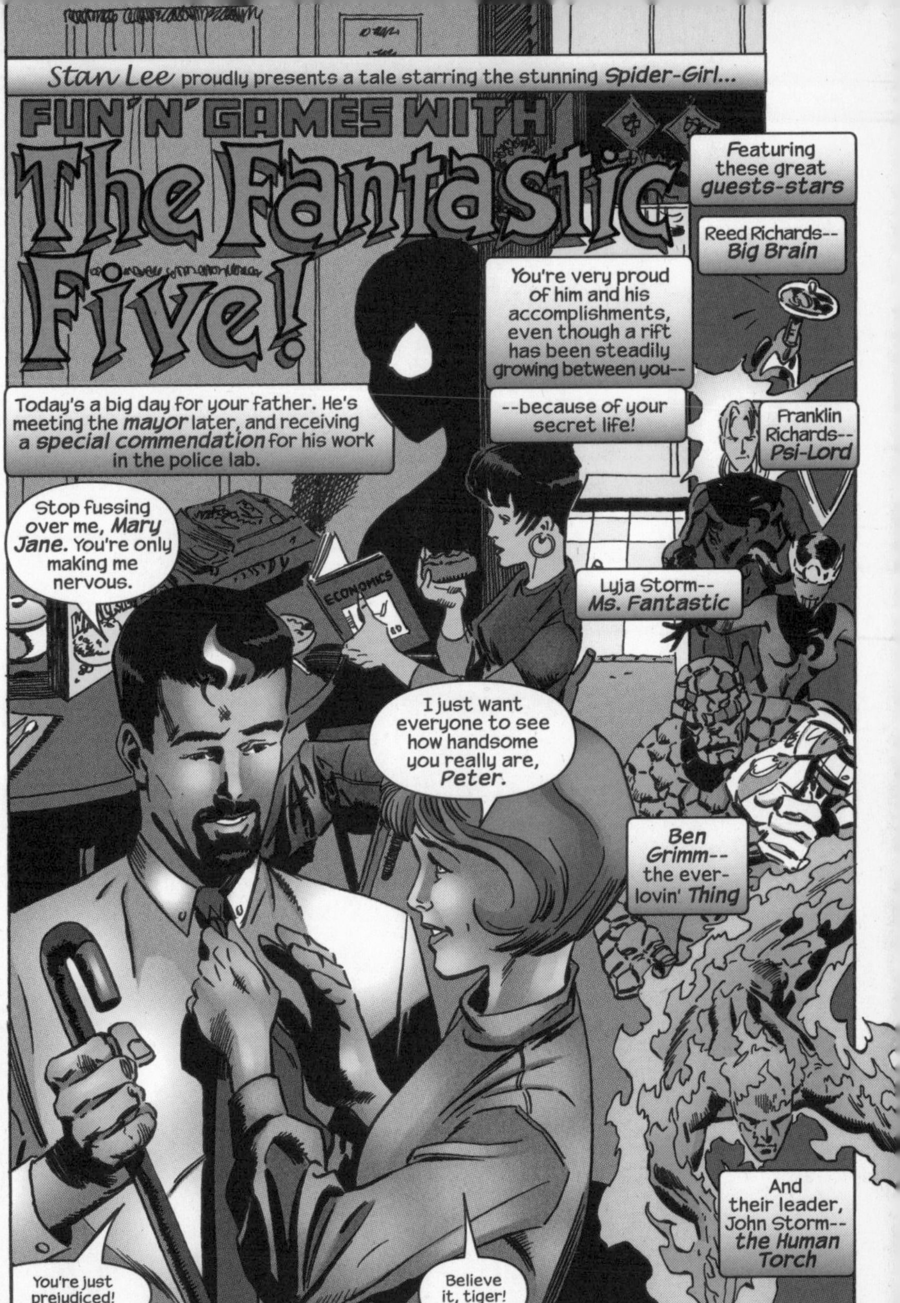

Stan Lee proudly presents a tale starring the stunning Spider-Girl...
FUN 'N' GAMES WITH The Fantastic Five!
Featuring these great guests-stars
Reed Richards-- Big Brain
You're very proud of him and his accomplishments, even though a rift has been steadily growing between you--
Today's a big day for your father. He's meeting the mayor later, and receiving a special commendation for his work in the police lab.
--because of your secret life!
Franklin Richards-- Psi-Lord
Stop fussing over me, Mary Jane. You're only making me nervous.
Lyja Storm-- Ms. Fantastic
ECONOMICS
I just want everyone to see how handsome you really are, Peter.
Ben Grimm-- the ever-lovin' Thing
And their leader, John Storm-- the Human Torch
You're just prejudiced!
Believe it, tiger!

Tom DeFalco writer | Pat Olliffe penciler | Al Williamson inker | Dave Sharpe letterer | Christie Scheele colorist | Bob Harras chief

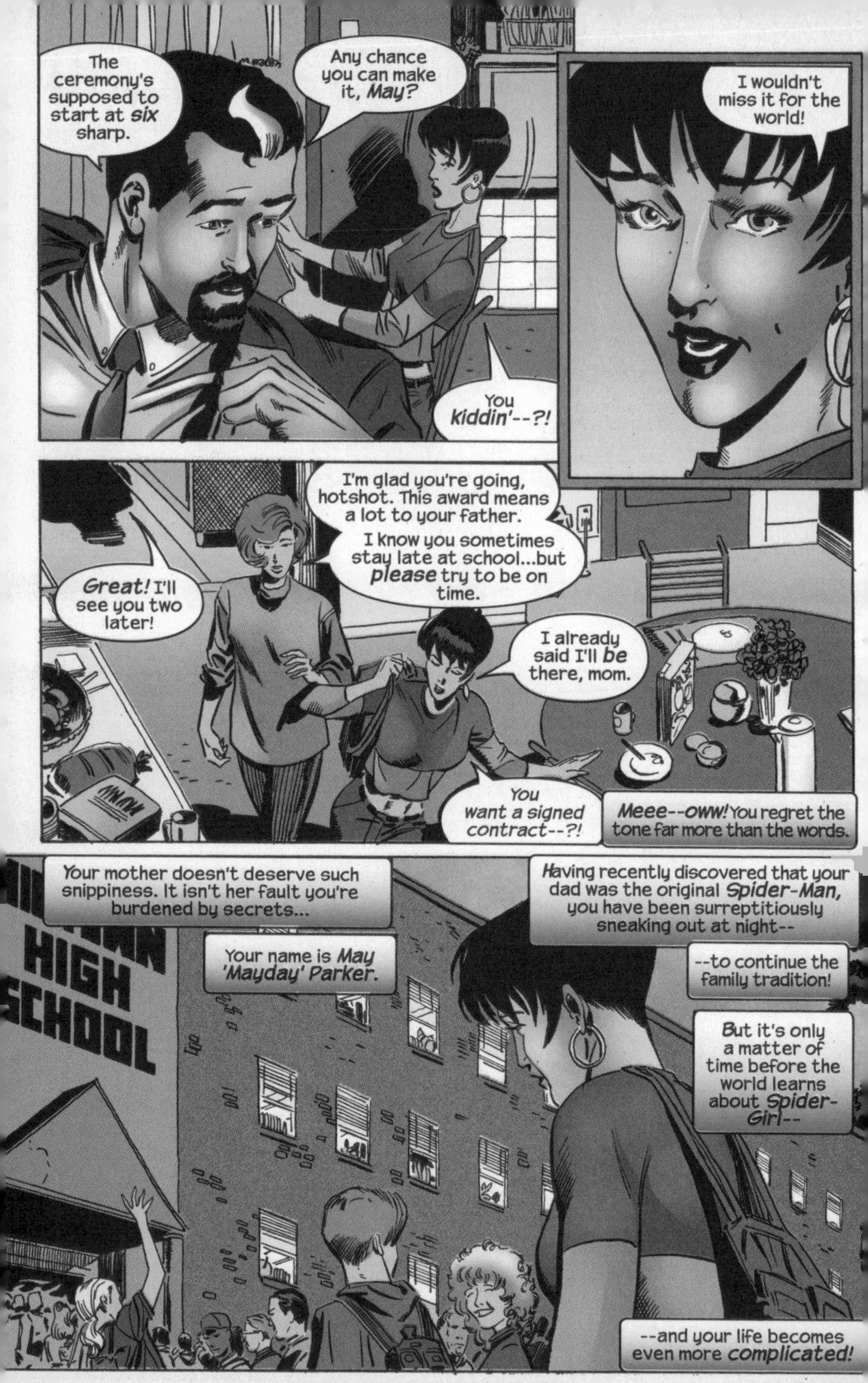

The ceremony's supposed to start at *six* sharp.
Any chance you can make it, *May?*
You *kiddin'*--?!
I wouldn't miss it for the world!
I'm glad you're going, hotshot. This award means a lot to your father.
I know you sometimes stay late at school...but *please* try to be on time.
Great! I'll see you two later!
I already said I'll *be* there, mom.
You want a signed contract--?!
Meee--oww! You regret the tone far more than the words.
Your mother doesn't deserve such snippiness. It isn't her fault you're burdened by secrets...
Your name is *May 'Mayday' Parker.*
Having recently discovered that your dad was the original *Spider-Man,* you have been surreptitiously sneaking out at night--
--to continue the family tradition!
But it's only a matter of time before the world learns about *Spider-Girl*--
--and your life becomes even more *complicated!*
HIGH SCHOOL

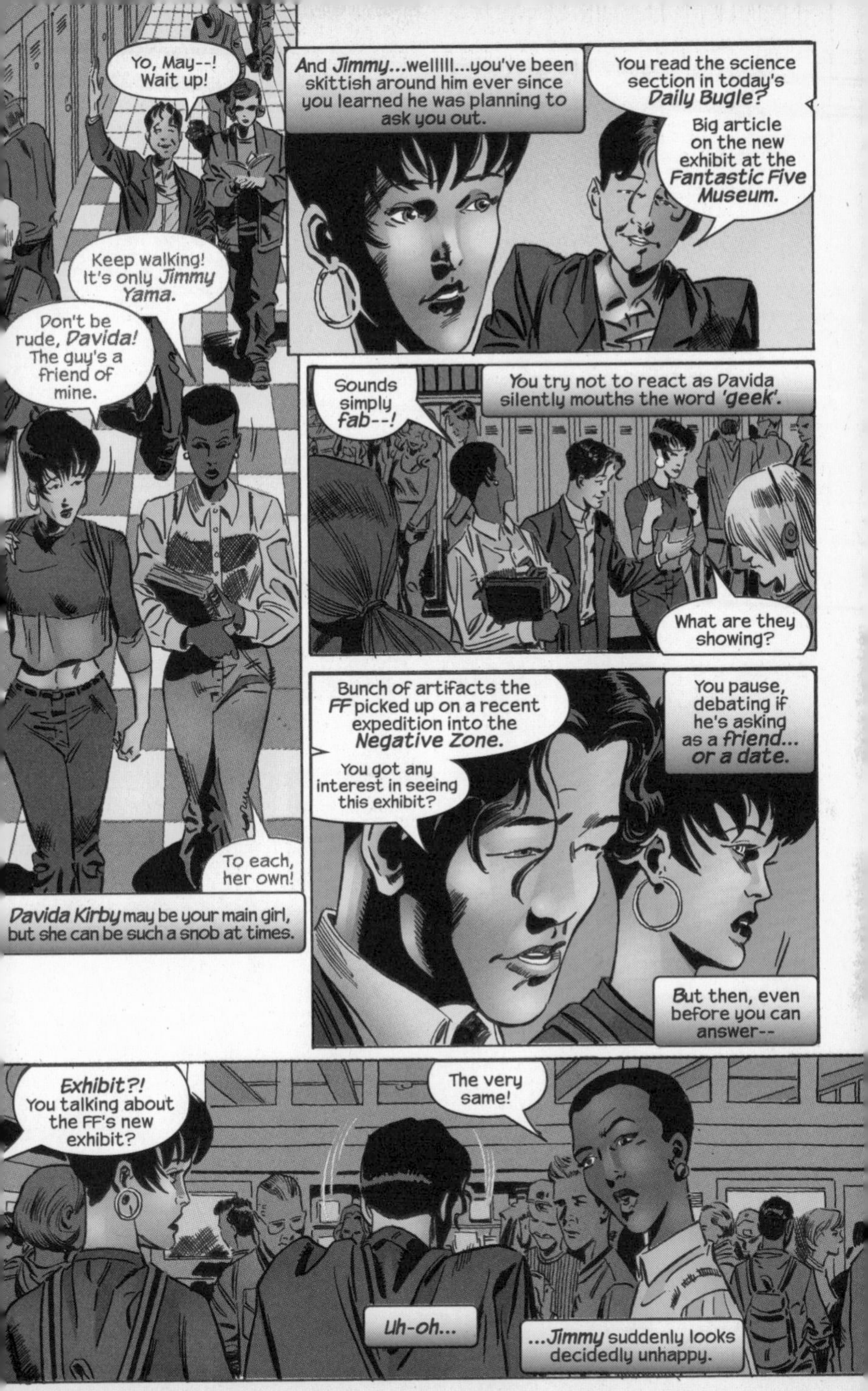
Yo, May--! Wait up!
Keep walking! It's only Jimmy Yama.
Don't be rude, Davida! The guy's a friend of mine.
To each, her own!
Davida Kirby may be your main girl, but she can be such a snob at times.
And Jimmy...wellll...you've been skittish around him ever since you learned he was planning to ask you out.
You read the science section in today's Daily Bugle?
Big article on the new exhibit at the Fantastic Five Museum.
Sounds simply fab--!
You try not to react as Davida silently mouths the word 'geek'.
What are they showing?
Bunch of artifacts the FF picked up on a recent expedition into the Negative Zone.
You got any interest in seeing this exhibit?
You pause, debating if he's asking as a friend... or a date.
But then, even before you can answer--
Exhibit?! You talking about the FF's new exhibit?
The very same!
Uh-oh...
...Jimmy suddenly looks decidedly unhappy.

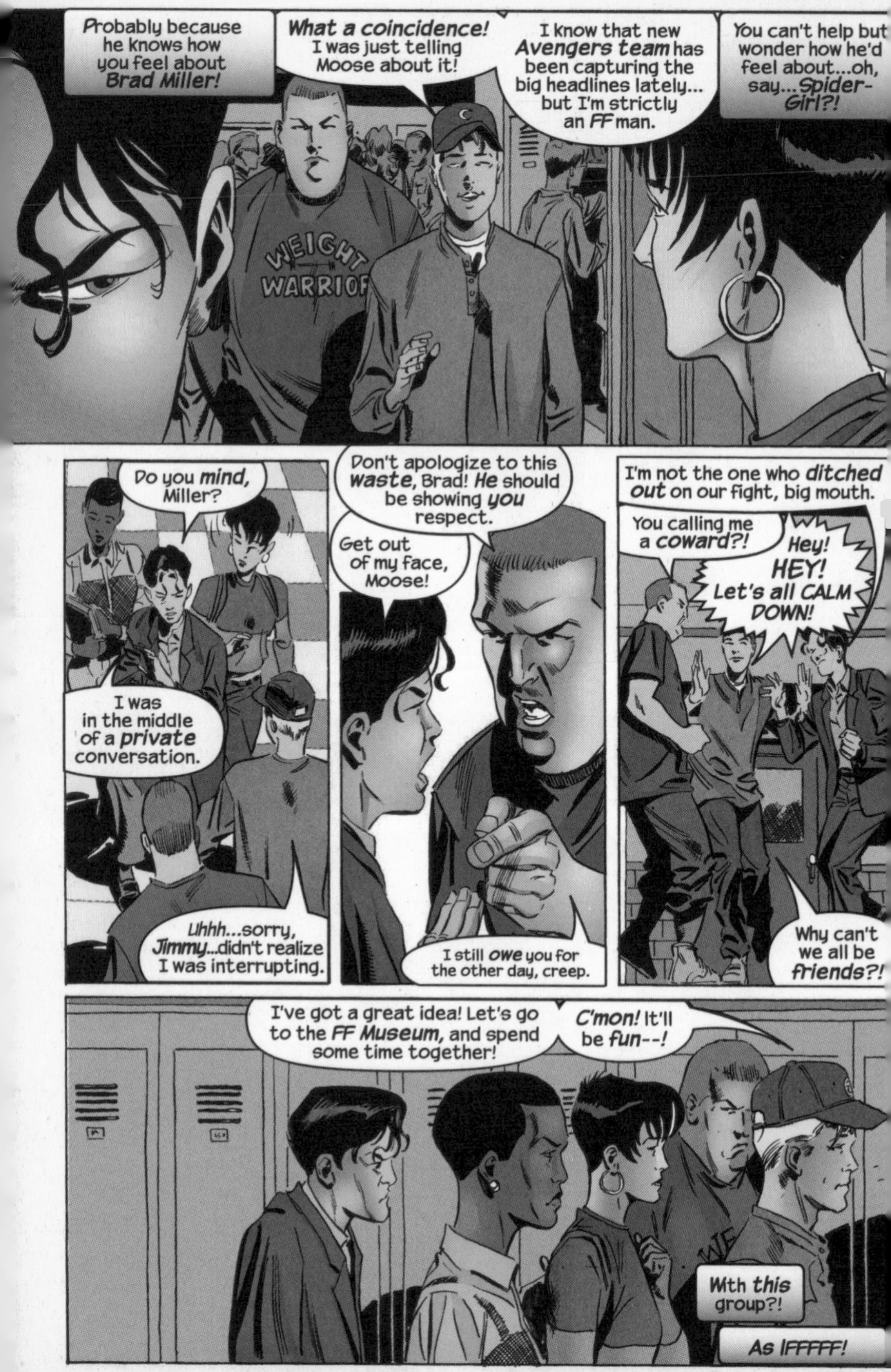
Probably because he knows how you feel about Brad Miller!
What a coincidence! I was just telling Moose about it!
I know that new Avengers team has been capturing the big headlines lately... but I'm strictly an FF man.
You can't help but wonder how he'd feel about...oh, say...Spider-Girl?!
WEIGHT WARRIOR
Do you mind, Miller?
I was in the middle of a private conversation.
Uhhh...sorry, Jimmy...didn't realize I was interrupting.
Don't apologize to this waste, Brad! He should be showing you respect.
Get out of my face, Moose!
I still owe you for the other day, creep.
I'm not the one who ditched out on our fight, big mouth.
You calling me a coward?!
Hey! HEY! Let's all CALM DOWN!
Why can't we all be friends?!
I've got a great idea! Let's go to the FF Museum, and spend some time together!
C'mon! It'll be fun--!
With this group?!
As IFFFFF!

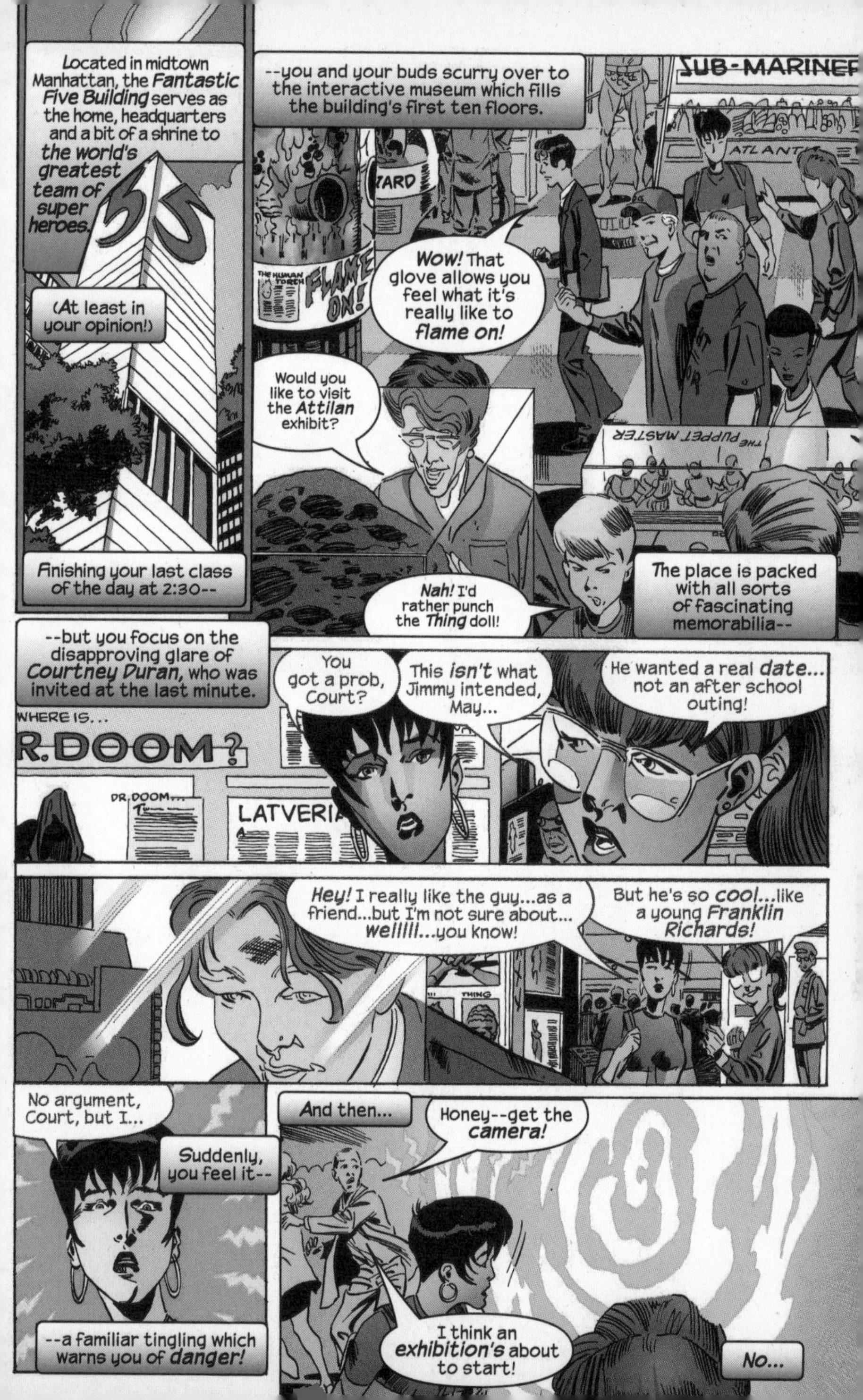
Located in midtown Manhattan, the Fantastic Five Building serves as the home, headquarters and a bit of a shrine to the world's greatest team of super heroes.
(At least in your opinion!)
Finishing your last class of the day at 2:30--
--you and your buds scurry over to the interactive museum which fills the building's first ten floors.
SUB-MARINER
ATLANTI
THE HUMAN TORCH
FLAME ON!
Wow! That glove allows you feel what it's really like to flame on!
Would you like to visit the Attilan exhibit?
THE PUPPET MASTER
Nah! I'd rather punch the Thing doll!
The place is packed with all sorts of fascinating memorabilia--
--but you focus on the disapproving glare of Courtney Duran, who was invited at the last minute.
WHERE IS...
R.DOOM?
DR. DOOM...
LATVERIA
You got a prob, Court?
This isn't what Jimmy intended, May...
He wanted a real date... not an after school outing!
Hey! I really like the guy...as a friend...but I'm not sure about... welllll...you know!
But he's so cool...like a young Franklin Richards!
THING
No argument, Court, but I...
Suddenly, you feel it--
--a familiar tingling which warns you of danger!
And then...
Honey--get the camera!
I think an exhibition's about to start!
No...

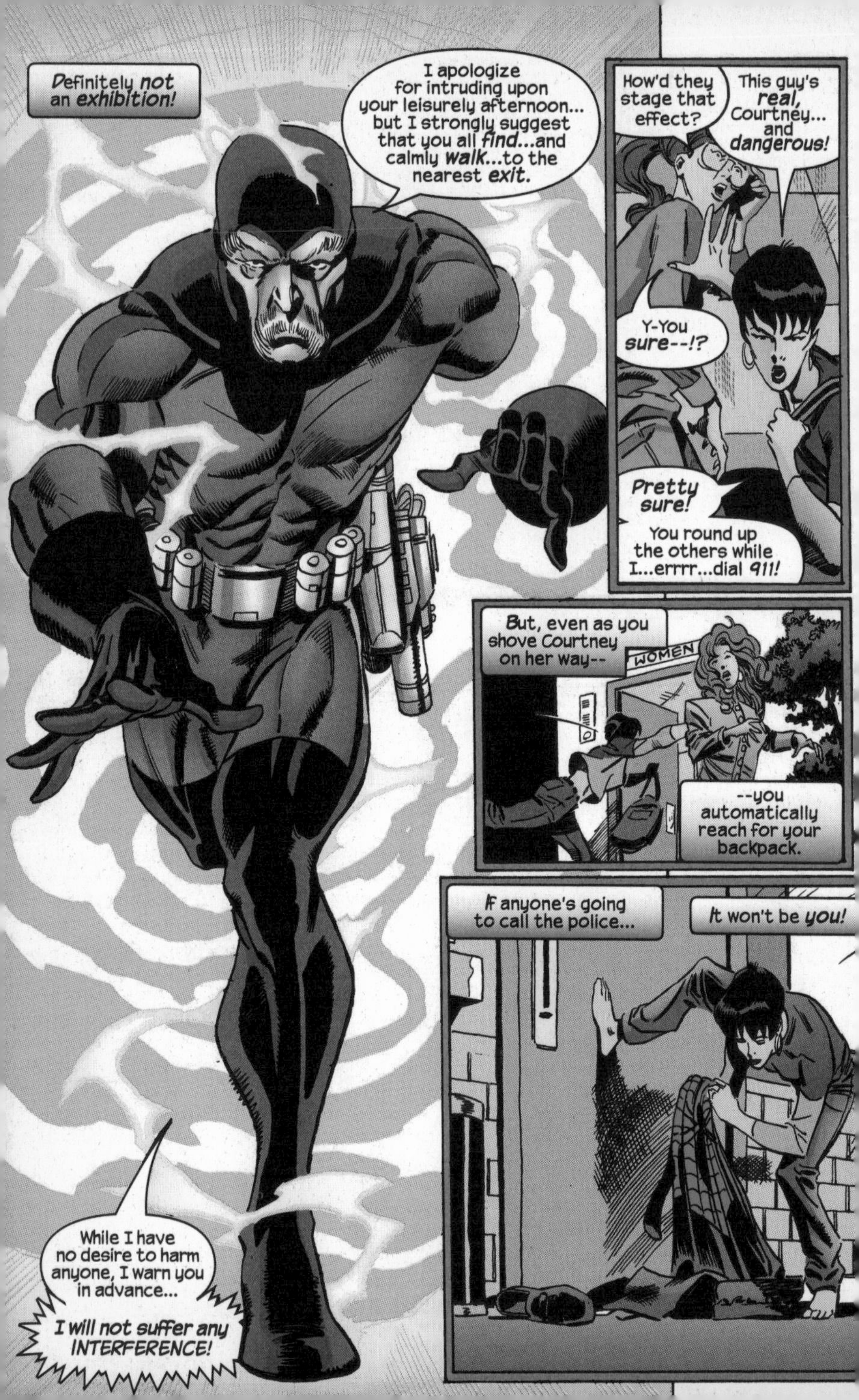
Definitely not an exhibition!
I apologize for intruding upon your leisurely afternoon... but I strongly suggest that you all find...and calmly walk...to the nearest exit.
While I have no desire to harm anyone, I warn you in advance...
I will not suffer any INTERFERENCE!
How'd they stage that effect?
This guy's real, Courtney... and dangerous!
Y-You sure--!?
Pretty sure!
You round up the others while I...errrr...dial 911!
But, even as you shove Courtney on her way--
WOMEN
--you automatically reach for your backpack.
If anyone's going to call the police...
It won't be you!

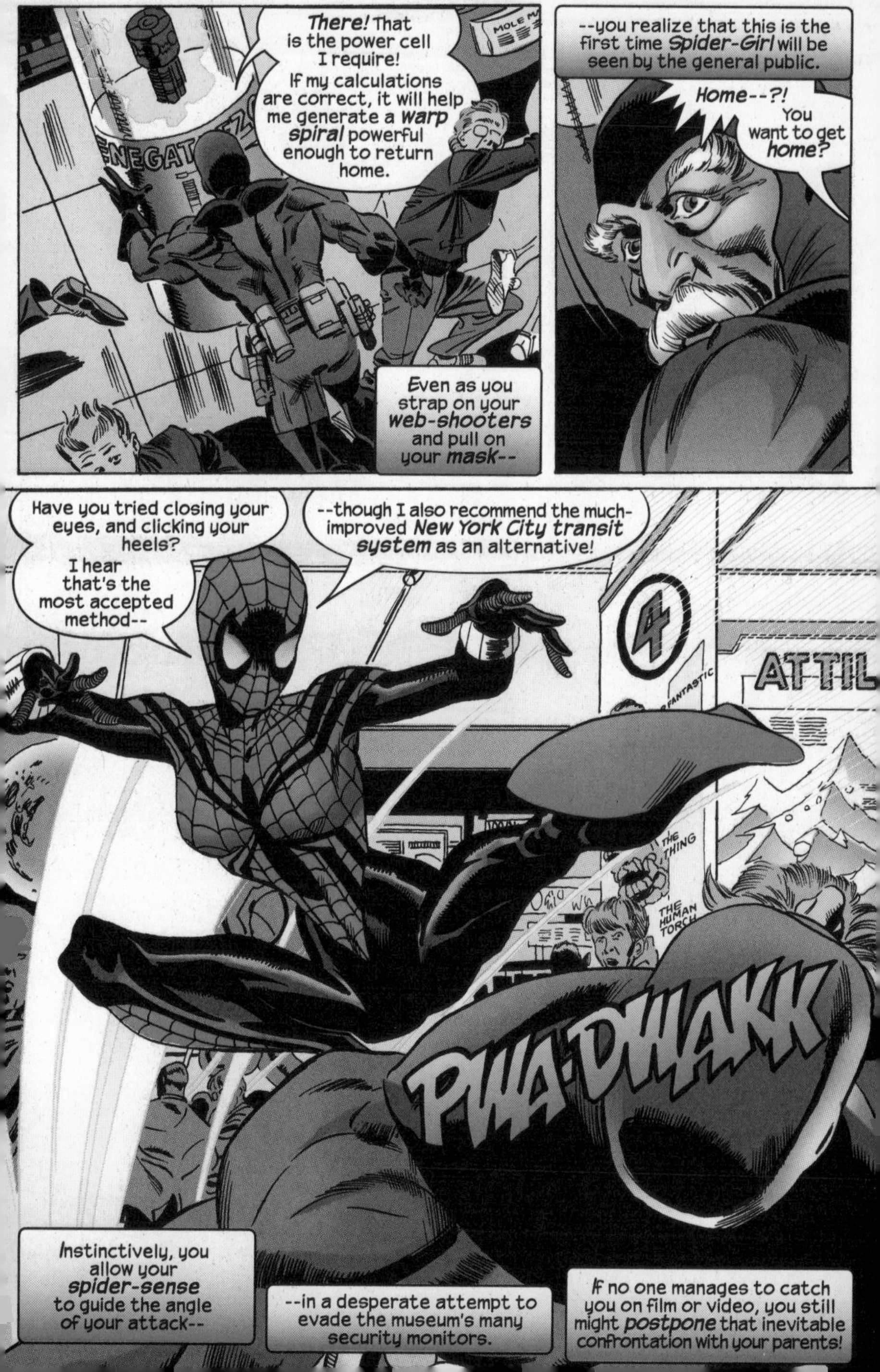

There! That is the power cell I require! If my calculations are correct, it will help me generate a warp spiral powerful enough to return home.
Even as you strap on your web-shooters and pull on your mask--
--you realize that this is the first time Spider-Girl will be seen by the general public.
Home--?! You want to get home?
Have you tried closing your eyes, and clicking your heels? I hear that's the most accepted method--
--though I also recommend the much-improved New York City transit system as an alternative!
FANTASTIC
ATTIL
THE THING
THE HUMAN TORCH
PWA-DWAKK
Instinctively, you allow your spider-sense to guide the angle of your attack--
--in a desperate attempt to evade the museum's many security monitors.
If no one manages to catch you on film or video, you still might postpone that inevitable confrontation with your parents!

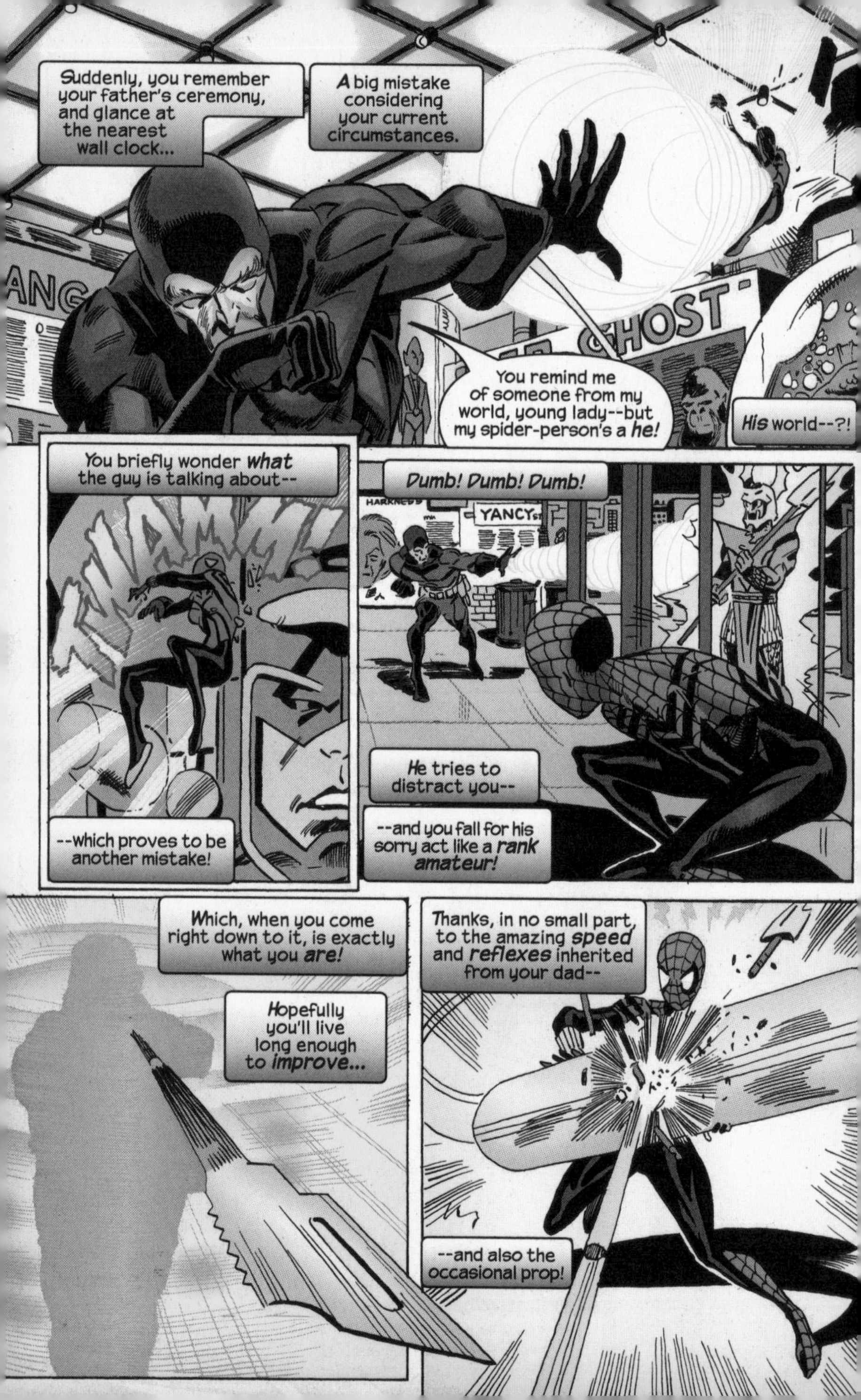
Suddenly, you remember your father's ceremony, and glance at the nearest wall clock...
A big mistake considering your current circumstances.
You remind me of someone from my world, young lady--but my spider-person's a he!
His world--?!
You briefly wonder what the guy is talking about--
--which proves to be another mistake!
Dumb! Dumb! Dumb!
YANCY ST
He tries to distract you--
--and you fall for his sorry act like a rank amateur!
Which, when you come right down to it, is exactly what you are!
Hopefully you'll live long enough to improve...
Thanks, in no small part, to the amazing speed and reflexes inherited from your dad--
--and also the occasional prop!

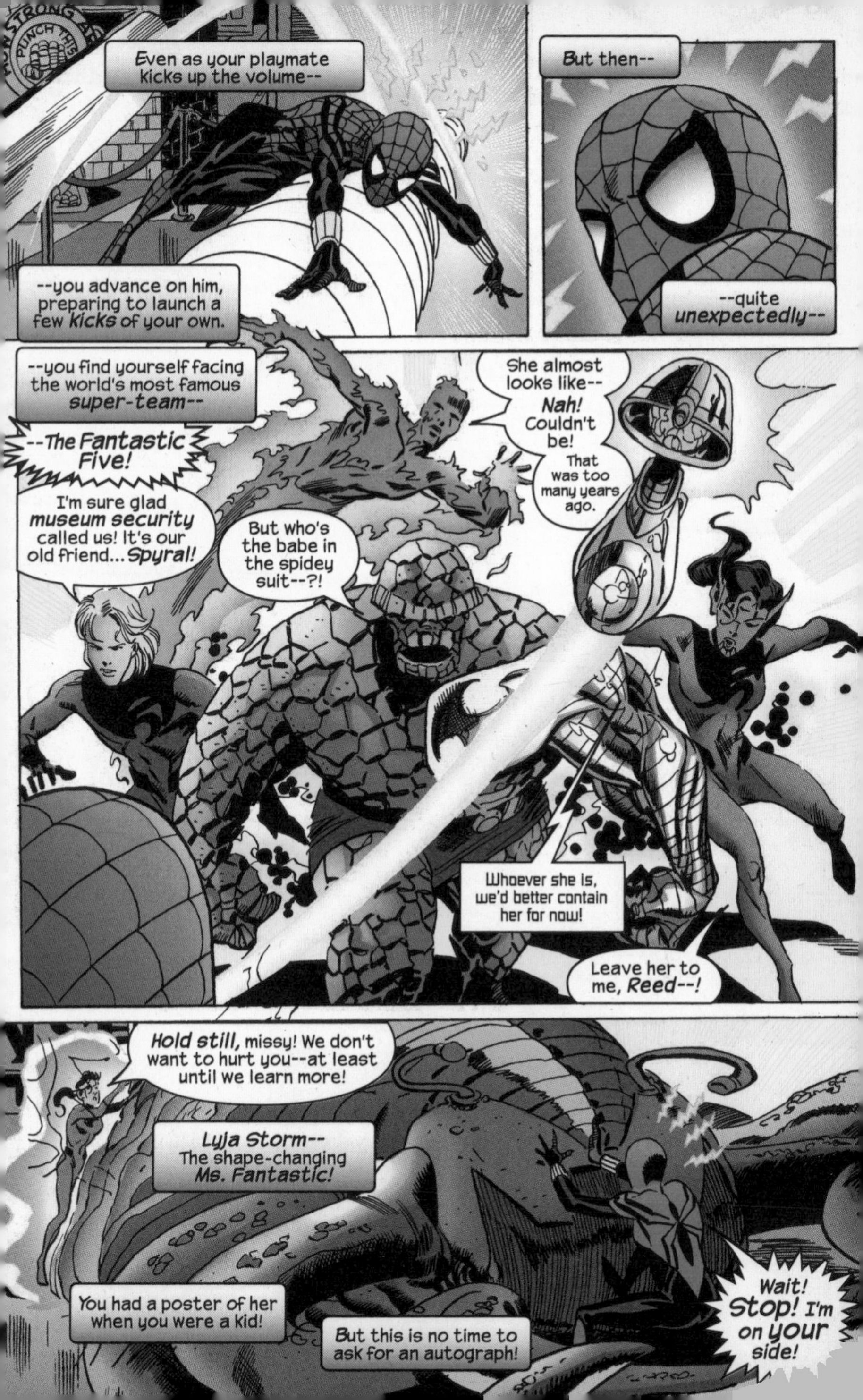

MONSTRONG AT
PUNCH THIS
Even as your playmate kicks up the volume--
--you advance on him, preparing to launch a few kicks of your own.
But then--
--quite unexpectedly--
--you find yourself facing the world's most famous super-team--
--The Fantastic Five!
She almost looks like-- Nah! Couldn't be!
That was too many years ago.
I'm sure glad museum security called us! It's our old friend... Spyral!
But who's the babe in the spidey suit--?!
Whoever she is, we'd better contain her for now!
Leave her to me, Reed--!
Hold still, missy! We don't want to hurt you--at least until we learn more!
Lyja Storm-- The shape-changing Ms. Fantastic!
You had a poster of her when you were a kid!
But this is no time to ask for an autograph!
Wait! Stop! I'm on your side!

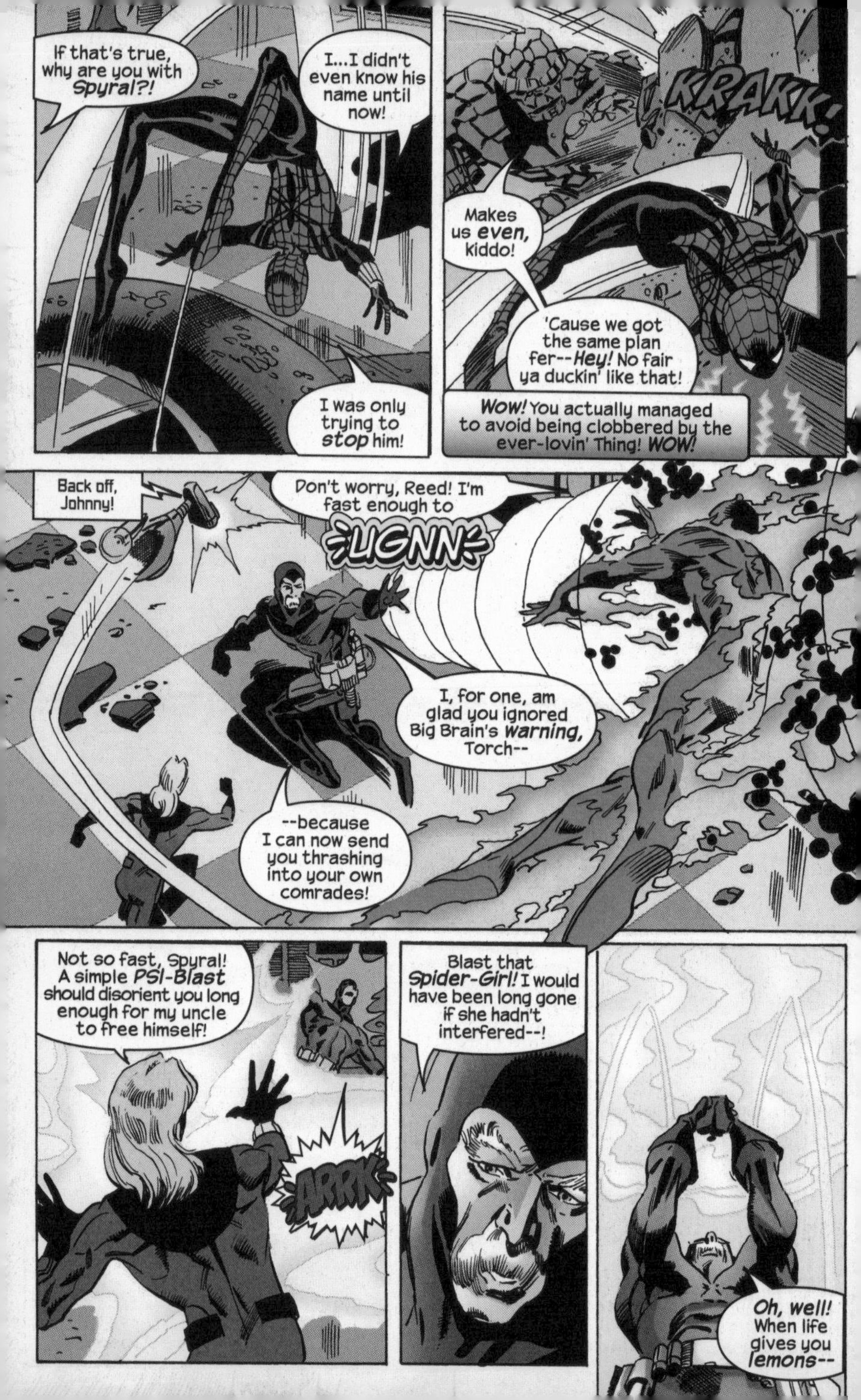
If that's true, why are you with Spyral?!
I...I didn't even know his name until now!
I was only trying to stop him!
KRAKK!
Makes us even, kiddo!
'Cause we got the same plan fer--Hey! No fair ya duckin' like that!
Wow! You actually managed to avoid being clobbered by the ever-lovin' Thing! WOW!
Back off, Johnny!
Don't worry, Reed! I'm fast enough to
UGNN
I, for one, am glad you ignored Big Brain's warning, Torch--
--because I can now send you thrashing into your own comrades!
Not so fast, Spyral! A simple PSI-Blast should disorient you long enough for my uncle to free himself!
ARRK
Blast that Spider-Girl! I would have been long gone if she hadn't interfered--!
Oh, well! When life gives you lemons--

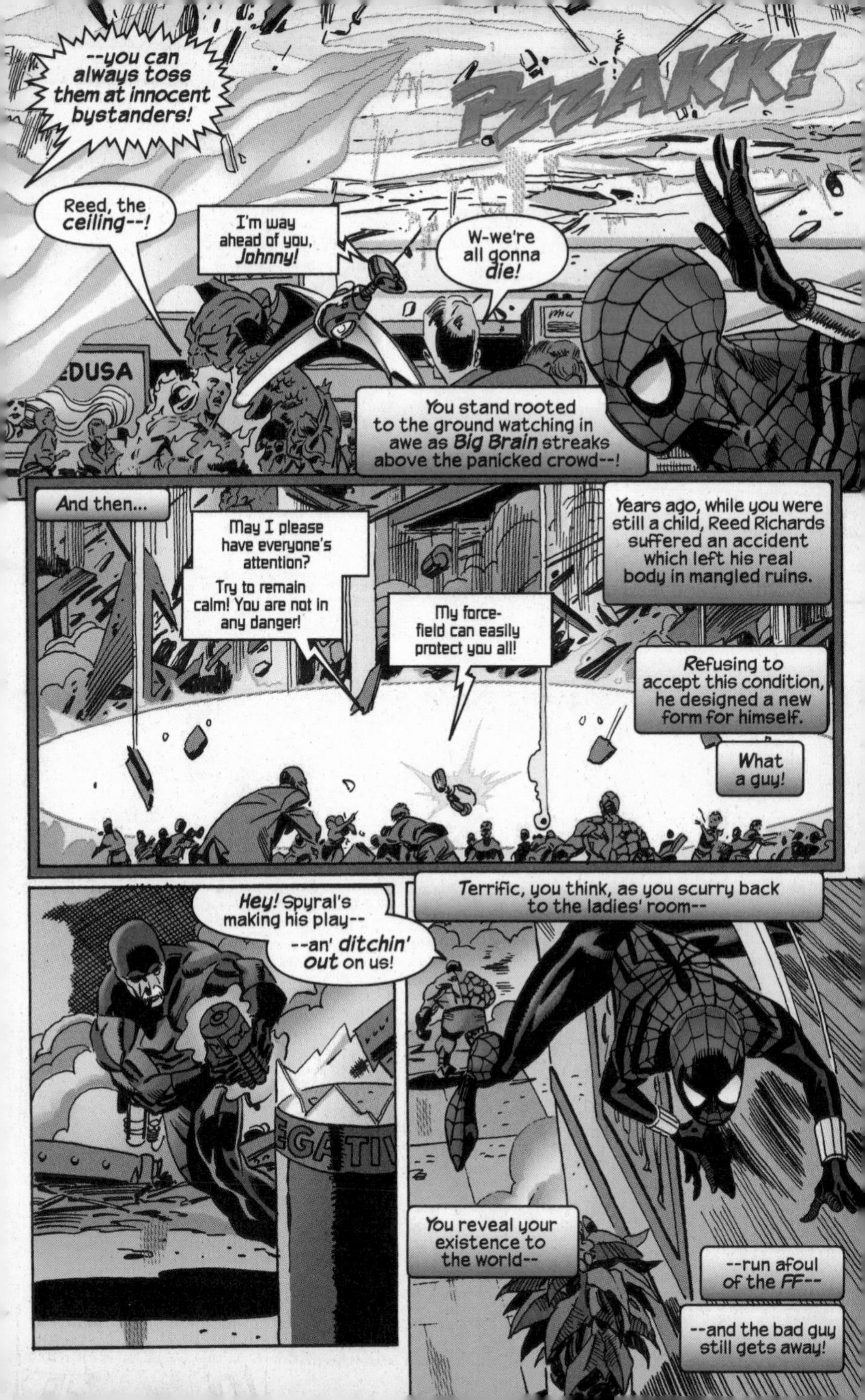
--you can always toss them at innocent bystanders!
PZZAKK!
Reed, the ceiling--!
I'm way ahead of you, Johnny!
W-we're all gonna die!
EDUSA
You stand rooted to the ground watching in awe as Big Brain streaks above the panicked crowd--!
And then...
May I please have everyone's attention?
Try to remain calm! You are not in any danger!
My force-field can easily protect you all!
Years ago, while you were still a child, Reed Richards suffered an accident which left his real body in mangled ruins.
Refusing to accept this condition, he designed a new form for himself.
What a guy!
Hey! Spyral's making his play--
--an' ditchin' out on us!
Terrific, you think, as you scurry back to the ladies' room--
You reveal your existence to the world--
--run afoul of the FF--
--and the bad guy still gets away!

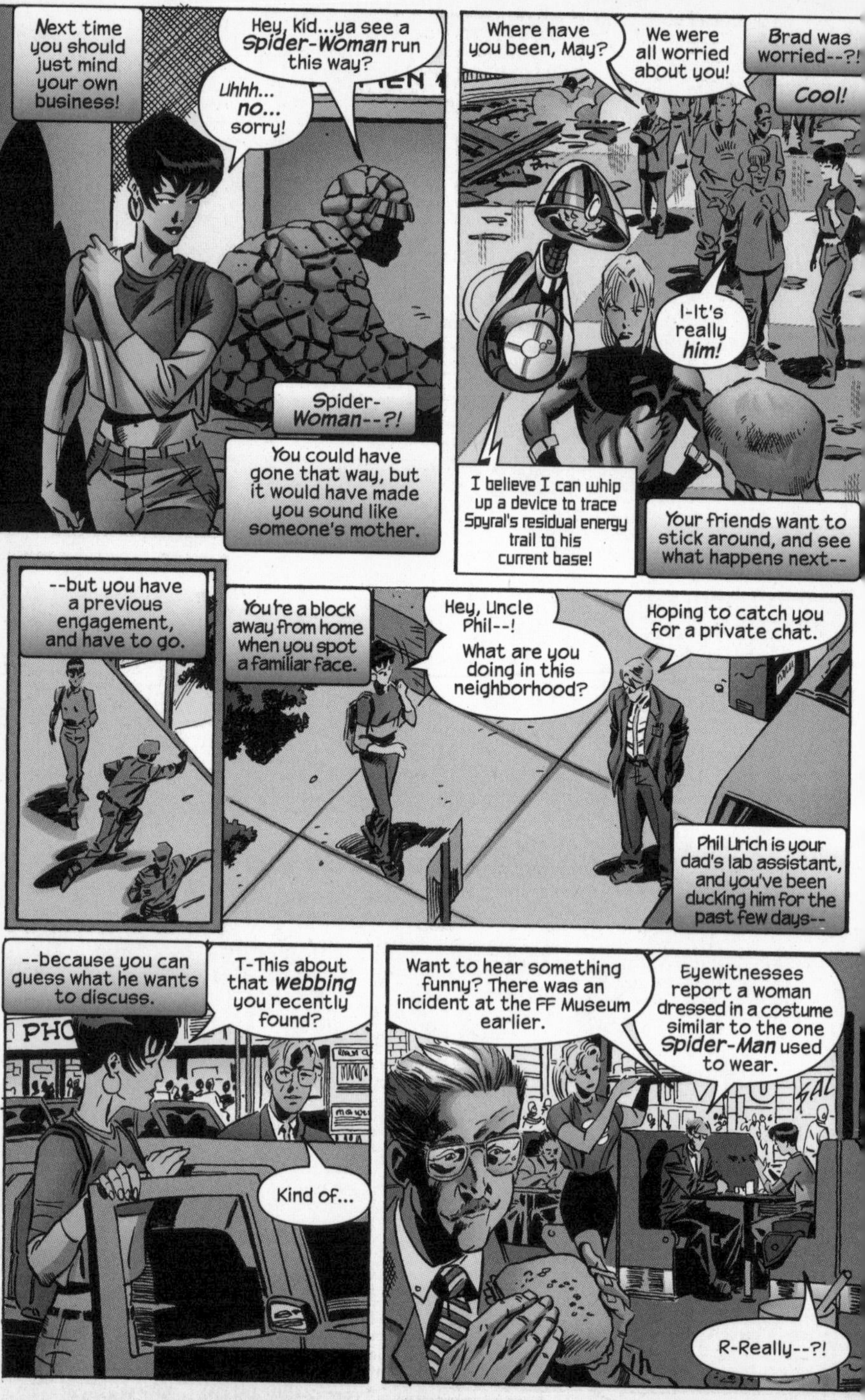
Next time you should just mind your own business!
Hey, kid...ya see a Spider-Woman run this way?
Uhhh... no... sorry!
Spider-Woman--?!
You could have gone that way, but it would have made you sound like someone's mother.
Where have you been, May?
We were all worried about you!
Brad was worried--?!
Cool!
I-It's really him!
I believe I can whip up a device to trace Spyral's residual energy trail to his current base!
Your friends want to stick around, and see what happens next--
--but you have a previous engagement, and have to go.
You're a block away from home when you spot a familiar face.
Hey, Uncle Phil--!
What are you doing in this neighborhood?
Hoping to catch you for a private chat.
Phil Urich is your dad's lab assistant, and you've been ducking him for the past few days--
--because you can guess what he wants to discuss.
T-This about that webbing you recently found?
Kind of...
Want to hear something funny? There was an incident at the FF Museum earlier.
Eyewitnesses report a woman dressed in a costume similar to the one Spider-Man used to wear.
R-Really--?!

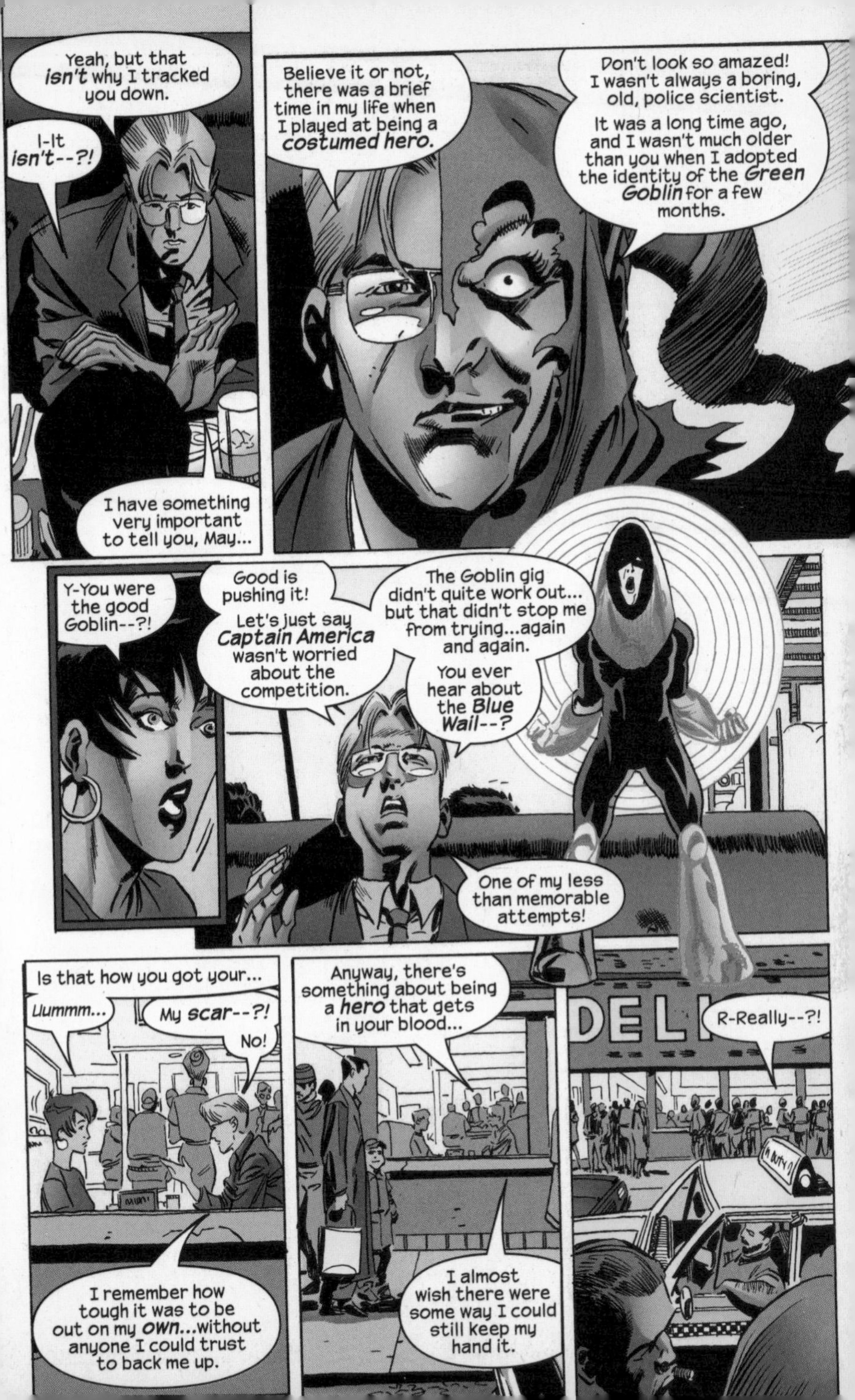
Yeah, but that isn't why I tracked you down.
I-It isn't--?!
I have something very important to tell you, May...
Believe it or not, there was a brief time in my life when I played at being a costumed hero.
Don't look so amazed! I wasn't always a boring, old, police scientist.
It was a long time ago, and I wasn't much older than you when I adopted the identity of the Green Goblin for a few months.
Y-You were the good Goblin--?!
Good is pushing it!
Let's just say Captain America wasn't worried about the competition.
The Goblin gig didn't quite work out... but that didn't stop me from trying...again and again.
You ever hear about the Blue Wail--?
One of my less than memorable attempts!
Is that how you got your...
Uummm...
My scar--?!
No!
I remember how tough it was to be out on my own...without anyone I could trust to back me up.
Anyway, there's something about being a hero that gets in your blood...
I almost wish there were some way I could still keep my hand it.
DELI
R-Really--?!

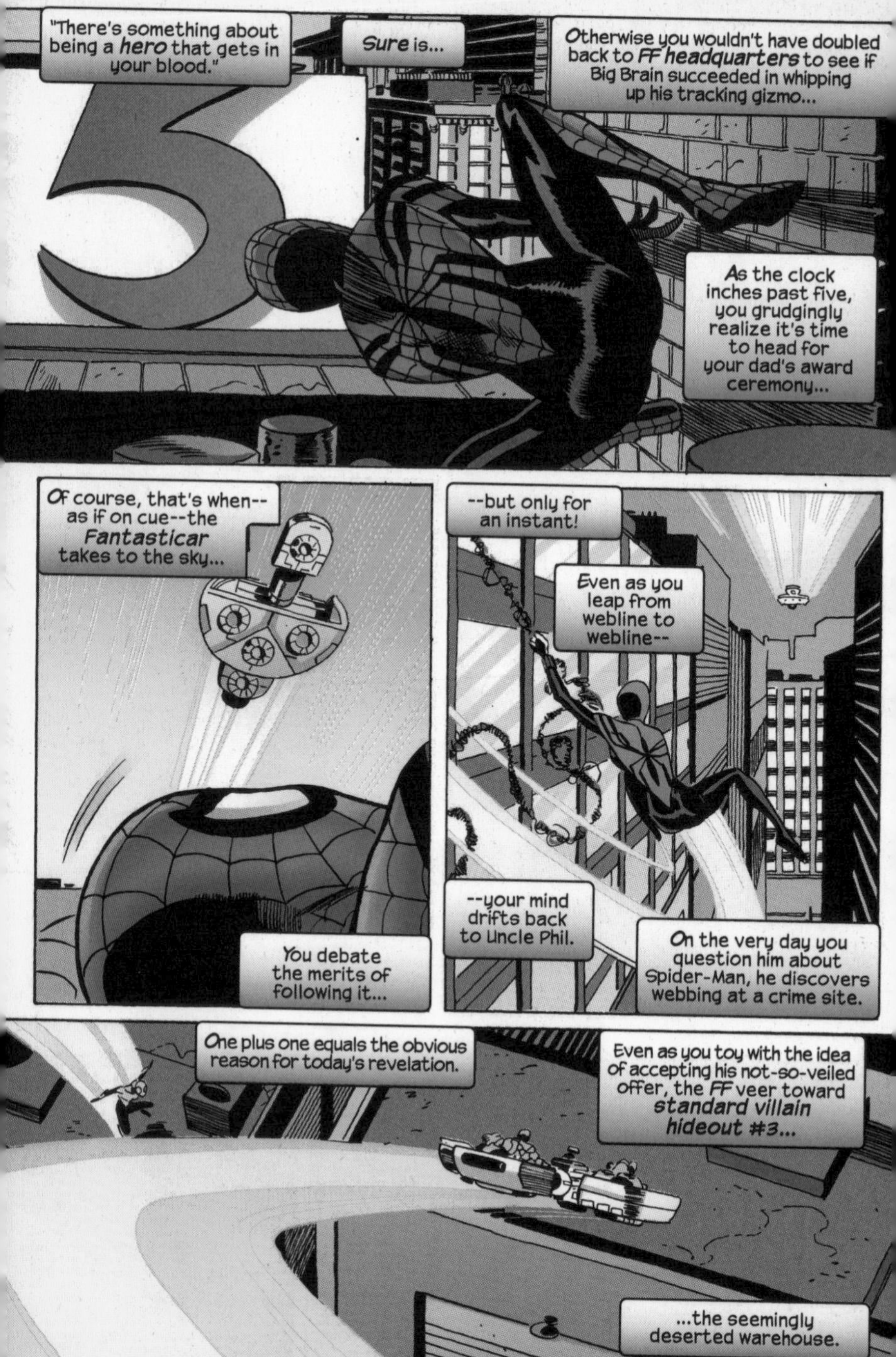

"There's something about being a hero that gets in your blood."
Sure is...
Otherwise you wouldn't have doubled back to FF headquarters to see if Big Brain succeeded in whipping up his tracking gizmo...
As the clock inches past five, you grudgingly realize it's time to head for your dad's award ceremony...
Of course, that's when-- as if on cue--the Fantasticar takes to the sky...
You debate the merits of following it...
--but only for an instant!
Even as you leap from webline to webline--
--your mind drifts back to Uncle Phil.
On the very day you question him about Spider-Man, he discovers webbing at a crime site.
One plus one equals the obvious reason for today's revelation.
Even as you toy with the idea of accepting his not-so-veiled offer, the FF veer toward standard villain hideout #3...
...the seemingly deserted warehouse.

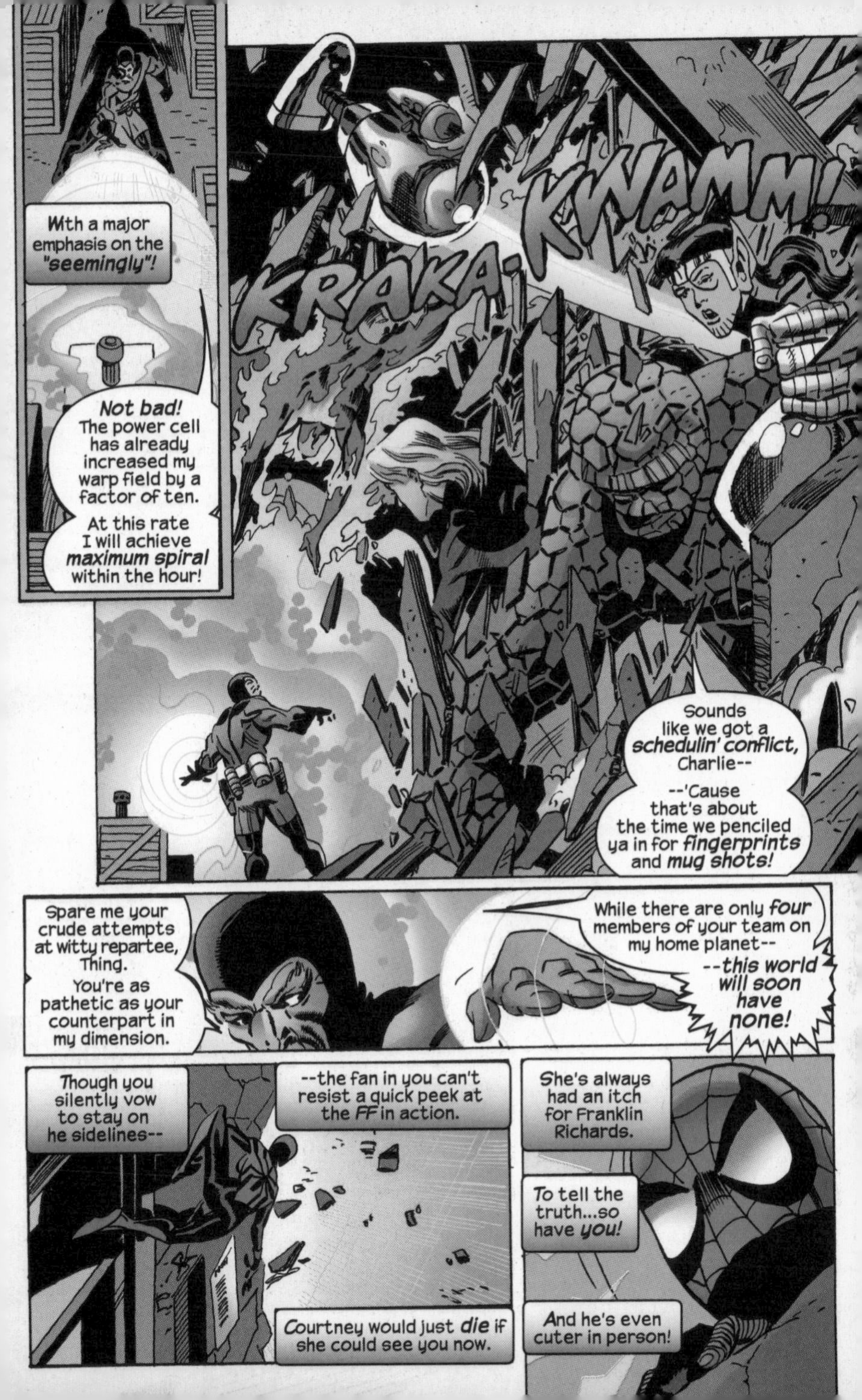
With a major emphasis on the "seemingly"!
KRAKA-KWAMM!
Not bad! The power cell has already increased my warp field by a factor of ten.
At this rate I will achieve maximum spiral within the hour!
Sounds like we got a schedulin' conflict, Charlie--
--'Cause that's about the time we penciled ya in for fingerprints and mug shots!
Spare me your crude attempts at witty repartee, Thing.
You're as pathetic as your counterpart in my dimension.
While there are only four members of your team on my home planet--
--this world will soon have none!
Though you silently vow to stay on he sidelines--
--the fan in you can't resist a quick peek at the FF in action.
Courtney would just die if she could see you now.
She's always had an itch for Franklin Richards.
To tell the truth...so have you!
And he's even cuter in person!

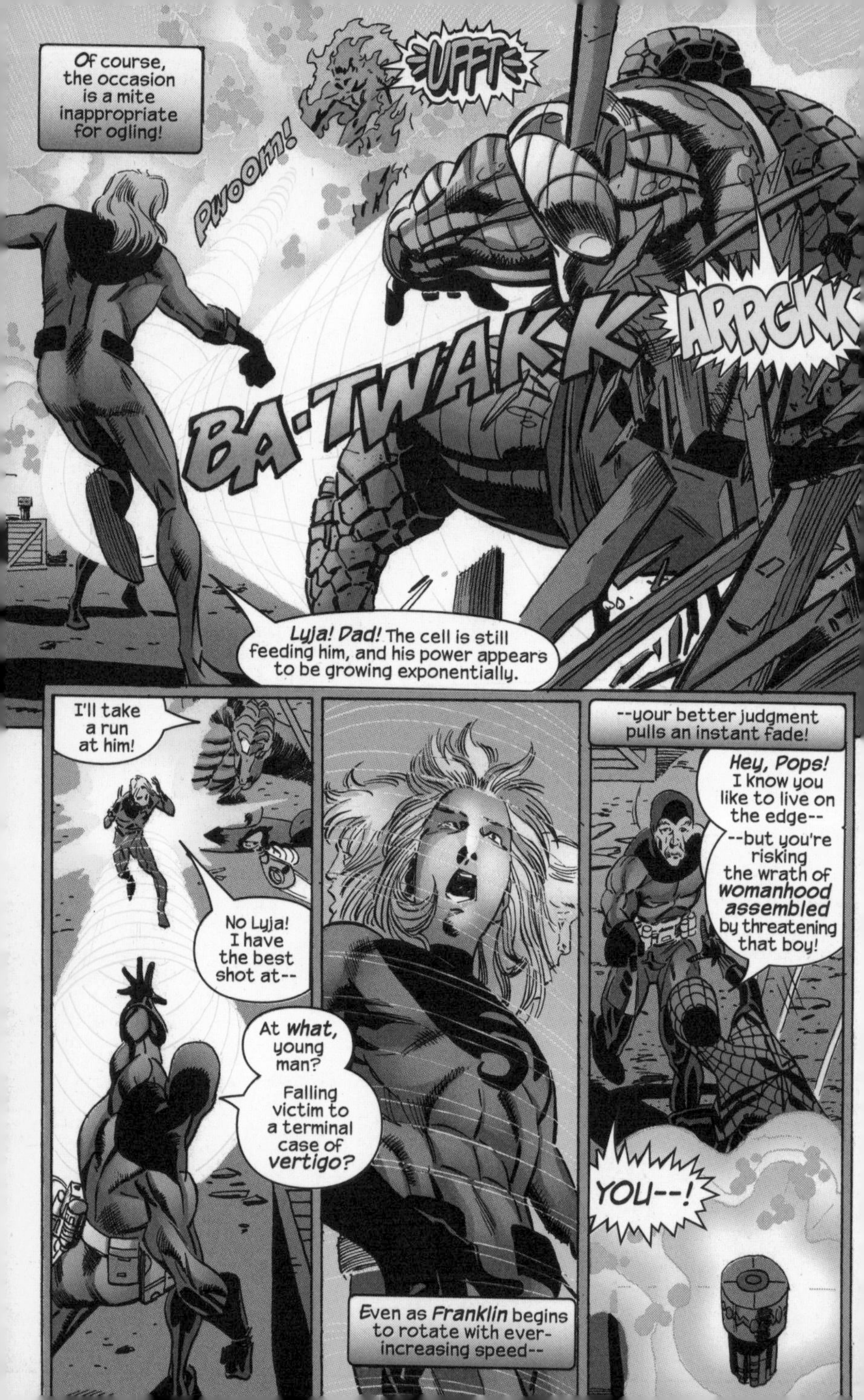
Of course, the occasion is a mite inappropriate for ogling!
UFFT
PWOOM!
BA-TWAKK
ARRGKK
Luja! Dad! The cell is still feeding him, and his power appears to be growing exponentially.
I'll take a run at him!
No Luja! I have the best shot at--
At what, young man?
Falling victim to a terminal case of vertigo?
Even as Franklin begins to rotate with ever-increasing speed--
--your better judgment pulls an instant fade!
Hey, Pops! I know you like to live on the edge--
--but you're risking the wrath of womanhood assembled by threatening that boy!
YOU--!

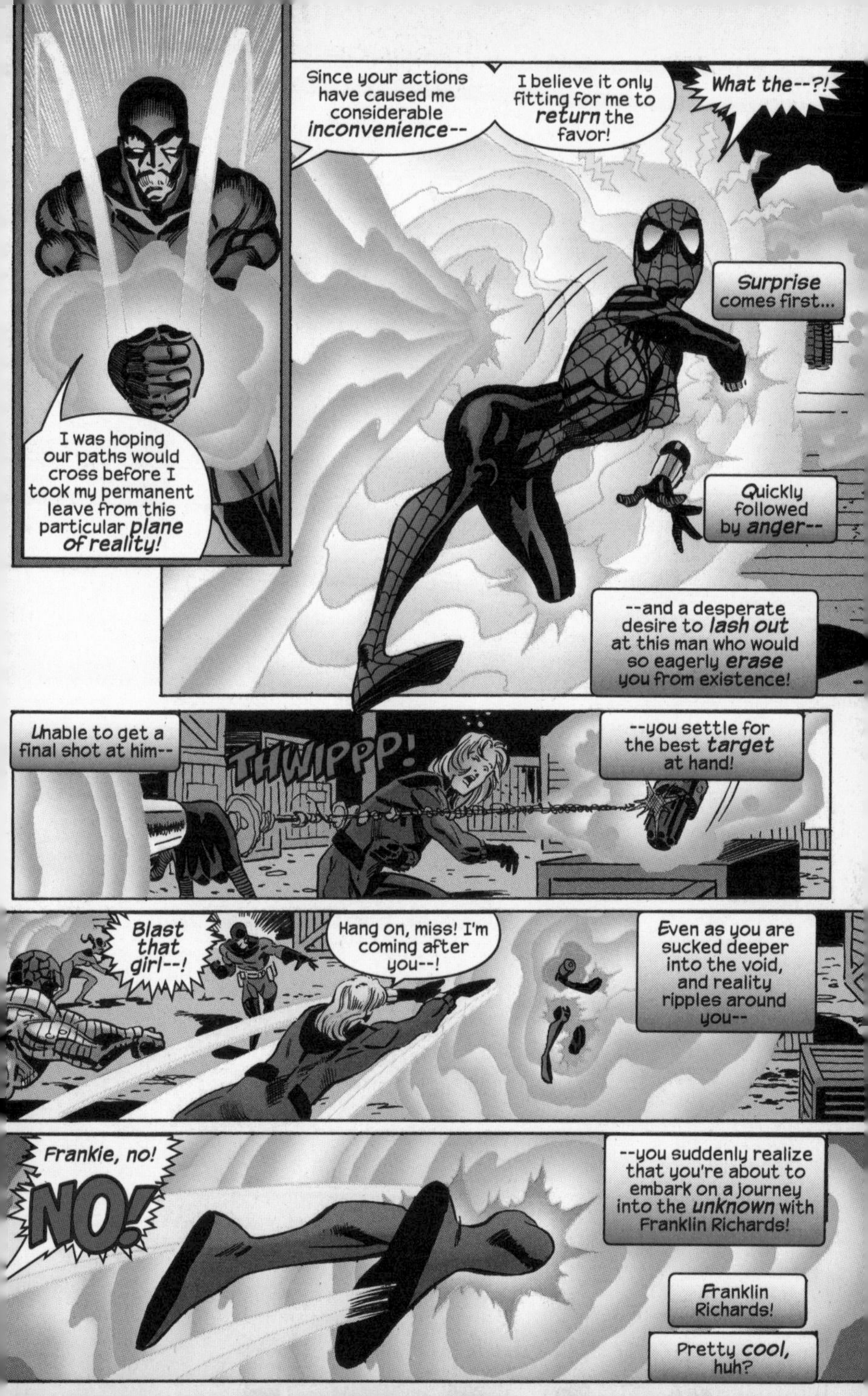

I was hoping our paths would cross before I took my permanent leave from this particular *plane of reality*!
Since your actions have caused me considerable *inconvenience*--
I believe it only fitting for me to *return* the favor!
What the--?!
Surprise comes first...
Quickly followed by *anger*--
--and a desperate desire to *lash out* at this man who would so eagerly *erase* you from existence!
Unable to get a final shot at him--
THWIPPP!
--you settle for the best *target* at hand!
Blast that girl--!
Hang on, miss! I'm coming after you--!
Even as you are sucked deeper into the void, and reality ripples around you--
Frankie, no!
NO!
--you suddenly realize that you're about to embark on a journey into the *unknown* with Franklin Richards!
Franklin Richards!
Pretty *cool*, huh?

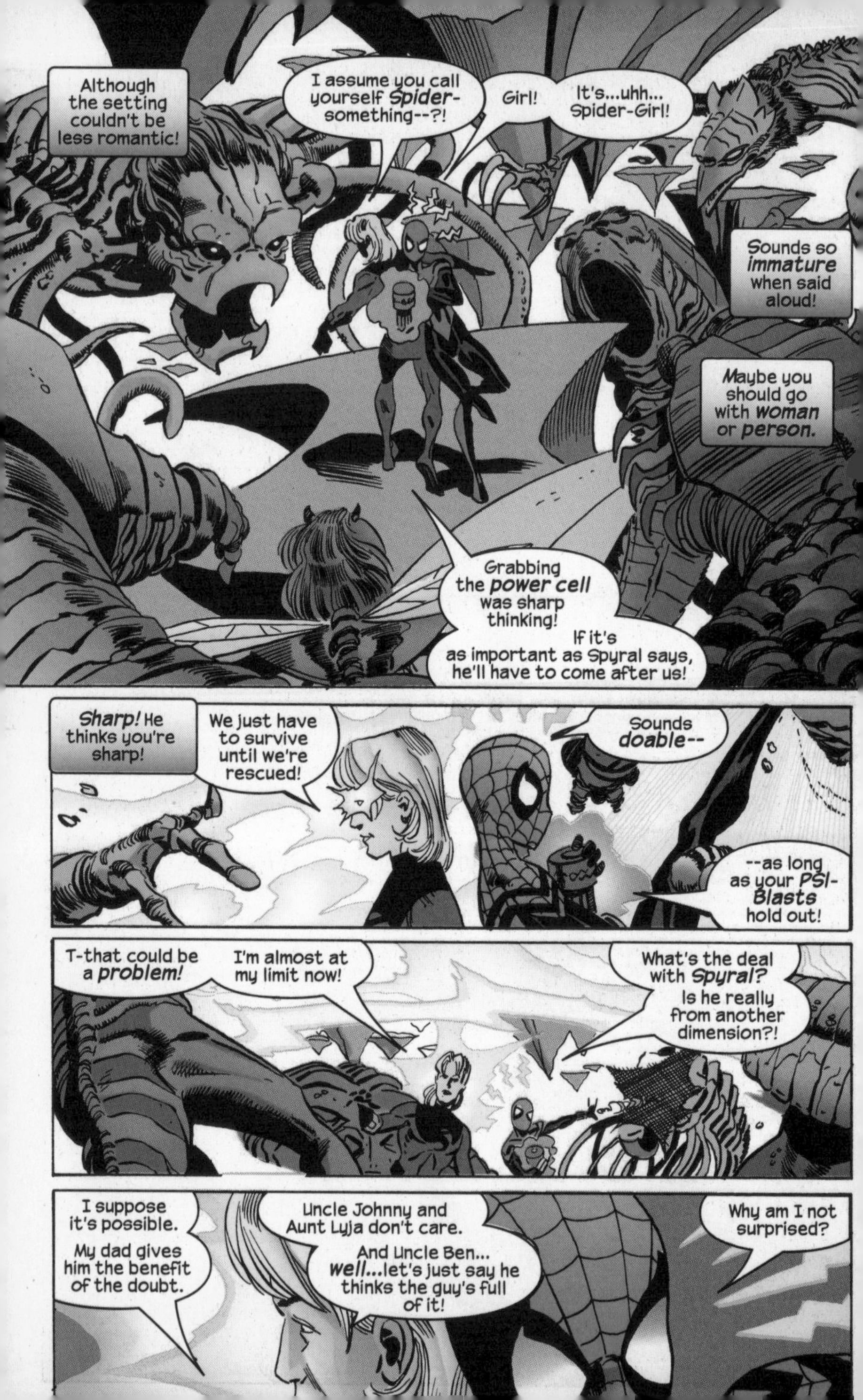
Although the setting couldn't be less romantic!
I assume you call yourself Spider-something--?!
Girl!
It's...uhh... Spider-Girl!
Sounds so immature when said aloud!
Maybe you should go with woman or person.
Grabbing the power cell was sharp thinking!
If it's as important as Spyral says, he'll have to come after us!
Sharp! He thinks you're sharp!
We just have to survive until we're rescued!
Sounds doable--
--as long as your PSI-Blasts hold out!
T-that could be a problem!
I'm almost at my limit now!
What's the deal with Spyral?
Is he really from another dimension?!
I suppose it's possible.
My dad gives him the benefit of the doubt.
Uncle Johnny and Aunt Lyja don't care.
And Uncle Ben... well...let's just say he thinks the guy's full of it!
Why am I not surprised?

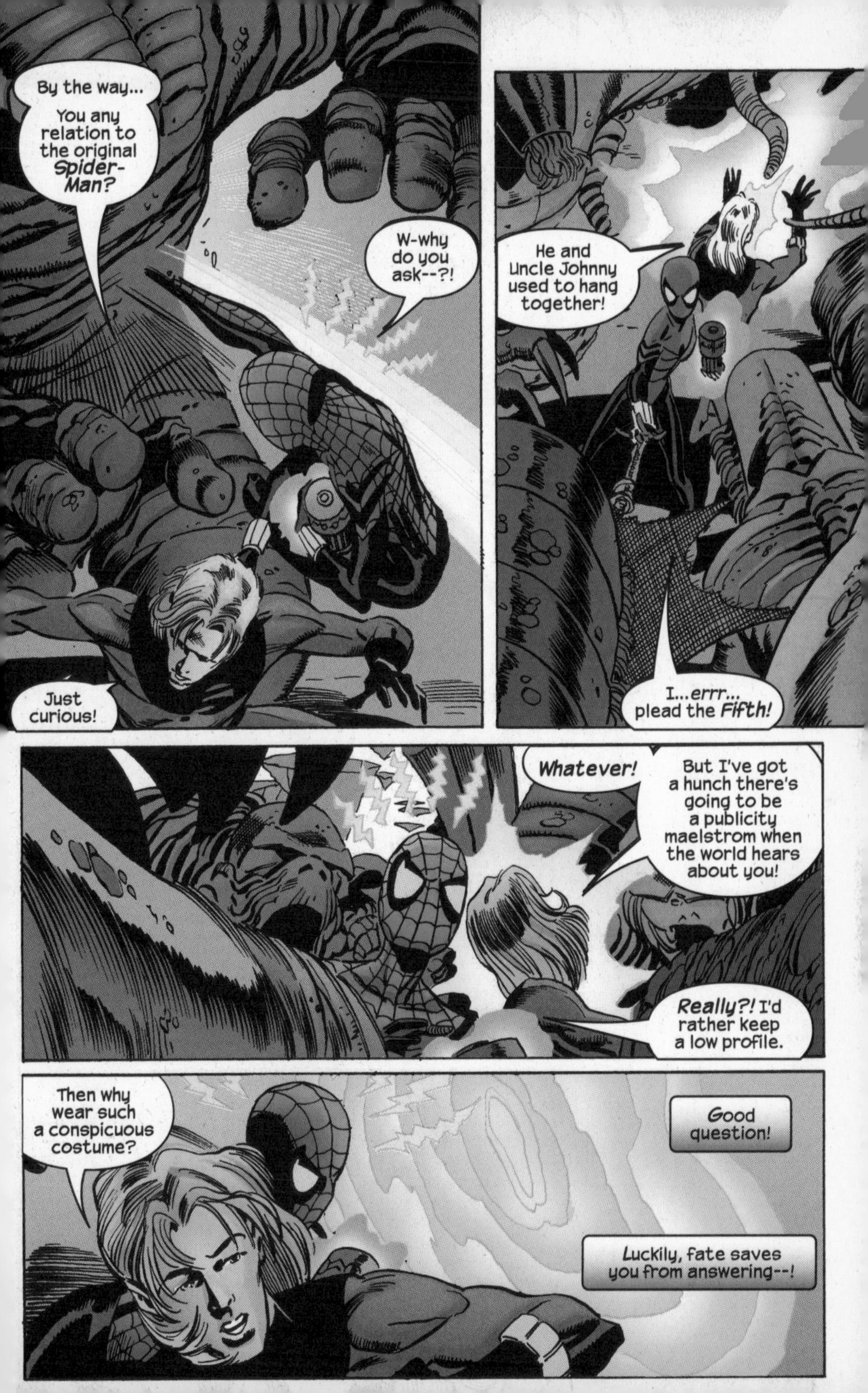
By the way... You any relation to the original Spider-Man?
W-why do you ask--?!
Just curious!
He and Uncle Johnny used to hang together!
I...errr... plead the Fifth!
Whatever!
But I've got a hunch there's going to be a publicity maelstrom when the world hears about you!
Really?! I'd rather keep a low profile.
Then why wear such a conspicuous costume?
Good question!
Luckily, fate saves you from answering--!

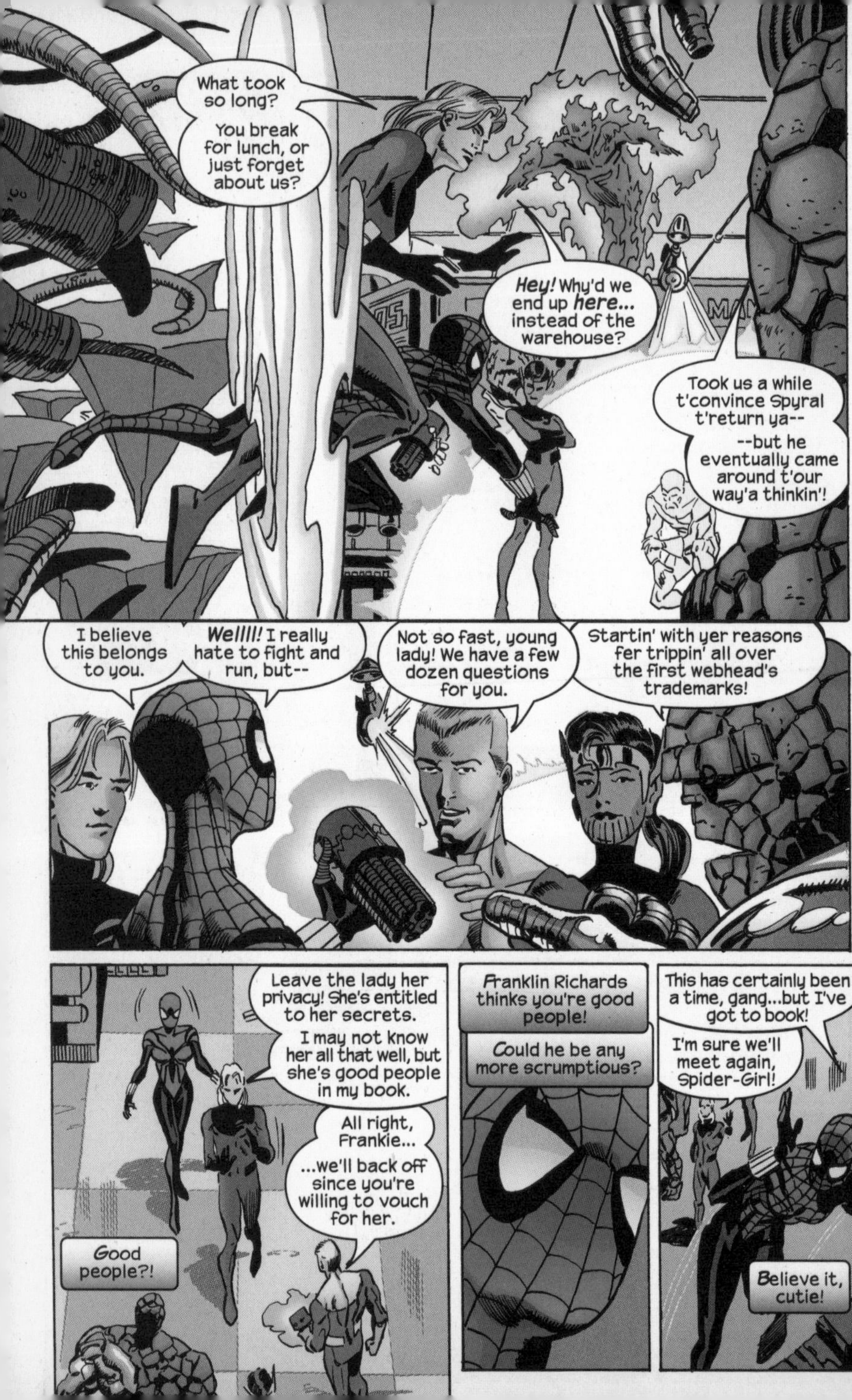
What took so long?
You break for lunch, or just forget about us?
Hey! Why'd we end up here... instead of the warehouse?
Took us a while t'convince Spyral t'return ya--
--but he eventually came around t'our way'a thinkin'!
I believe this belongs to you.
Wellll! I really hate to fight and run, but--
Not so fast, young lady! We have a few dozen questions for you.
Startin' with yer reasons fer trippin' all over the first webhead's trademarks!
Leave the lady her privacy! She's entitled to her secrets.
I may not know her all that well, but she's good people in my book.
All right, Frankie...
...we'll back off since you're willing to vouch for her.
Good people?!
Franklin Richards thinks you're good people!
Could he be any more scrumptious?
This has certainly been a time, gang...but I've got to book!
I'm sure we'll meet again, Spider-Girl!
Believe it, cutie!

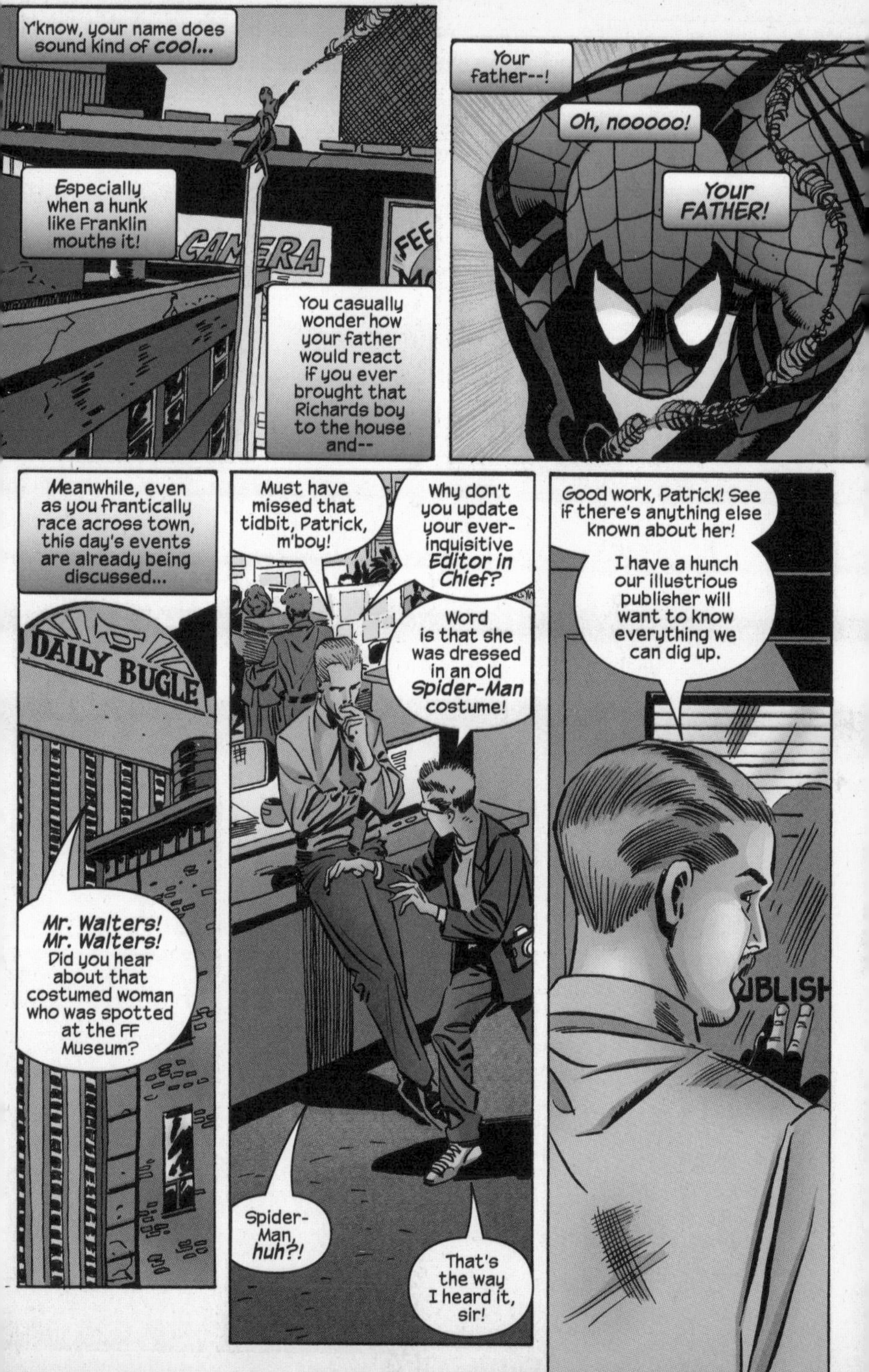

Y'know, your name does sound kind of cool...
Especially when a hunk like Franklin mouths it!
CAMERA
You casually wonder how your father would react if you ever brought that Richards boy to the house and--
Your father--!
Oh, nooooo!
Your FATHER!
Meanwhile, even as you frantically race across town, this day's events are already being discussed...
DAILY BUGLE
Mr. Walters! Mr. Walters! Did you hear about that costumed woman who was spotted at the FF Museum?
Must have missed that tidbit, Patrick, m'boy!
Why don't you update your ever-inquisitive Editor in Chief?
Word is that she was dressed in an old Spider-Man costume!
Spider-Man, huh?!
That's the way I heard it, sir!
Good work, Patrick! See if there's anything else known about her!
I have a hunch our illustrious publisher will want to know everything we can dig up.

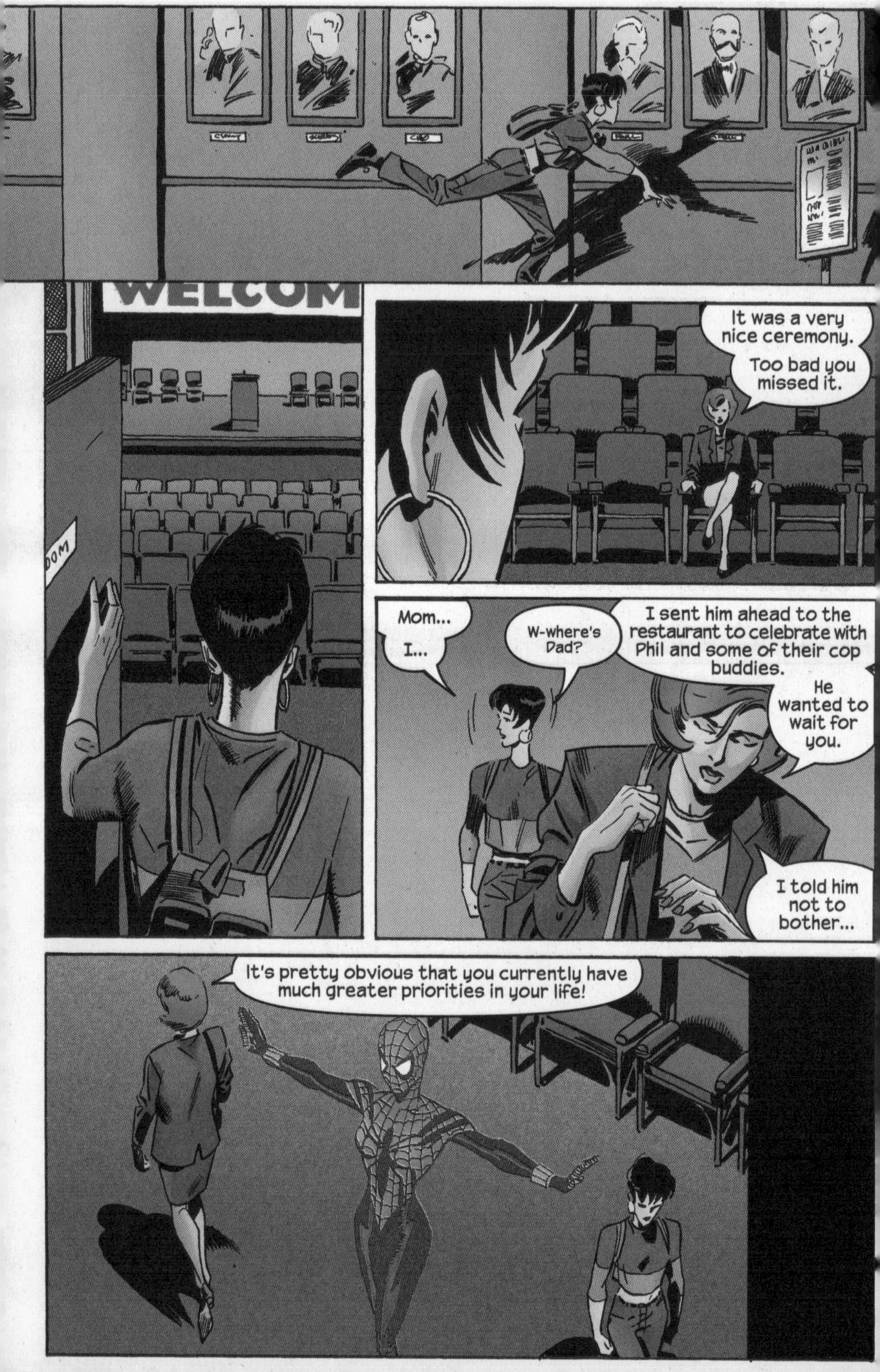
WELCOM
It was a very nice ceremony.
Too bad you missed it.
Mom...
I...
W-where's Dad?
I sent him ahead to the restaurant to celebrate with Phil and some of their cop buddies.
He wanted to wait for you.
I told him not to bother...
It's pretty obvious that you currently have much greater priorities in your life!

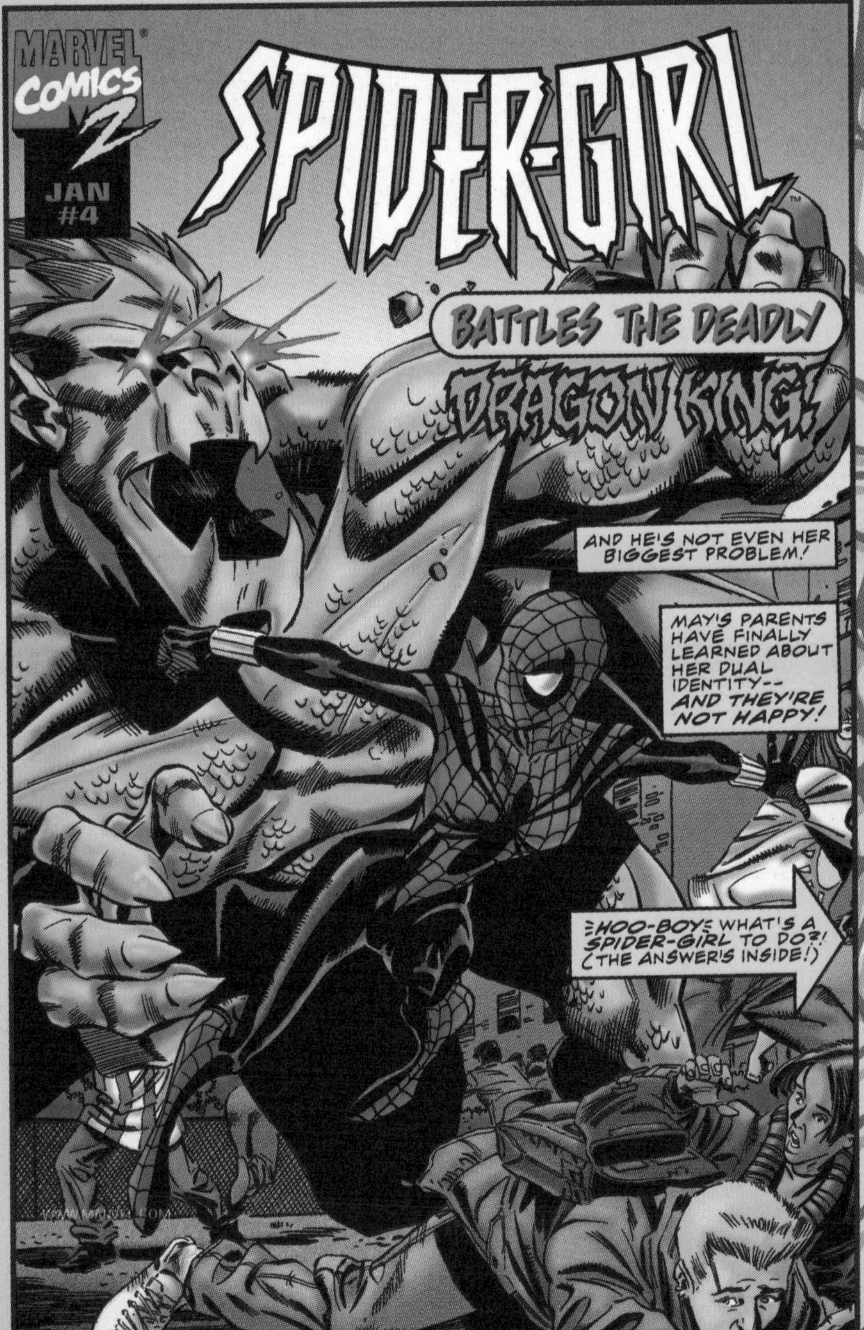
MARVEL COMICS 2
JAN #4
SPIDER-GIRL
BATTLES THE DEADLY
DRAGON KING!
AND HE'S NOT EVEN HER BIGGEST PROBLEM!
MAY'S PARENTS HAVE FINALLY LEARNED ABOUT HER DUAL IDENTITY-- AND THEY'RE NOT HAPPY!
HOO-BOY! WHAT'S A SPIDER-GIRL TO DO?! (THE ANSWER'S INSIDE!)
DEFALCO • OLLIFFE • WILLIAMSON

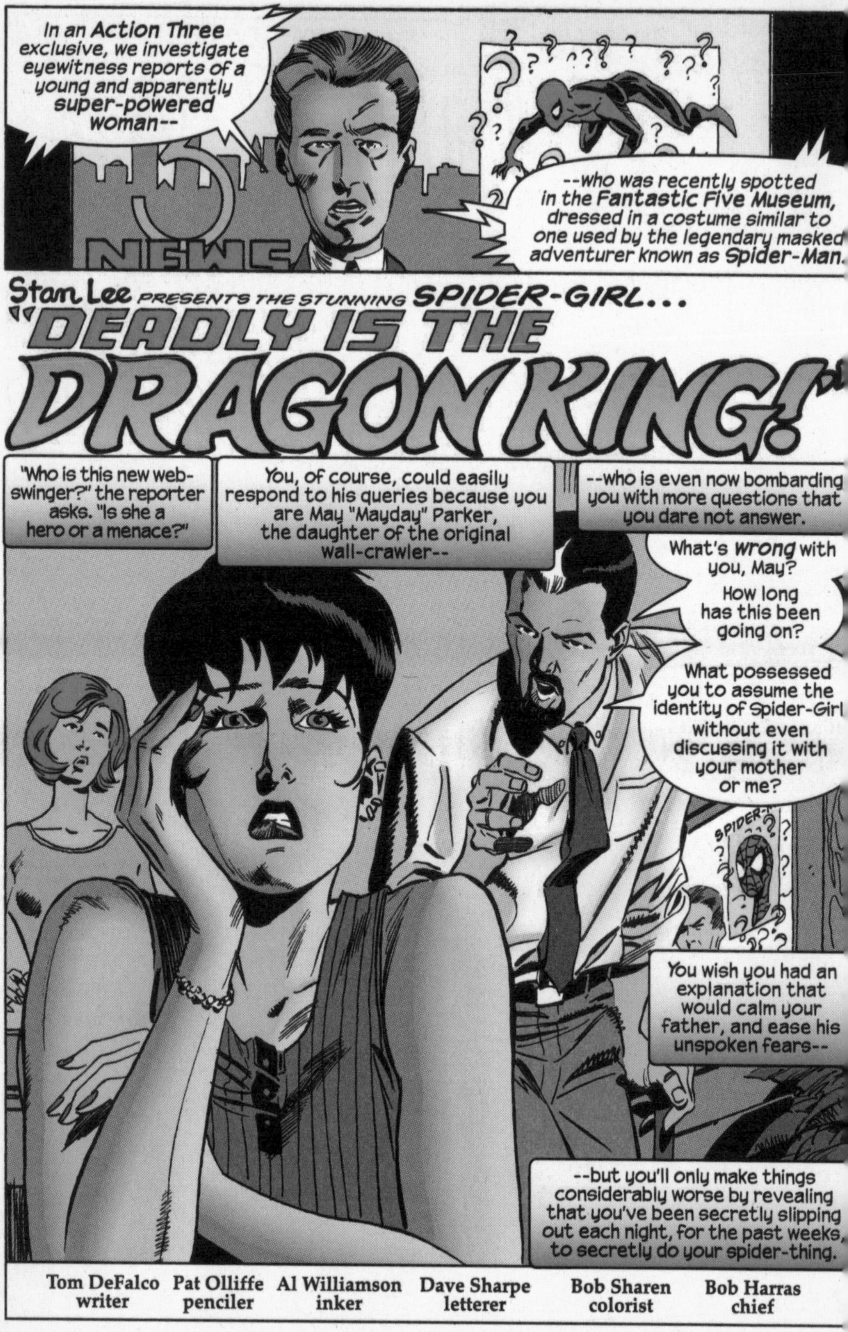
In an Action Three exclusive, we investigate eyewitness reports of a young and apparently super-powered woman--
--who was recently spotted in the Fantastic Five Museum, dressed in a costume similar to one used by the legendary masked adventurer known as Spider-Man.
NEWS
Stan Lee PRESENTS THE STUNNING SPIDER-GIRL...
"DEADLY IS THE DRAGON KING!"
"Who is this new web-swinger?" the reporter asks. "Is she a hero or a menace?"
You, of course, could easily respond to his queries because you are May "Mayday" Parker, the daughter of the original wall-crawler--
--who is even now bombarding you with more questions that you dare not answer.
What's wrong with you, May? How long has this been going on?
What possessed you to assume the identity of Spider-Girl without even discussing it with your mother or me?
SPIDER-
You wish you had an explanation that would calm your father, and ease his unspoken fears--
--but you'll only make things considerably worse by revealing that you've been secretly slipping out each night, for the past weeks, to secretly do your spider-thing.
Tom DeFalco writer
Pat Olliffe penciler
Al Williamson inker
Dave Sharpe letterer
Bob Sharen colorist
Bob Harras chief

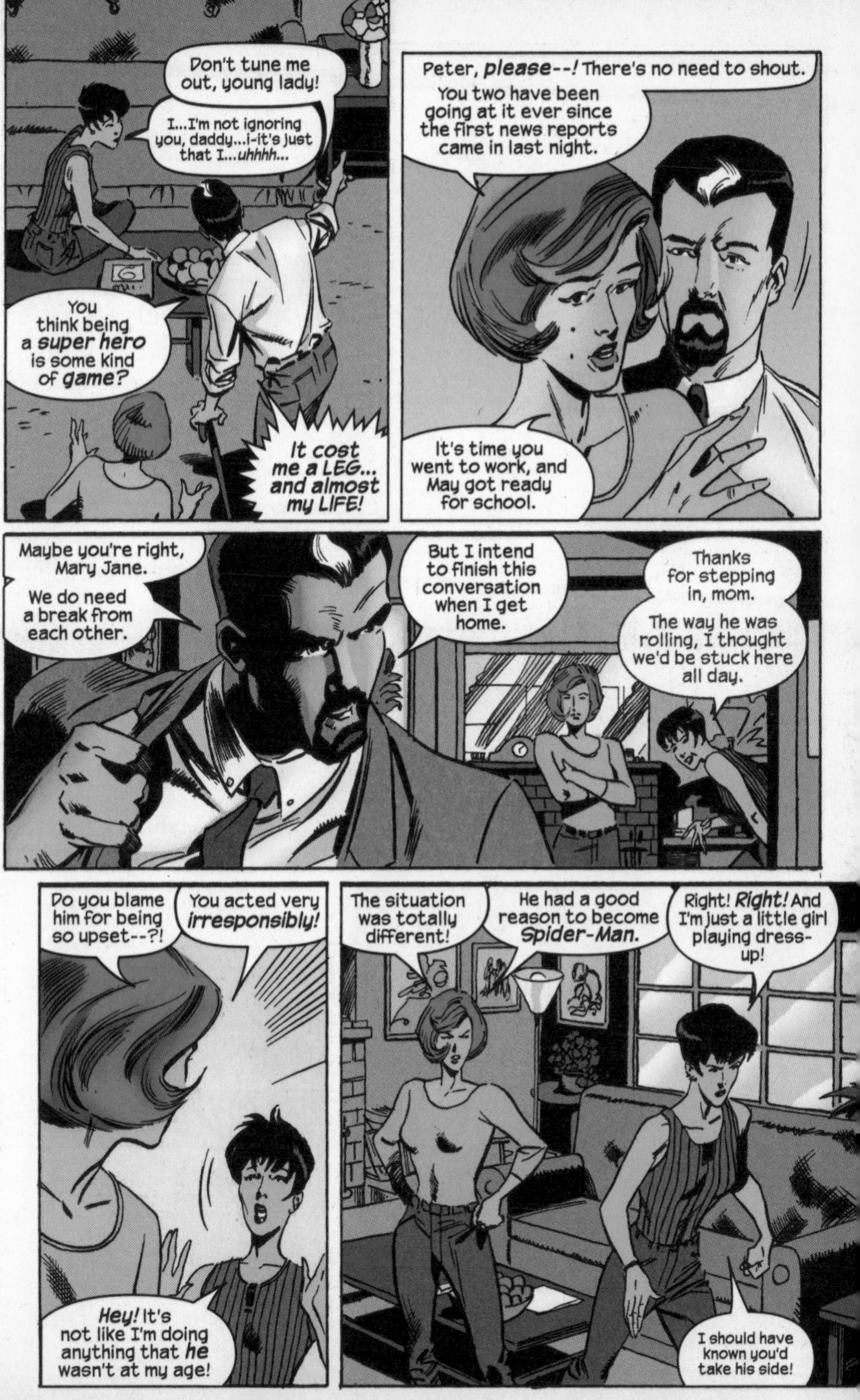
Don't tune me out, young lady!
I...I'm not ignoring you, daddy...i-it's just that I...*uhhhh*...
You think being a *super hero* is some kind of *game?*
It cost me a LEG... and almost my LIFE!
Peter, *please--!* There's no need to shout.
You two have been going at it ever since the first news reports came in last night.
It's time you went to work, and May got ready for school.
Maybe you're right, Mary Jane.
We do need a break from each other.
But I intend to finish this conversation when I get home.
Thanks for stepping in, mom.
The way he was rolling, I thought we'd be stuck here all day.
Do you blame him for being so upset--?!
You acted very *irresponsibly!*
Hey! It's not like I'm doing anything that *he* wasn't at my age!
The situation was totally different!
He had a good reason to become *Spider-Man.*
Right! *Right!* And I'm just a little girl playing dress-up!
I should have known you'd take his side!

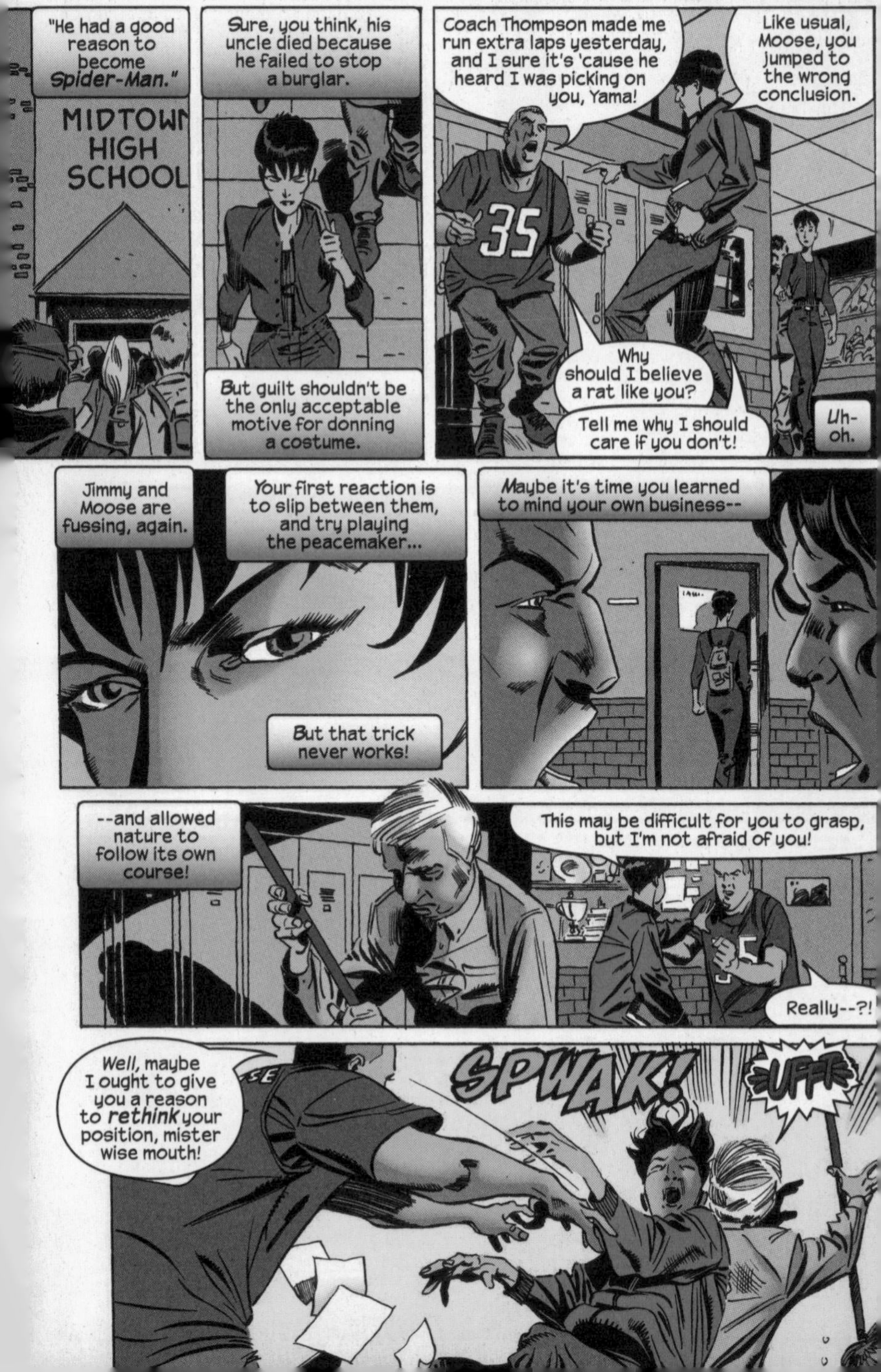
"He had a good reason to become Spider-Man."
MIDTOWN HIGH SCHOOL
Sure, you think, his uncle died because he failed to stop a burglar.
But guilt shouldn't be the only acceptable motive for donning a costume.
Coach Thompson made me run extra laps yesterday, and I sure it's 'cause he heard I was picking on you, Yama!
Like usual, Moose, you jumped to the wrong conclusion.
Why should I believe a rat like you?
Tell me why I should care if you don't!
Uh-oh.
Jimmy and Moose are fussing, again.
Your first reaction is to slip between them, and try playing the peacemaker...
But that trick never works!
Maybe it's time you learned to mind your own business--
--and allowed nature to follow its own course!
This may be difficult for you to grasp, but I'm not afraid of you!
Really--?!
Well, maybe I ought to give you a reason to rethink your position, mister wise mouth!
SPWAK!
UFF!

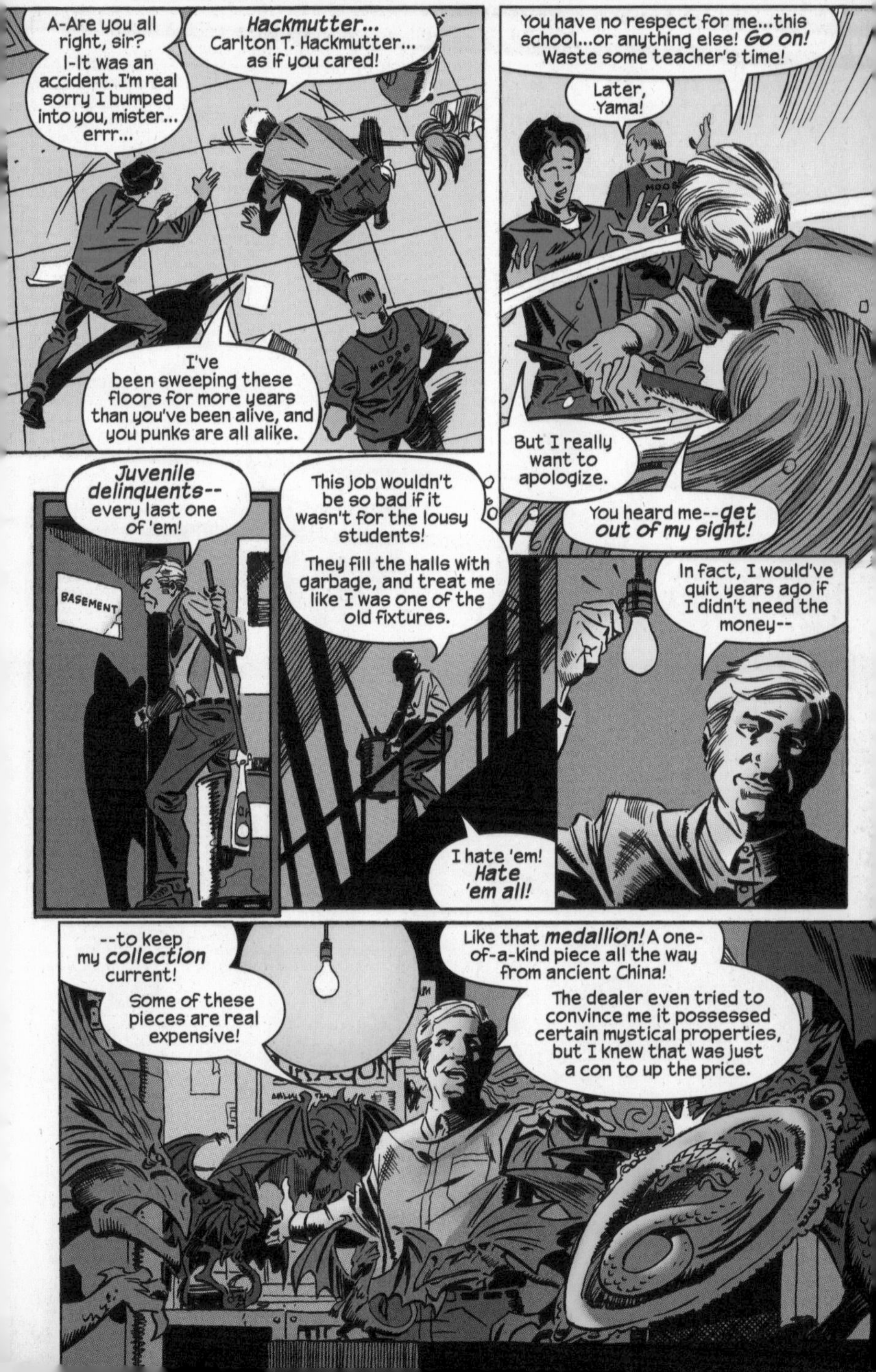
A-Are you all right, sir? I-It was an accident. I'm real sorry I bumped into you, mister... errr...
Hackmutter... Carlton T. Hackmutter... as if you cared!
I've been sweeping these floors for more years than you've been alive, and you punks are all alike.
You have no respect for me...this school...or anything else! Go on! Waste some teacher's time!
Later, Yama!
But I really want to apologize.
You heard me--get out of my sight!
Juvenile delinquents-- every last one of 'em!
BASEMENT
This job wouldn't be so bad if it wasn't for the lousy students!
They fill the halls with garbage, and treat me like I was one of the old fixtures.
I hate 'em! Hate 'em all!
In fact, I would've quit years ago if I didn't need the money--
--to keep my collection current!
Some of these pieces are real expensive!
Like that medallion! A one-of-a-kind piece all the way from ancient China!
The dealer even tried to convince me it possessed certain mystical properties, but I knew that was just a con to up the price.

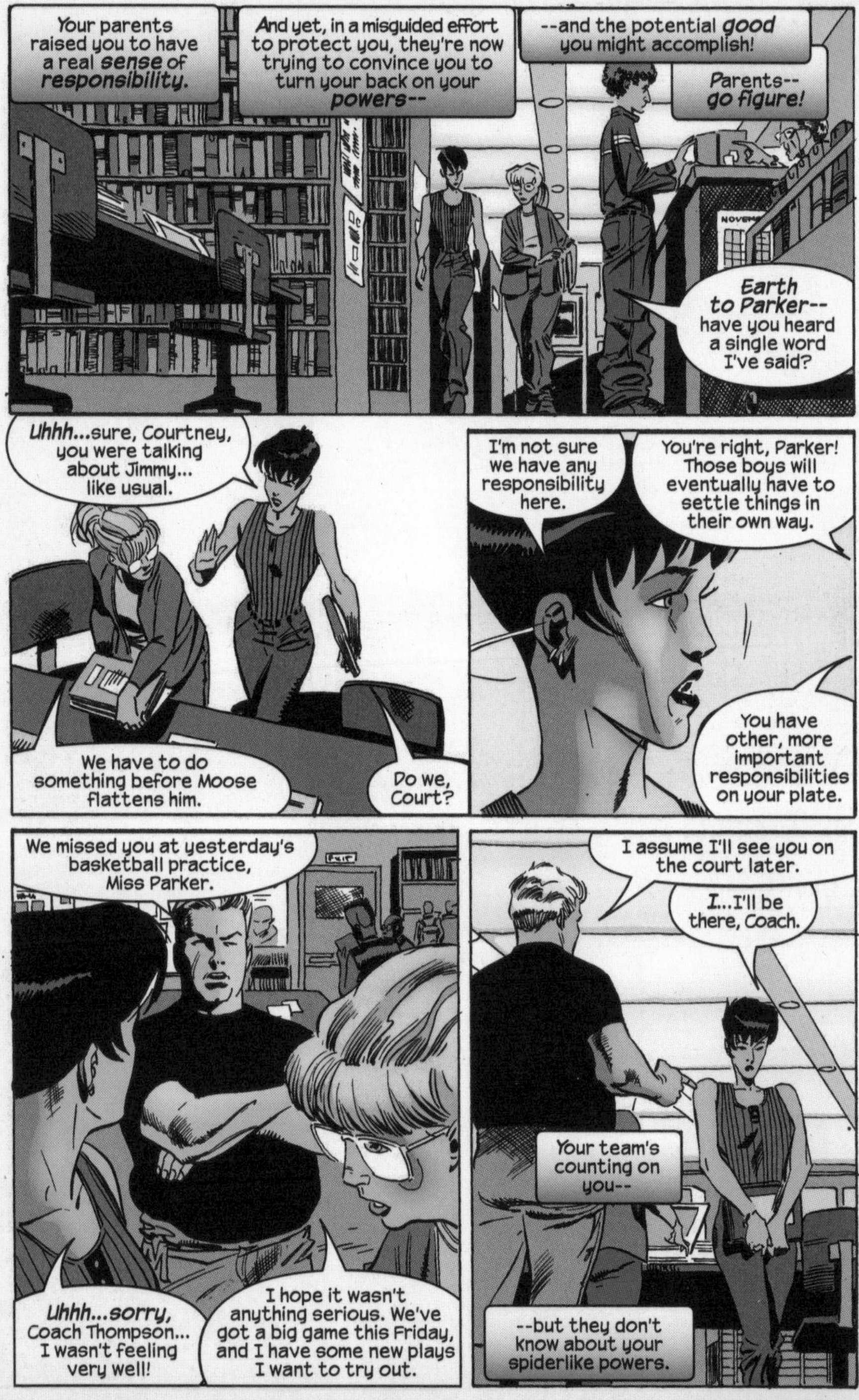
Your parents raised you to have a real sense of responsibility.
And yet, in a misguided effort to protect you, they're now trying to convince you to turn your back on your powers--
--and the potential good you might accomplish!
Parents-- go figure!
NOVEM
Earth to Parker-- have you heard a single word I've said?
Uhhh...sure, Courtney, you were talking about Jimmy... like usual.
We have to do something before Moose flattens him.
Do we, Court?
I'm not sure we have any responsibility here.
You're right, Parker! Those boys will eventually have to settle things in their own way.
You have other, more important responsibilities on your plate.
We missed you at yesterday's basketball practice, Miss Parker.
Uhhh...sorry, Coach Thompson... I wasn't feeling very well!
I hope it wasn't anything serious. We've got a big game this Friday, and I have some new plays I want to try out.
I assume I'll see you on the court later.
I...I'll be there, Coach.
Your team's counting on you--
--but they don't know about your spiderlike powers.

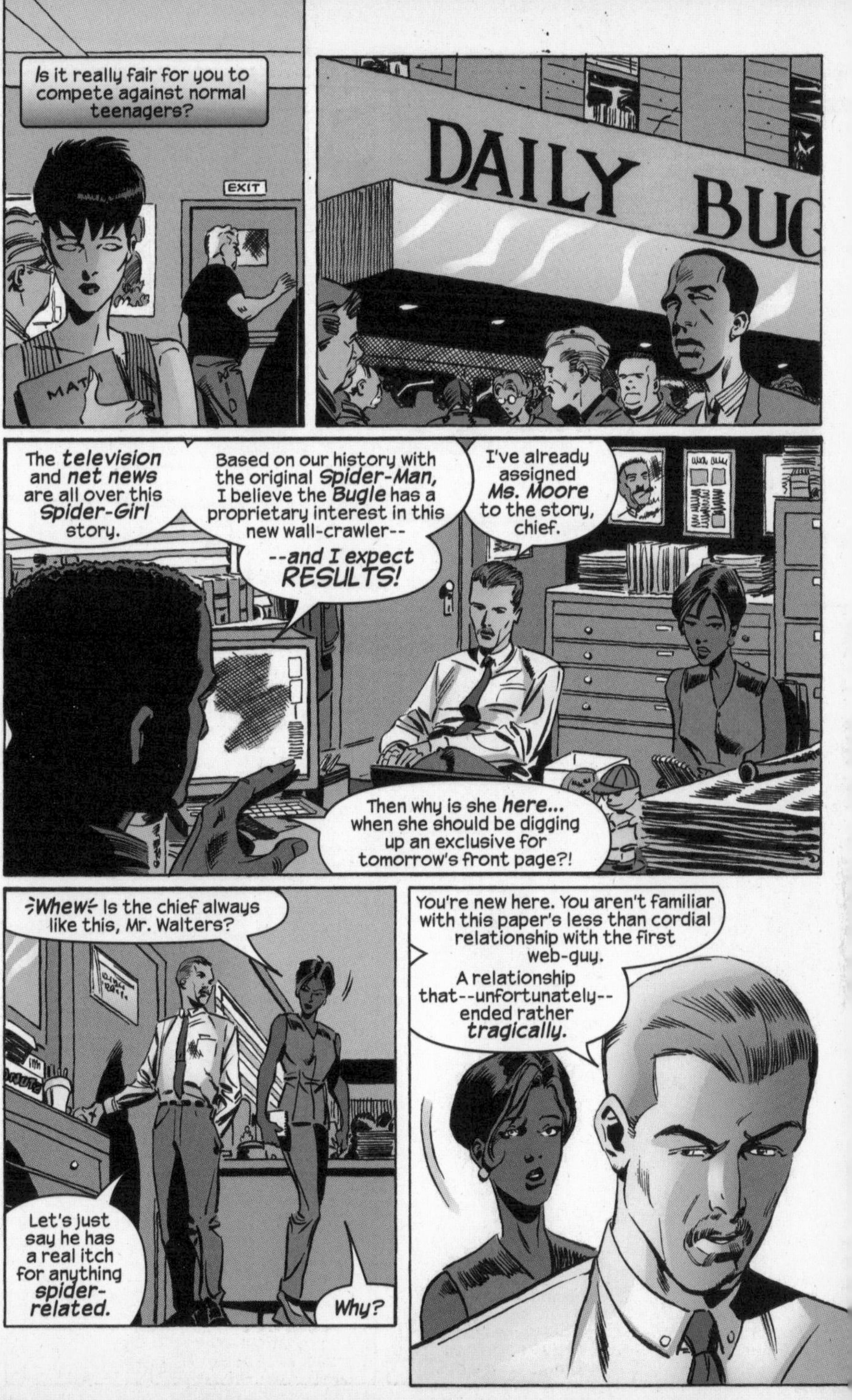

Is it really fair for you to compete against normal teenagers?
EXIT
DAILY BUG
The television and net news are all over this Spider-Girl story.
Based on our history with the original Spider-Man, I believe the Bugle has a proprietary interest in this new wall-crawler--
--and I expect RESULTS!
I've already assigned Ms. Moore to the story, chief.
Then why is she here... when she should be digging up an exclusive for tomorrow's front page?!
Whew! Is the chief always like this, Mr. Walters?
Let's just say he has a real itch for anything spider-related.
Why?
You're new here. You aren't familiar with this paper's less than cordial relationship with the first web-guy.
A relationship that--unfortunately--ended rather tragically.

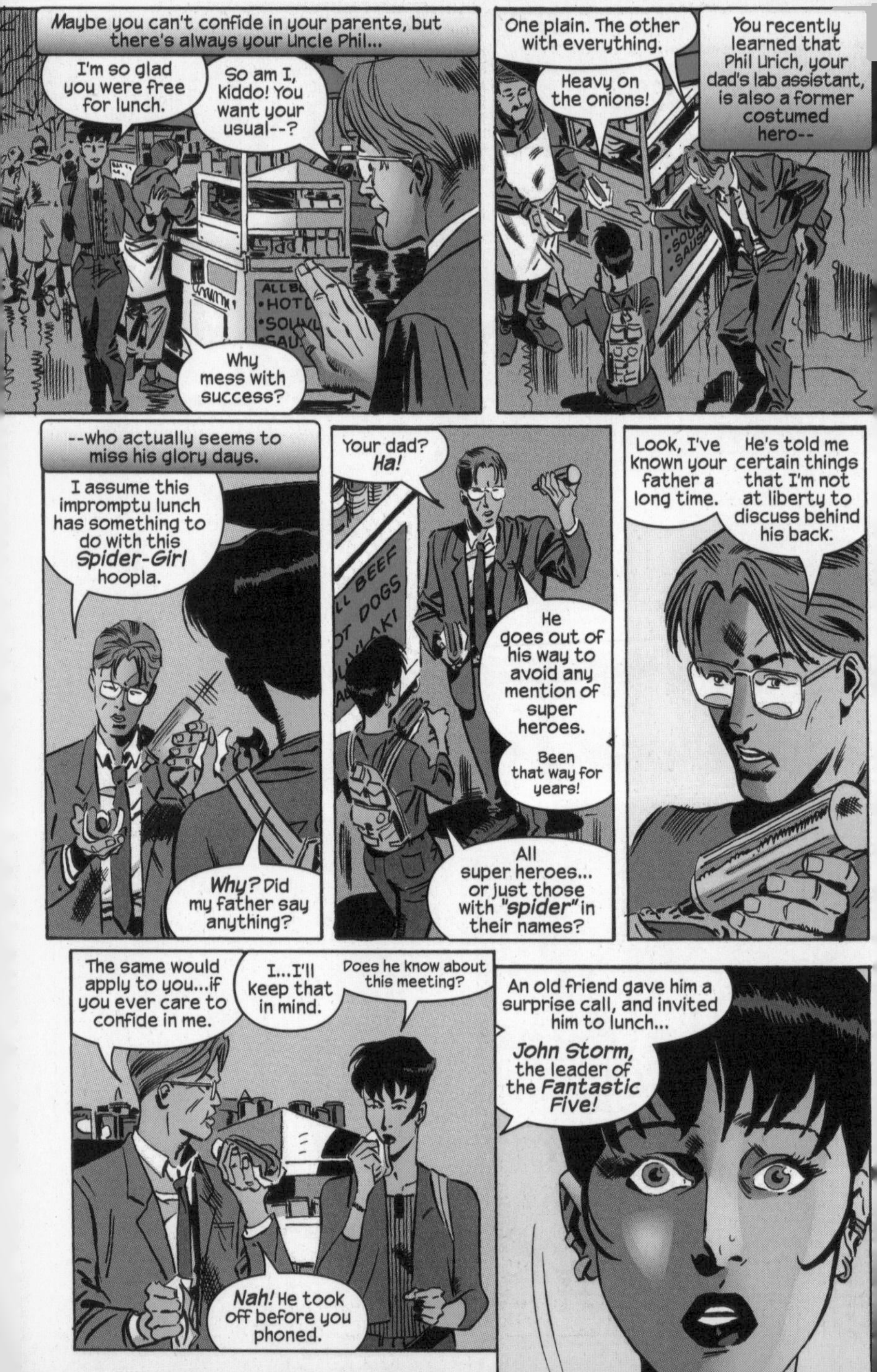
Maybe you can't confide in your parents, but there's always your Uncle Phil...
I'm so glad you were free for lunch.
So am I, kiddo! You want your usual--?
Why mess with success?
One plain. The other with everything.
Heavy on the onions!
You recently learned that Phil Urich, your dad's lab assistant, is also a former costumed hero--
--who actually seems to miss his glory days.
I assume this impromptu lunch has something to do with this Spider-Girl hoopla.
Why? Did my father say anything?
Your dad? Ha!
He goes out of his way to avoid any mention of super heroes.
Been that way for years!
All super heroes... or just those with "spider" in their names?
Look, I've known your father a long time.
He's told me certain things that I'm not at liberty to discuss behind his back.
The same would apply to you...if you ever care to confide in me.
I...I'll keep that in mind.
Does he know about this meeting?
Nah! He took off before you phoned.
An old friend gave him a surprise call, and invited him to lunch...
John Storm, the leader of the Fantastic Five!

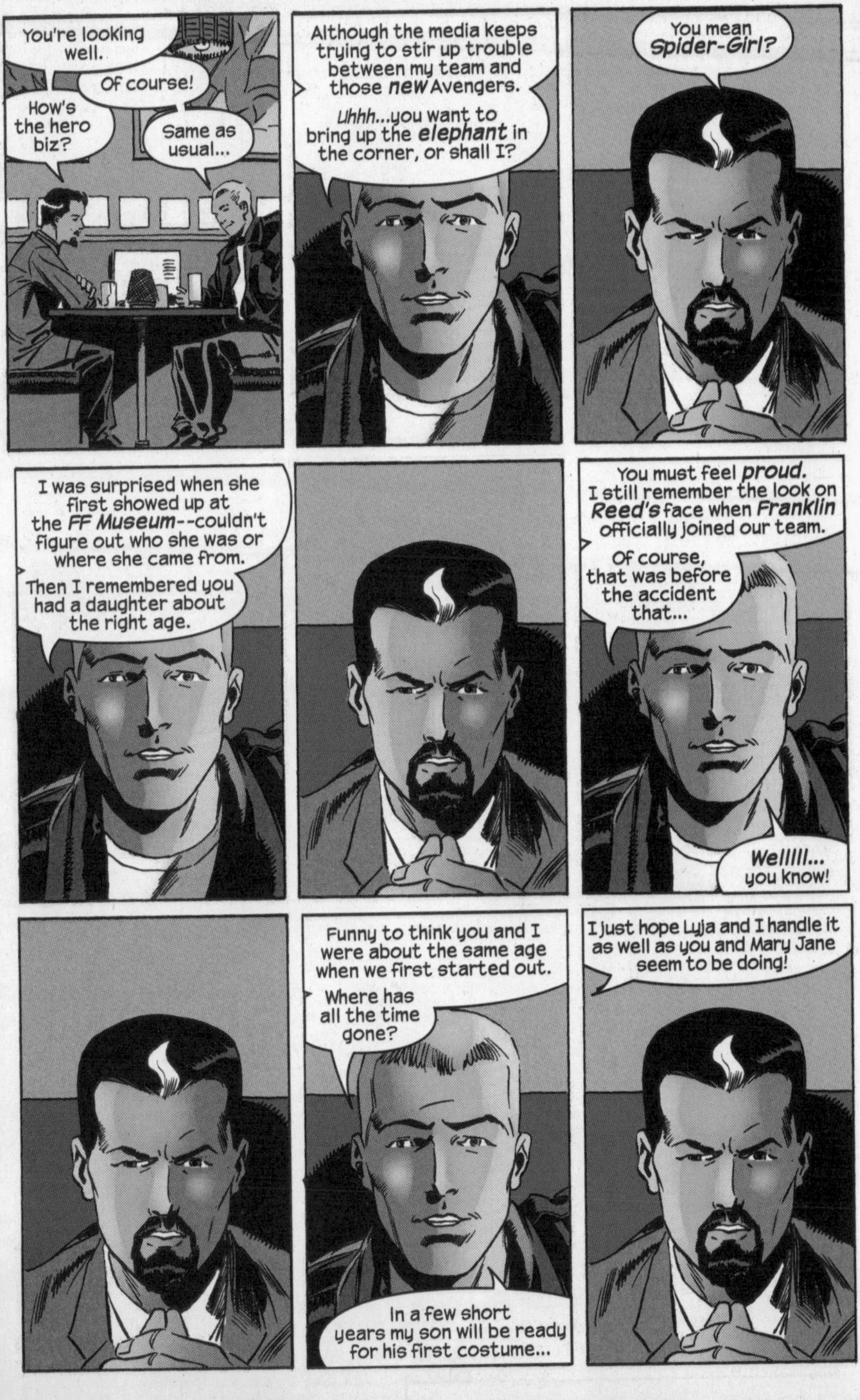

You're looking well.
Of course!
How's the hero biz?
Same as usual...
Although the media keeps trying to stir up trouble between my team and those *new* Avengers.
Uhhh...you want to bring up the *elephant* in the corner, or shall I?
You mean *Spider-Girl?*
I was surprised when she first showed up at the *FF Museum*--couldn't figure out who she was or where she came from.
Then I remembered you had a daughter about the right age.
You must feel *proud*. I still remember the look on *Reed's* face when *Franklin* officially joined our team.
Of course, that was before the accident that...
Welllll... you know!
Funny to think you and I were about the same age when we first started out.
Where has all the time gone?
In a few short years my son will be ready for his first costume...
I just hope Lyja and I handle it as well as you and Mary Jane seem to be doing!

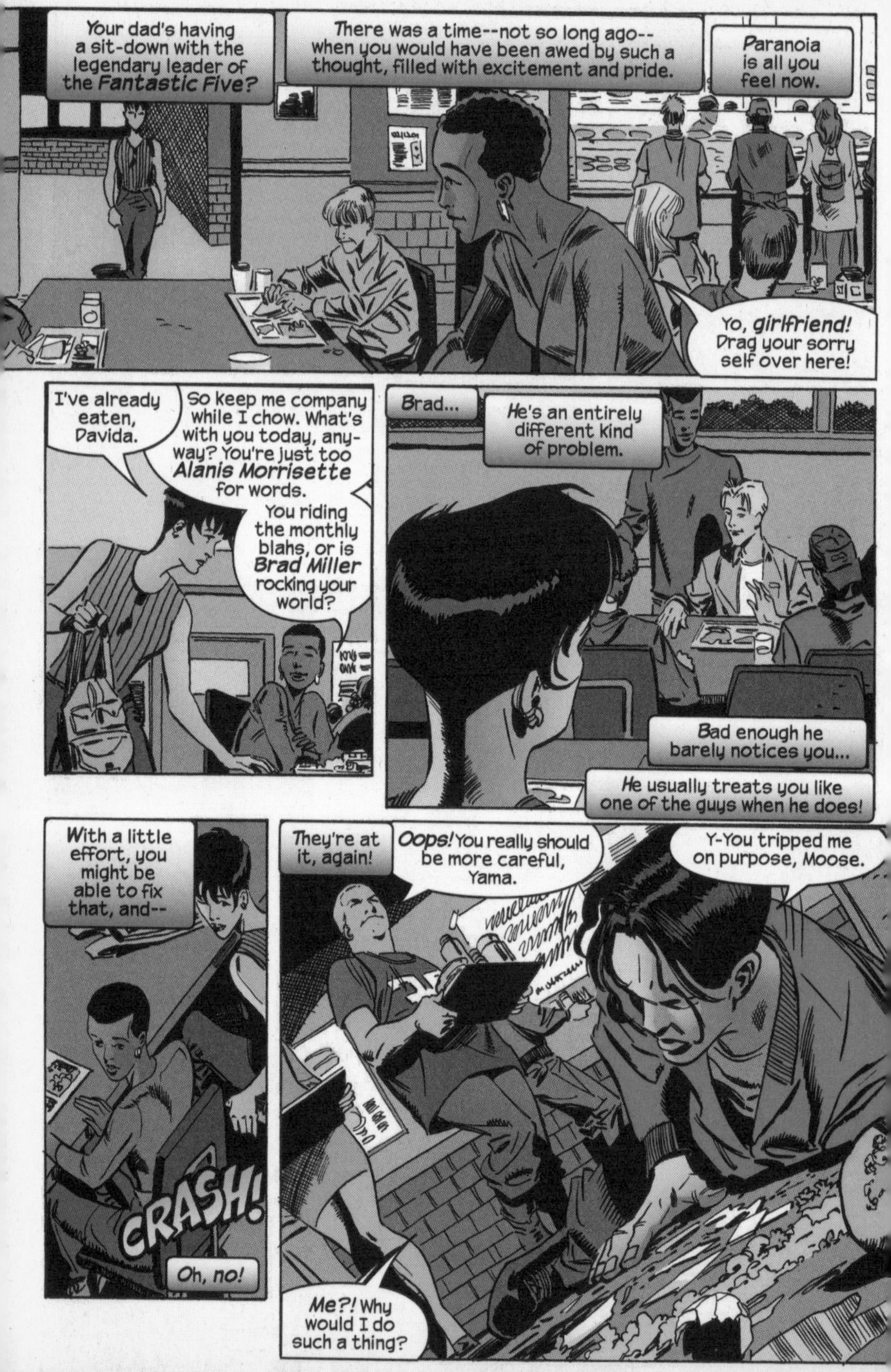

Your dad's having a sit-down with the legendary leader of the *Fantastic Five?*
There was a time--not so long ago--when you would have been awed by such a thought, filled with excitement and pride.
Paranoia is all you feel now.
Yo, *girlfriend!* Drag your sorry self over here!
I've already eaten, Davida.
So keep me company while I chow. What's with you today, any-way? You're just too *Alanis Morrisette* for words.
You riding the monthly blahs, or is *Brad Miller* rocking your world?
Brad...
He's an entirely different kind of problem.
Bad enough he barely notices you...
He usually treats you like one of the guys when he does!
With a little effort, you might be able to fix that, and--
CRASH!
Oh, no!
They're at it, again!
Oops! You really should be more careful, Yama.
Y-You tripped me on purpose, Moose.
Me?! Why would I do such a thing?

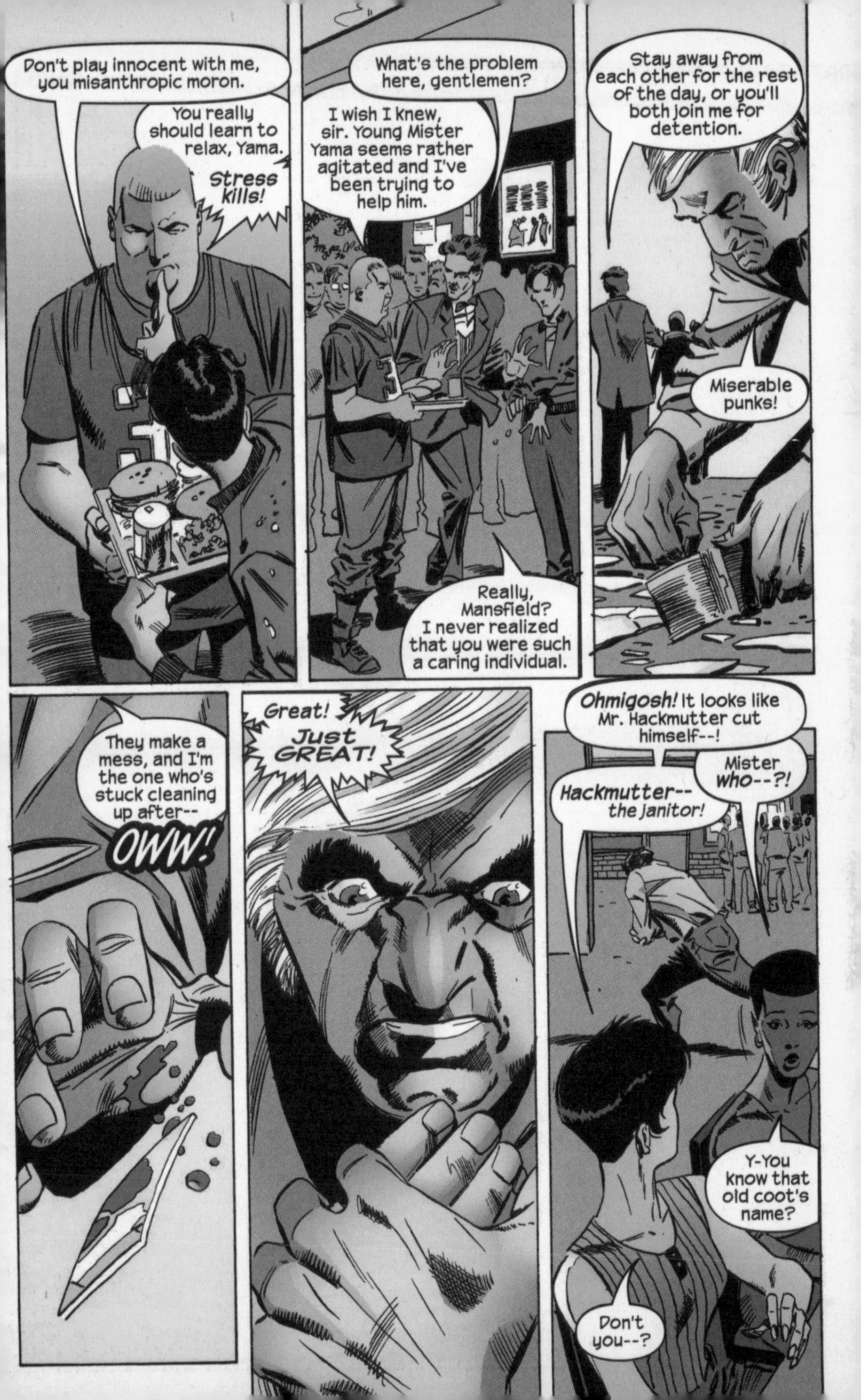

Don't play innocent with me, you misanthropic moron.
You really should learn to relax, Yama.
Stress kills!
What's the problem here, gentlemen?
I wish I knew, sir. Young Mister Yama seems rather agitated and I've been trying to help him.
Really, Mansfield? I never realized that you were such a caring individual.
Stay away from each other for the rest of the day, or you'll both join me for detention.
Miserable punks!
They make a mess, and I'm the one who's stuck cleaning up after--
OWW!
Great!
Just GREAT!
Ohmigosh! It looks like Mr. Hackmutter cut himself--!
Mister who--?!
Hackmutter-- the janitor!
Y-You know that old coot's name?
Don't you--?

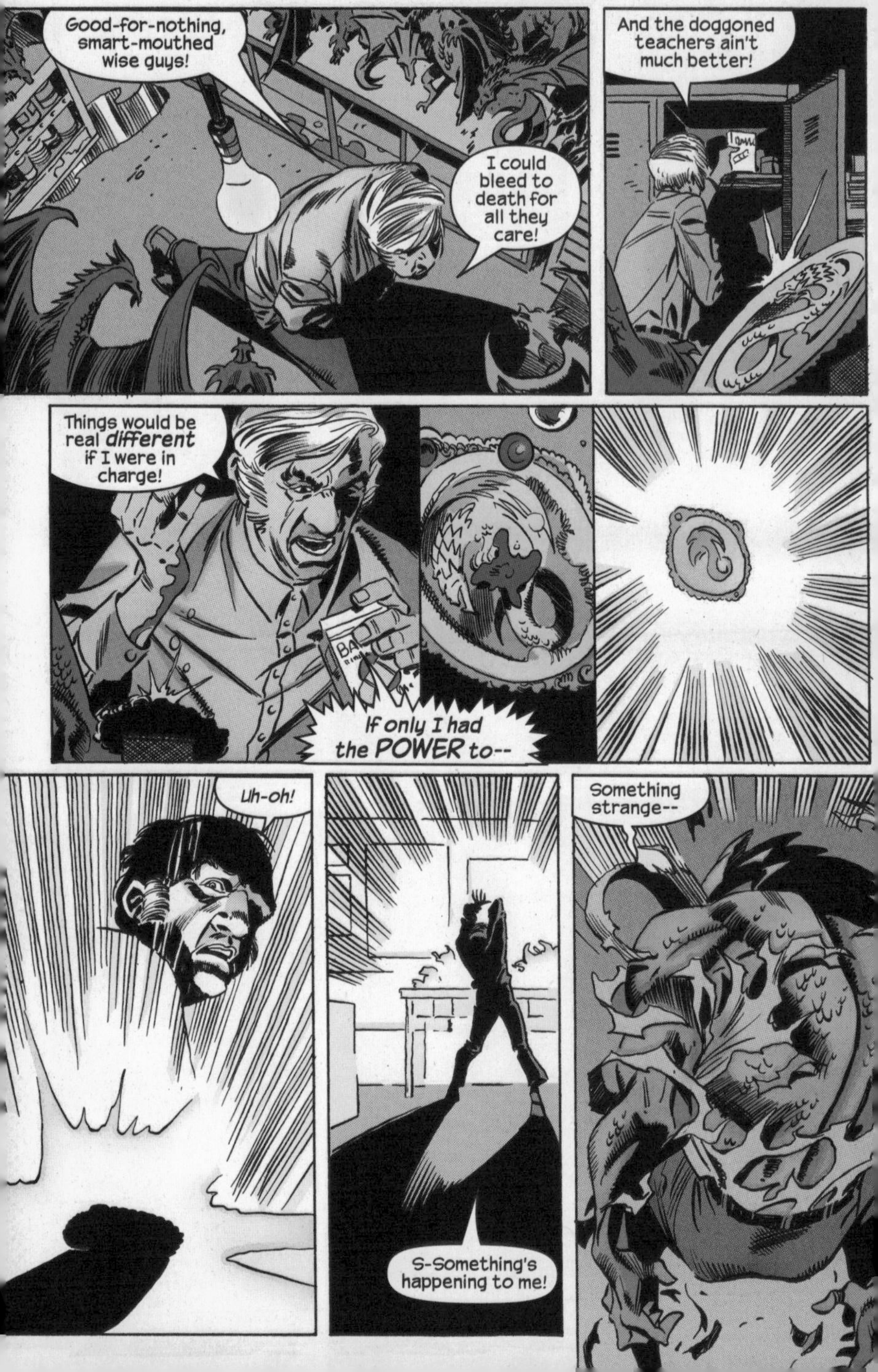
Good-for-nothing, smart-mouthed wise guys!
I could bleed to death for all they care!
And the doggoned teachers ain't much better!
Things would be real *different* if I were in charge!
If only I had the POWER to--
Uh-oh!
S-Something's happening to me!
Something strange--

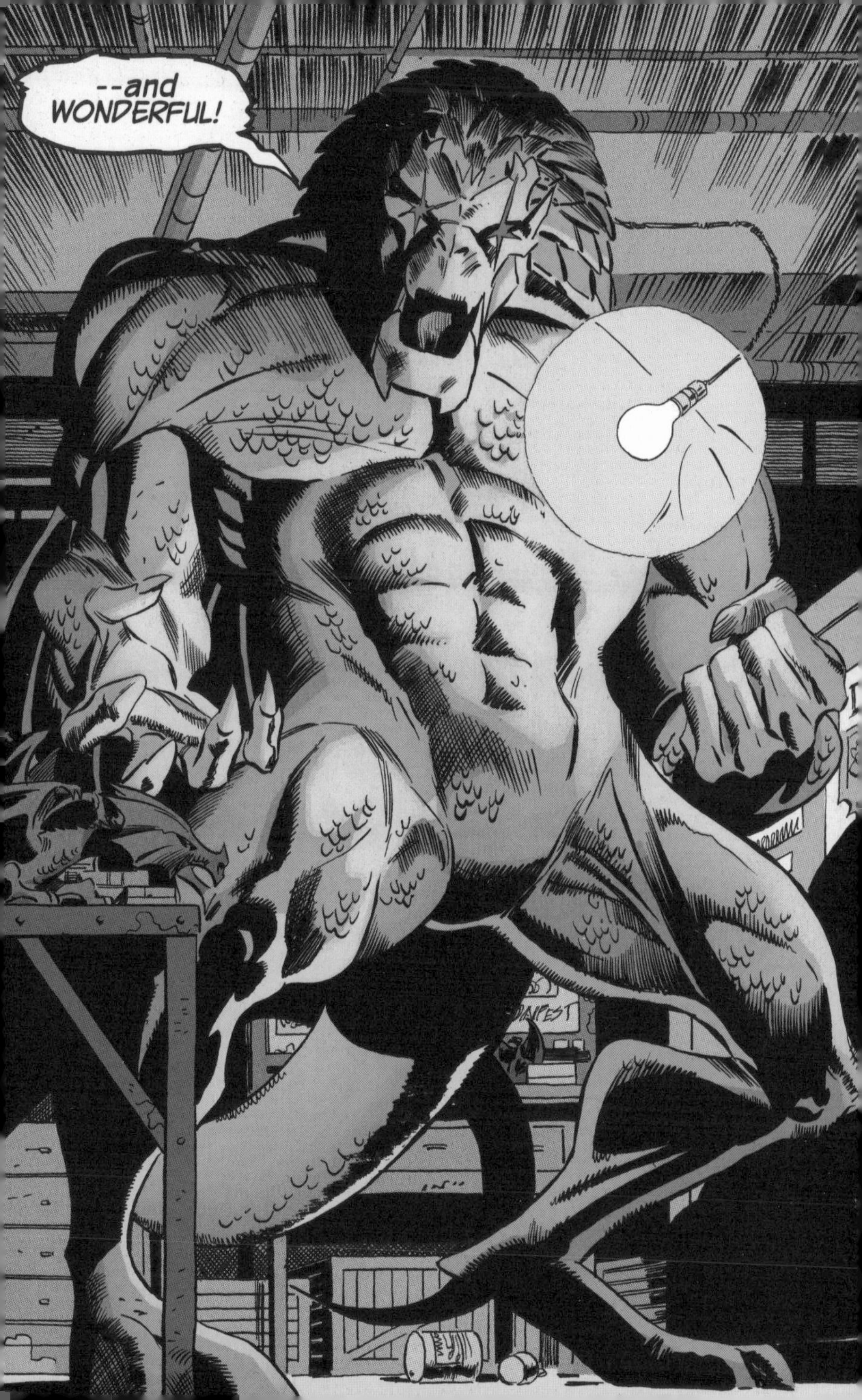
--and WONDERFUL!

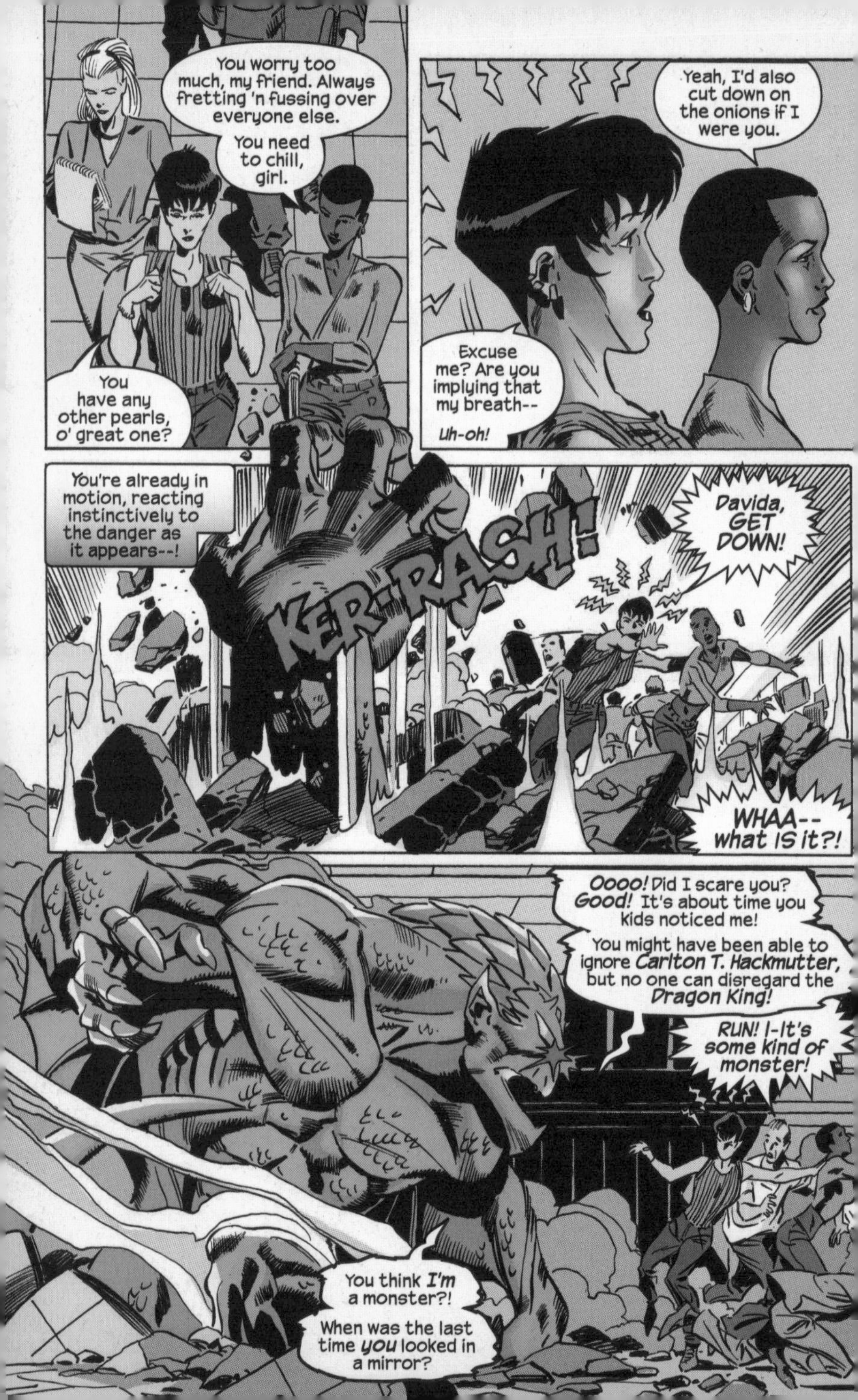

You worry too much, my friend. Always fretting 'n fussing over everyone else.
You need to chill, girl.
You have any other pearls, o' great one?
Yeah, I'd also cut down on the onions if I were you.
Excuse me? Are you implying that my breath--
Uh-oh!
You're already in motion, reacting instinctively to the danger as it appears--!
KER-RASH!
Davida, GET DOWN!
WHAA-- what IS it?!
Oooo! Did I scare you? Good! It's about time you kids noticed me!
You might have been able to ignore Carlton T. Hackmutter, but no one can disregard the Dragon King!
RUN! I-It's some kind of monster!
You think I'm a monster?!
When was the last time you looked in a mirror?

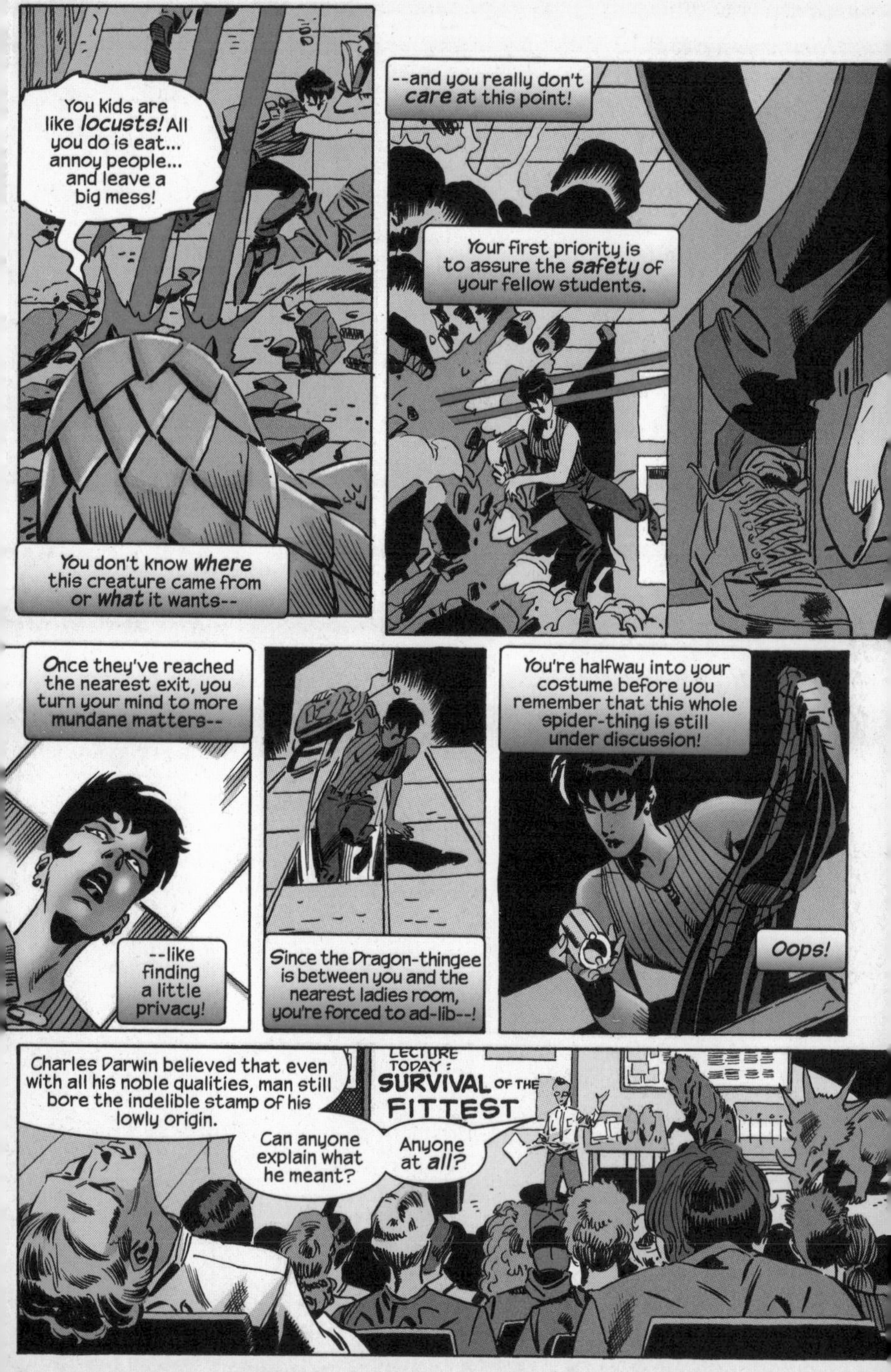
You kids are like locusts! All you do is eat... annoy people... and leave a big mess!
You don't know where this creature came from or what it wants--
--and you really don't care at this point!
Your first priority is to assure the safety of your fellow students.
Once they've reached the nearest exit, you turn your mind to more mundane matters--
--like finding a little privacy!
Since the Dragon-thingee is between you and the nearest ladies room, you're forced to ad-lib--!
You're halfway into your costume before you remember that this whole spider-thing is still under discussion!
Oops!
LECTURE TODAY: SURVIVAL OF THE FITTEST
Charles Darwin believed that even with all his noble qualities, man still bore the indelible stamp of his lowly origin.
Can anyone explain what he meant?
Anyone at all?

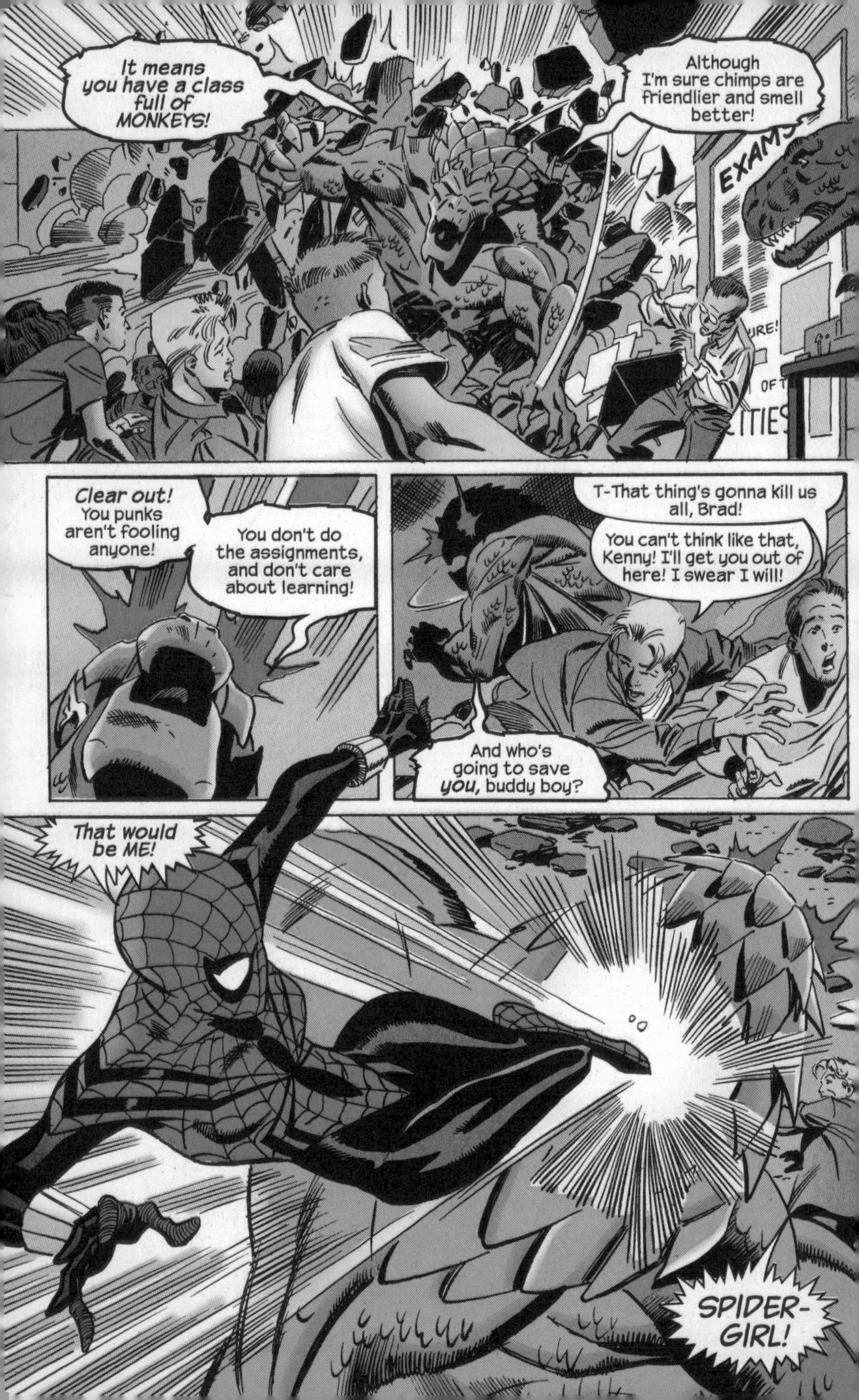
It means you have a class full of MONKEYS!
Although I'm sure chimps are friendlier and smell better!
EXAMS
Clear out! You punks aren't fooling anyone!
You don't do the assignments, and don't care about learning!
T-That thing's gonna kill us all, Brad!
You can't think like that, Kenny! I'll get you out of here! I swear I will!
And who's going to save you, buddy boy?
That would be ME!
SPIDER-GIRL!

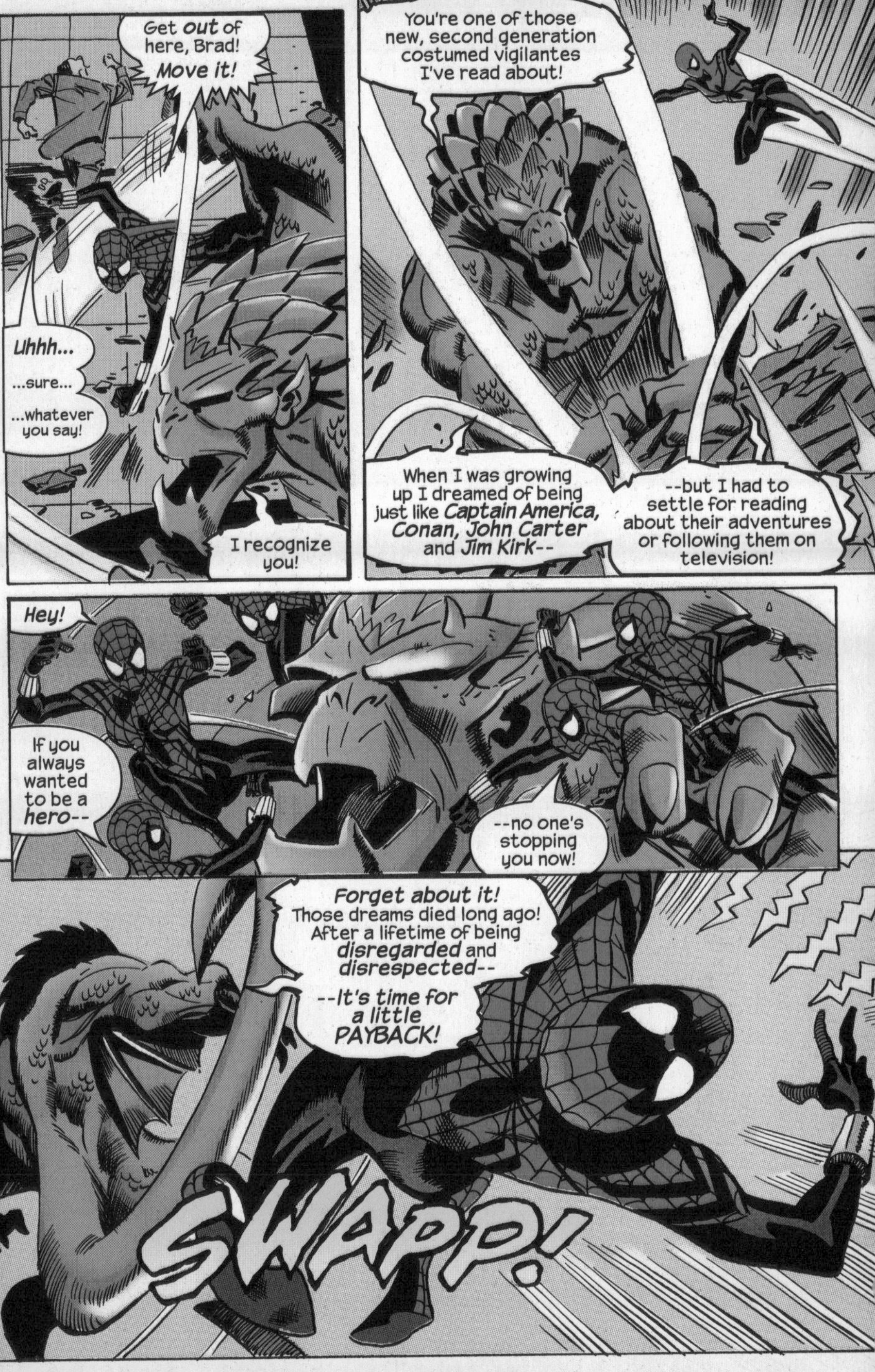
Get out of here, Brad! Move it!
Uhhh...
...sure...
...whatever you say!
I recognize you!
You're one of those new, second generation costumed vigilantes I've read about!
When I was growing up I dreamed of being just like Captain America, Conan, John Carter and Jim Kirk--
--but I had to settle for reading about their adventures or following them on television!
Hey!
If you always wanted to be a hero--
--no one's stopping you now!
Forget about it! Those dreams died long ago! After a lifetime of being disregarded and disrespected--
--It's time for a little PAYBACK!
SWAPP!

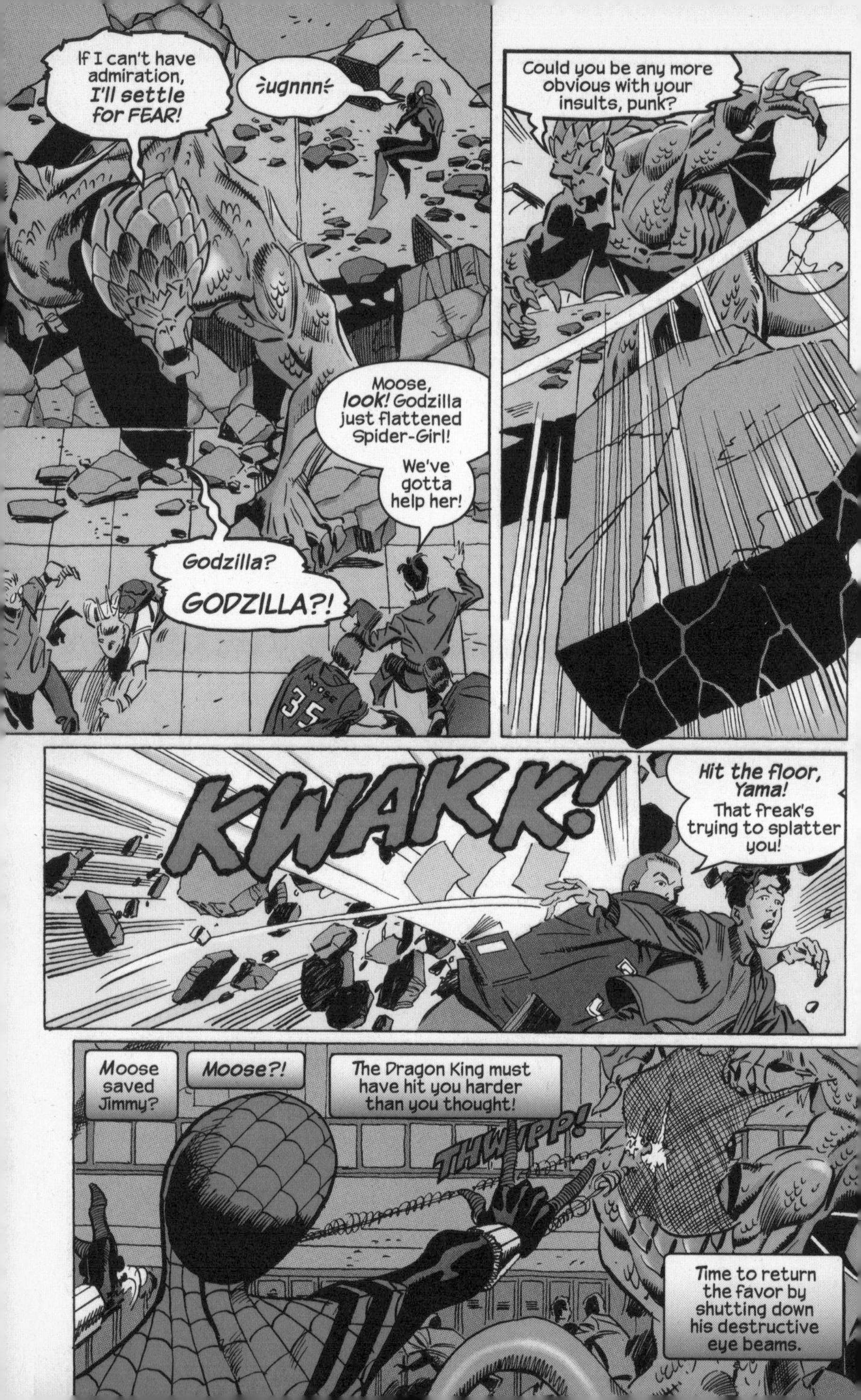

If I can't have admiration, I'll settle for FEAR!
-ugnnn-
Moose, look! Godzilla just flattened Spider-Girl!
We've gotta help her!
Godzilla?
GODZILLA?!
Could you be any more obvious with your insults, punk?
KWAKK!
Hit the floor, Yama!
That freak's trying to splatter you!
Moose saved Jimmy?
Moose?!
The Dragon King must have hit you harder than you thought!
THWIPP!
Time to return the favor by shutting down his destructive eye beams.

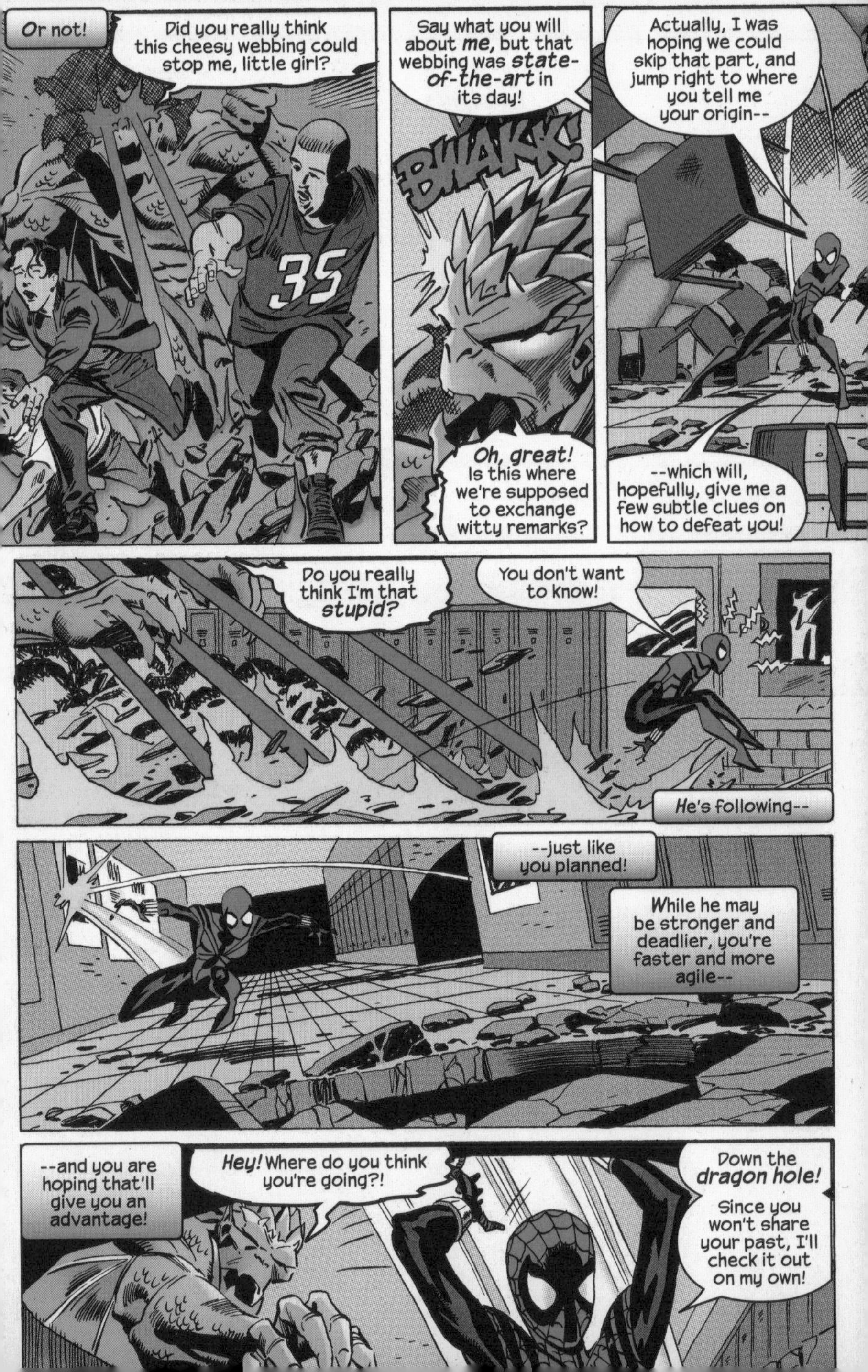
Or not!
Did you really think this cheesy webbing could stop me, little girl?
Say what you will about *me*, but that webbing was *state-of-the-art* in its day!
BWAKK!
Oh, great! Is this where we're supposed to exchange witty remarks?
Actually, I was hoping we could skip that part, and jump right to where you tell me your origin--
--which will, hopefully, give me a few subtle clues on how to defeat you!
Do you really think I'm that *stupid?*
You don't want to know!
He's following--
--just like you planned!
While he may be stronger and deadlier, you're faster and more agile--
--and you are hoping that'll give you an advantage!
Hey! Where do you think you're going?!
Down the *dragon hole!*
Since you won't share your past, I'll check it out on my own!

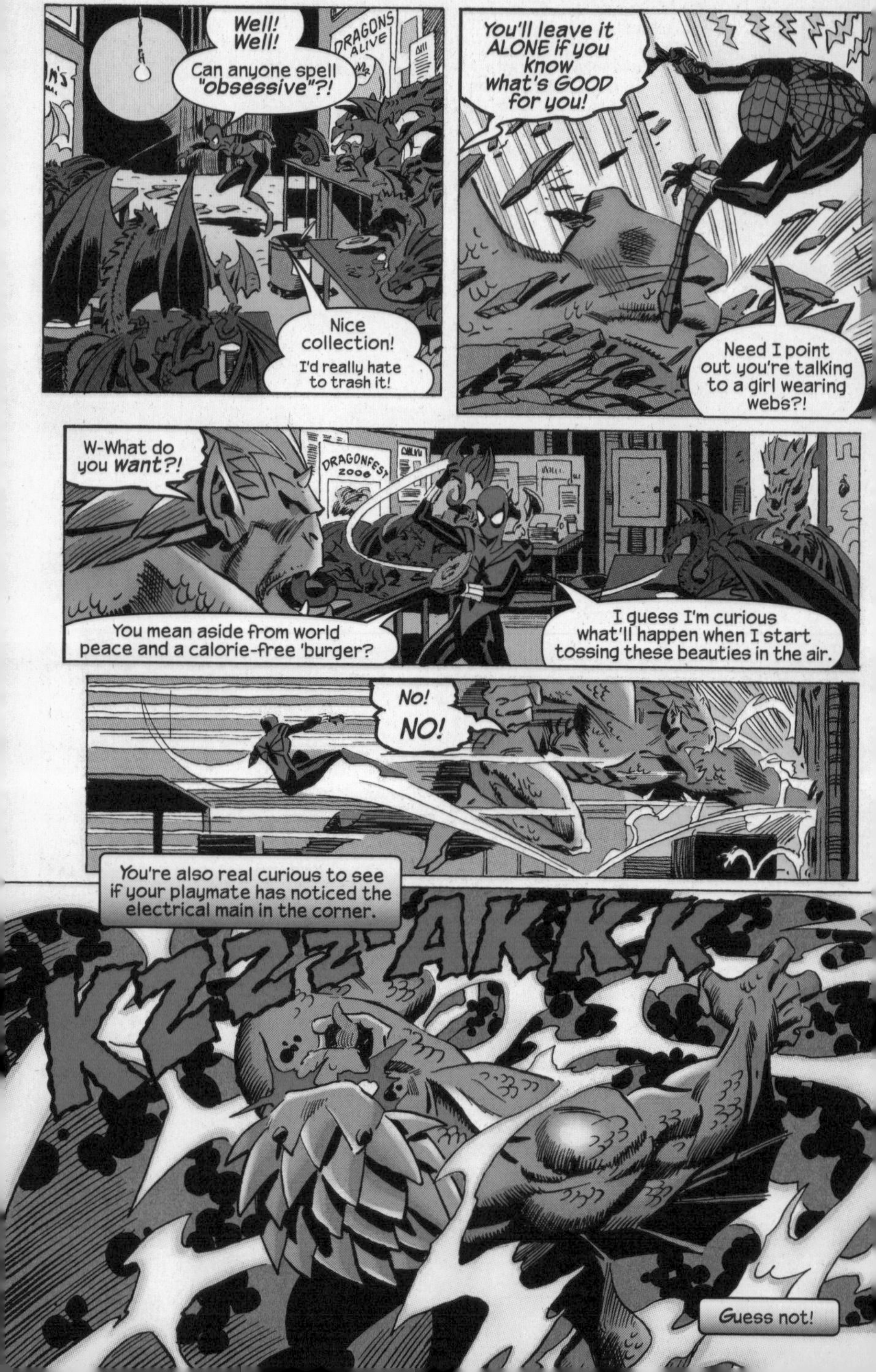
Well! Well!
Can anyone spell "obsessive"?!
DRAGONS ALIVE
Nice collection!
I'd really hate to trash it!
You'll leave it ALONE if you know what's GOOD for you!
Need I point out you're talking to a girl wearing webs?!
W-What do you want?!
DRAGONFEST 2006
You mean aside from world peace and a calorie-free 'burger?
I guess I'm curious what'll happen when I start tossing these beauties in the air.
No! NO!
You're also real curious to see if your playmate has noticed the electrical main in the corner.
KZZZ-AKKK
Guess not!

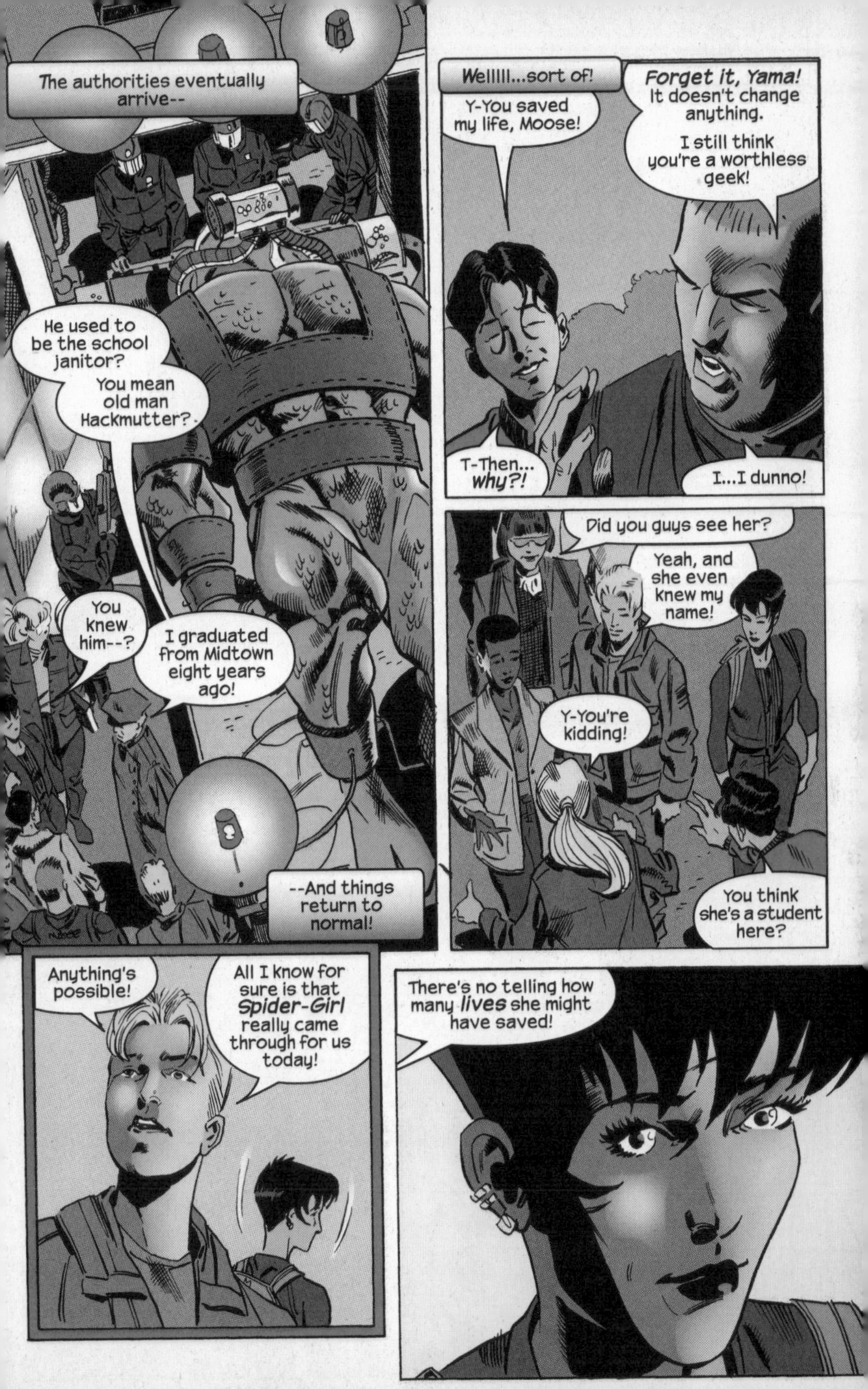
The authorities eventually arrive--
He used to be the school janitor?
You mean old man Hackmutter?
You knew him--?
I graduated from Midtown eight years ago!
--And things return to normal!
Wellllll...sort of!
Y-You saved my life, Moose!
Forget it, Yama! It doesn't change anything.
I still think you're a worthless geek!
T-Then... why?!
I...I dunno!
Did you guys see her?
Yeah, and she even knew my name!
Y-You're kidding!
You think she's a student here?
Anything's possible!
All I know for sure is that Spider-Girl really came through for us today!
There's no telling how many lives she might have saved!

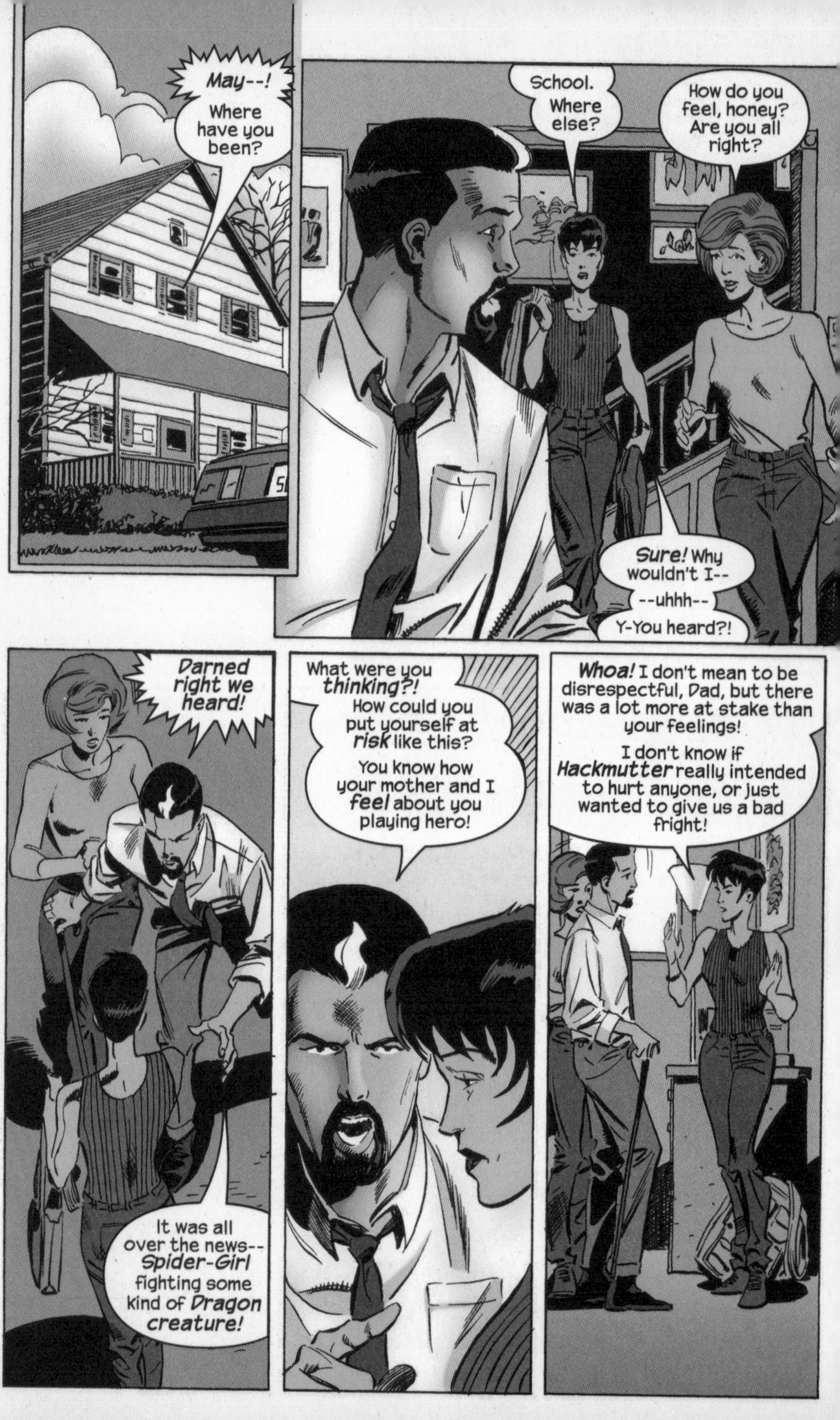
May--! Where have you been?
School. Where else?
How do you feel, honey? Are you all right?
Sure! Why wouldn't I--
--uhhh--
Y-You heard?!
Darned right we heard!
It was all over the news-- Spider-Girl fighting some kind of Dragon creature!
What were you thinking?! How could you put yourself at risk like this?
You know how your mother and I feel about you playing hero!
Whoa! I don't mean to be disrespectful, Dad, but there was a lot more at stake than your feelings!
I don't know if Hackmutter really intended to hurt anyone, or just wanted to give us a bad fright!

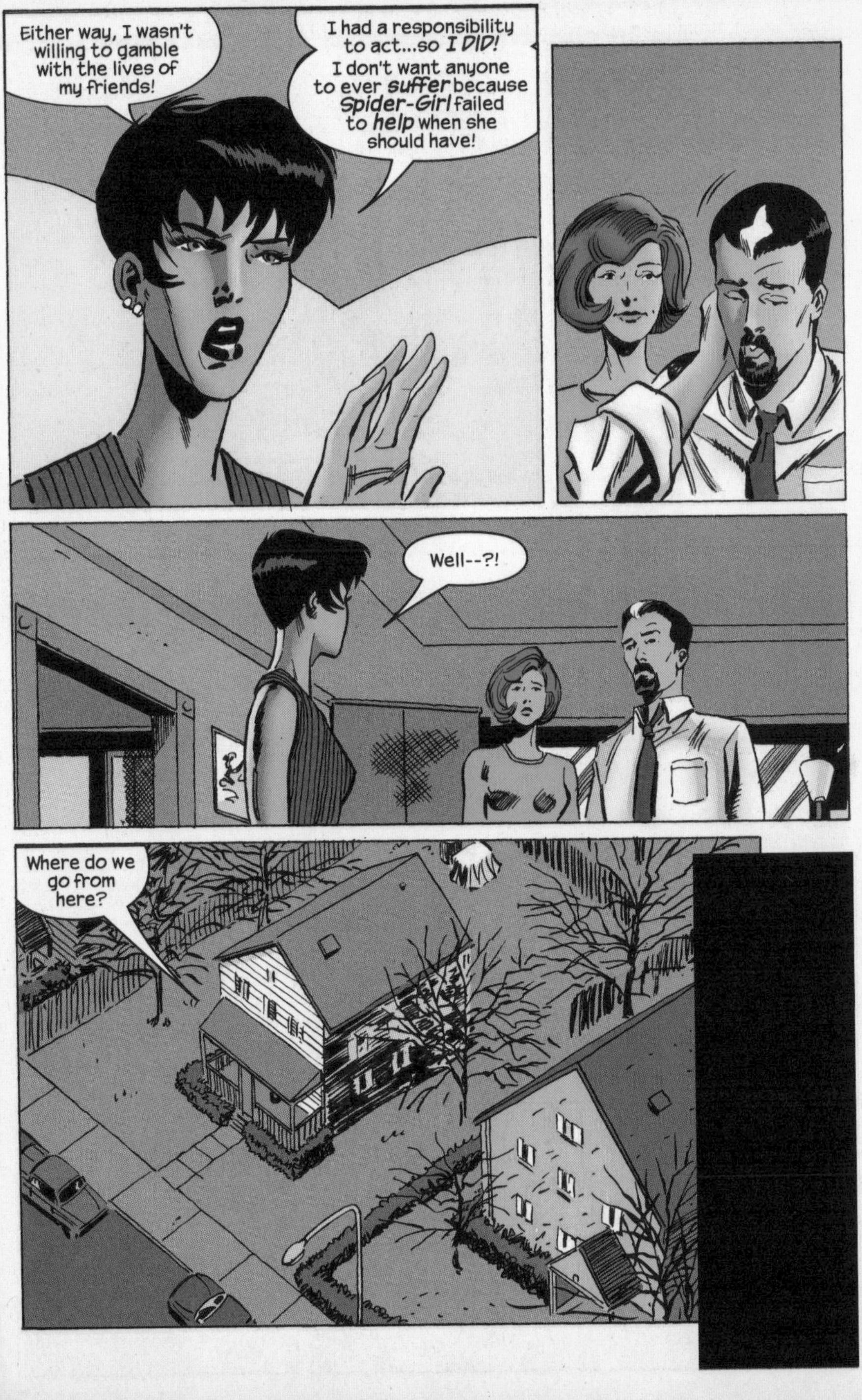
Either way, I wasn't willing to gamble with the lives of my friends!
I had a responsibility to act...so I DID!
I don't want anyone to ever suffer because Spider-Girl failed to help when she should have!
Well--?!
Where do we go from here?

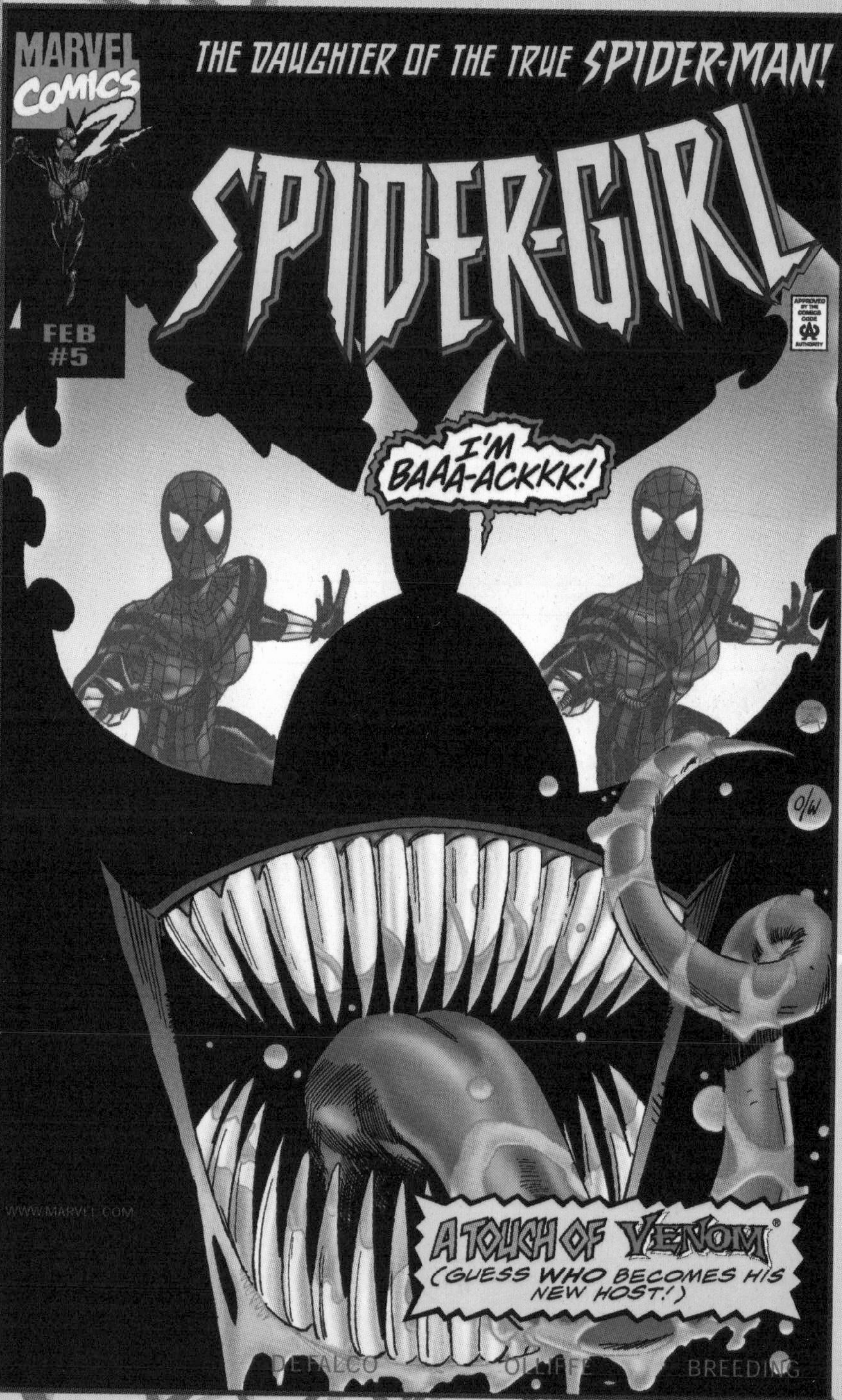
MARVEL COMICS
THE DAUGHTER OF THE TRUE SPIDER-MAN!
SPIDER-GIRL
FEB #5
APPROVED BY THE COMICS CODE AUTHORITY
I'M BAAA-ACKKK!
WWW.MARVEL.COM
A TOUCH OF VENOM®
(GUESS WHO BECOMES HIS NEW HOST!)
DEFALCO
OLLIFFE
BREEDING

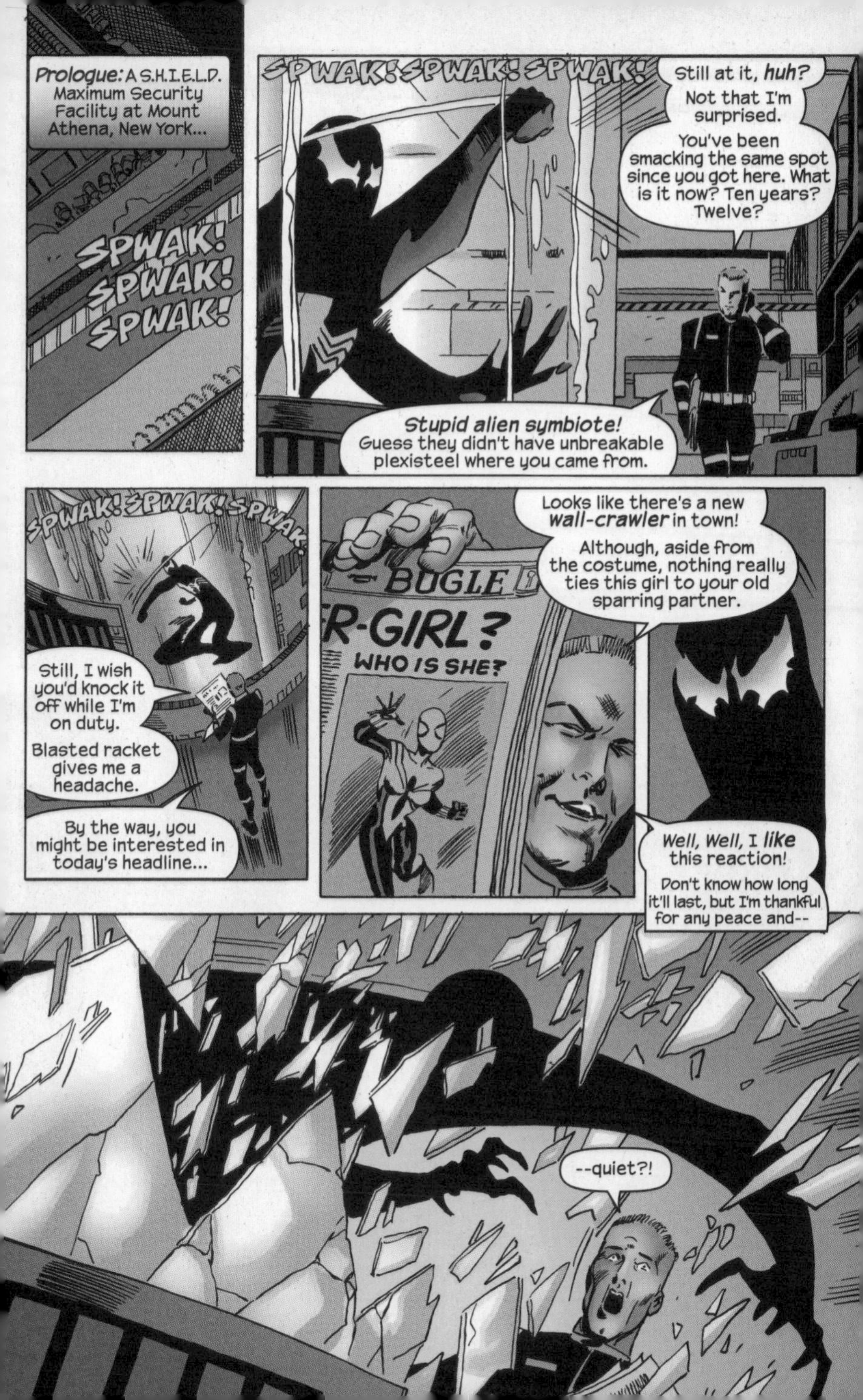
Prologue: A S.H.I.E.L.D. Maximum Security Facility at Mount Athena, New York...
SPWAK! SPWAK! SPWAK!
SPWAK! SPWAK! SPWAK!
Still at it, huh?
Not that I'm surprised.
You've been smacking the same spot since you got here. What is it now? Ten years? Twelve?
Stupid alien symbiote! Guess they didn't have unbreakable plexisteel where you came from.
SPWAK! SPWAK! SPWAK!
Still, I wish you'd knock it off while I'm on duty.
Blasted racket gives me a headache.
By the way, you might be interested in today's headline...
BUGLE
R-GIRL?
WHO IS SHE?
Looks like there's a new wall-crawler in town!
Although, aside from the costume, nothing really ties this girl to your old sparring partner.
Well, Well, I like this reaction!
Don't know how long it'll last, but I'm thankful for any peace and--
--quiet?!

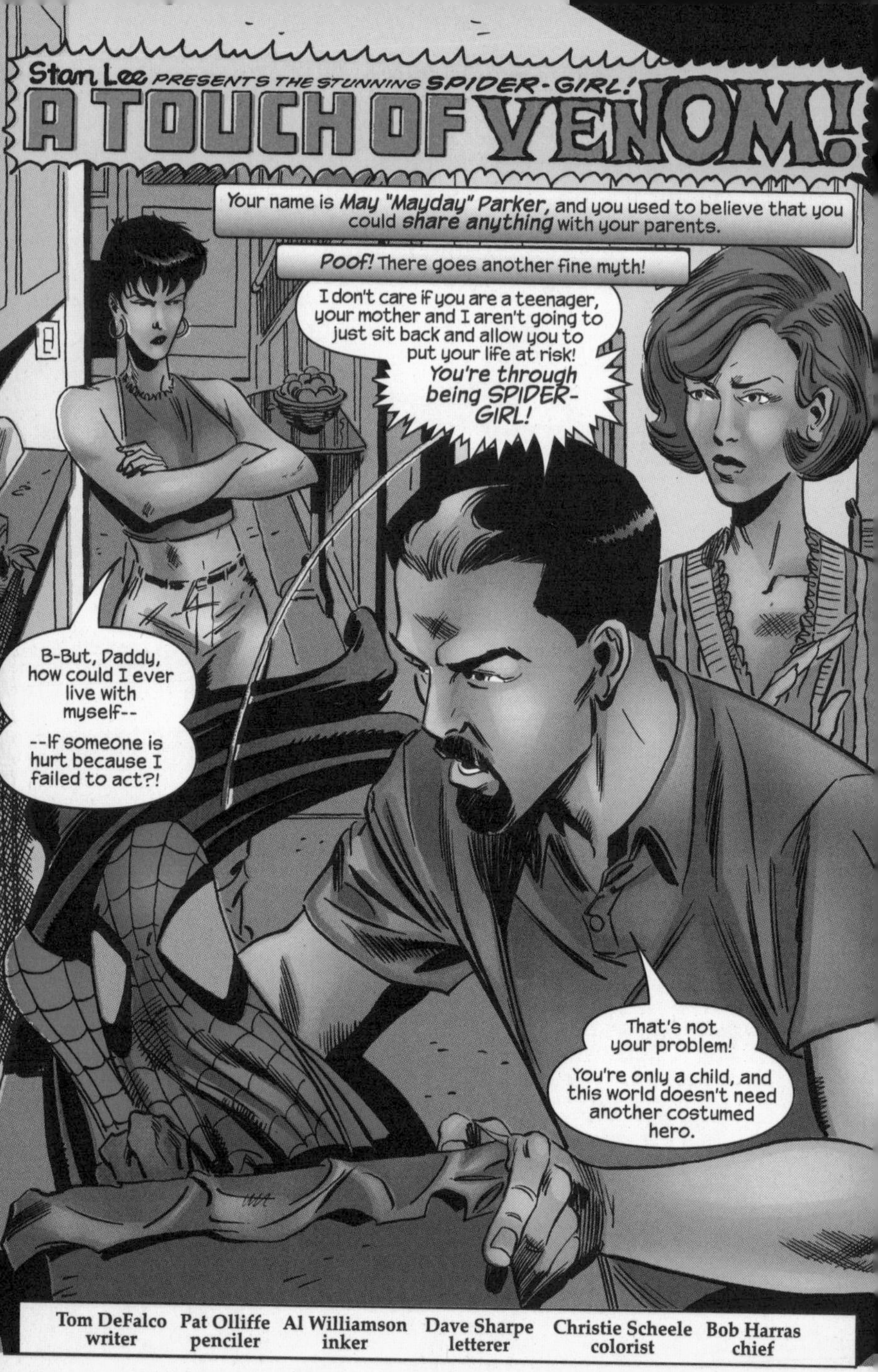
Stan Lee PRESENTS THE STUNNING SPIDER-GIRL!
A TOUCH OF VENOM!
Your name is May "Mayday" Parker, and you used to believe that you could share anything with your parents.
POOF! There goes another fine myth!
I don't care if you are a teenager, your mother and I aren't going to just sit back and allow you to put your life at risk!
You're through being SPIDER-GIRL!
B-But, Daddy, how could I ever live with myself--
--If someone is hurt because I failed to act?!
That's not your problem!
You're only a child, and this world doesn't need another costumed hero.
Tom DeFalco writer
Pat Olliffe penciler
Al Williamson inker
Dave Sharpe letterer
Christie Scheele colorist
Bob Harras chief

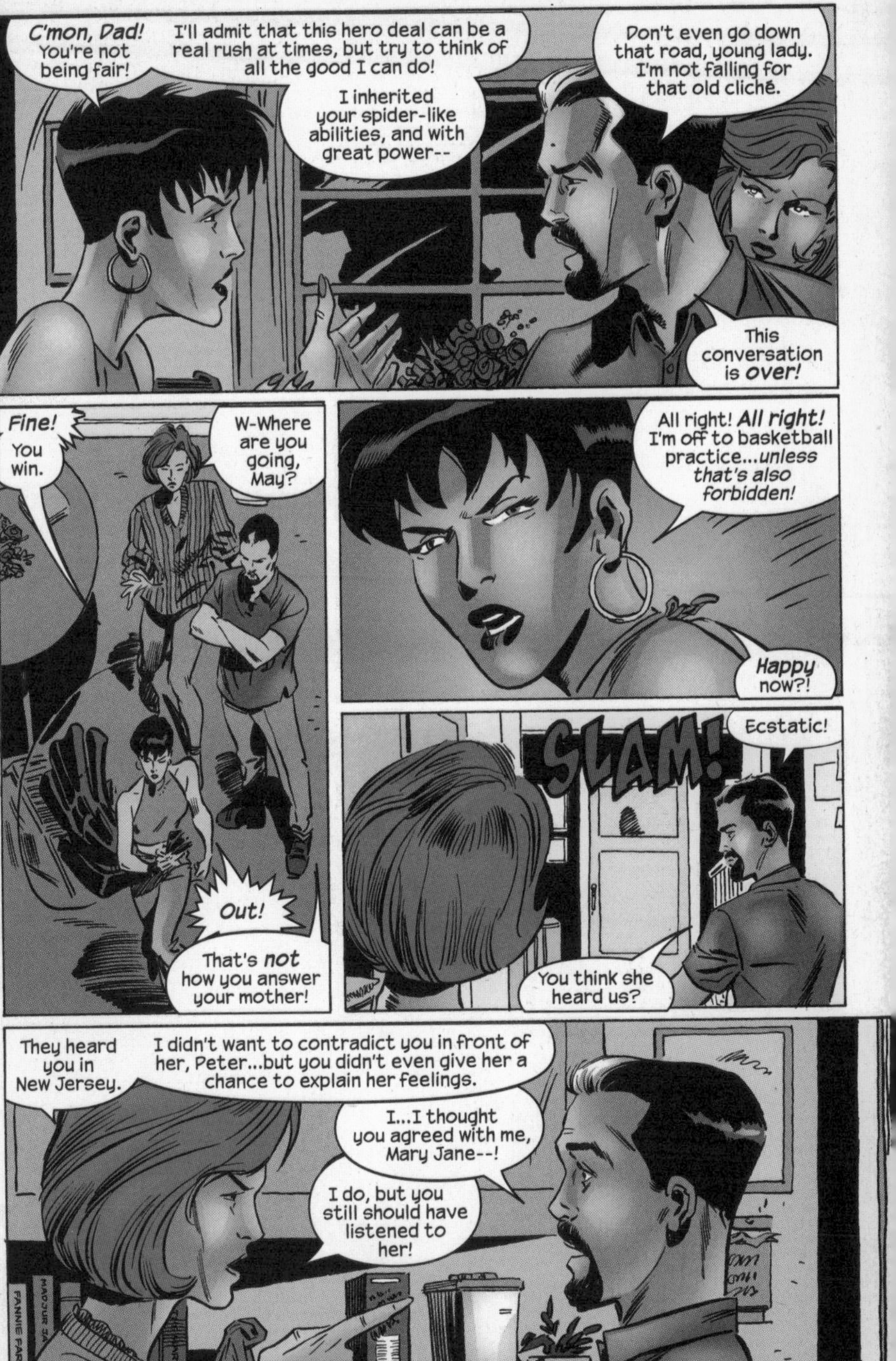
C'mon, Dad! You're not being fair!
I'll admit that this hero deal can be a real rush at times, but try to think of all the good I can do!
I inherited your spider-like abilities, and with great power--
Don't even go down that road, young lady. I'm not falling for that old cliché.
This conversation is over!
Fine! You win.
W-Where are you going, May?
Out!
That's not how you answer your mother!
All right! All right! I'm off to basketball practice...unless that's also forbidden!
Happy now?!
SLAM!
Ecstatic!
You think she heard us?
They heard you in New Jersey.
I didn't want to contradict you in front of her, Peter...but you didn't even give her a chance to explain her feelings.
I...I thought you agreed with me, Mary Jane--!
I do, but you still should have listened to her!
FANNIE FARMER

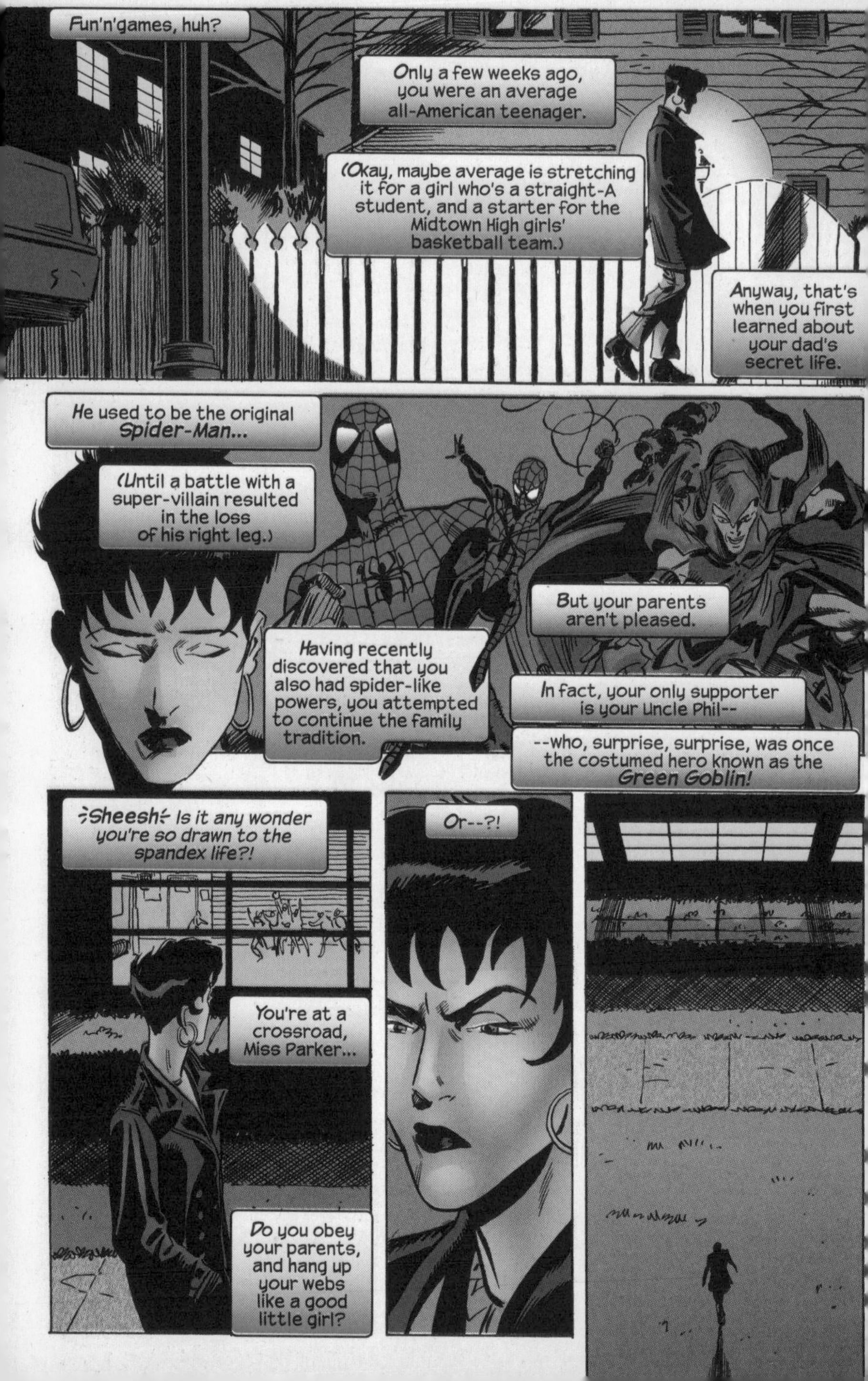
Fun'n'games, huh?
Only a few weeks ago, you were an average all-American teenager.
(Okay, maybe average is stretching it for a girl who's a straight-A student, and a starter for the Midtown High girls' basketball team.)
Anyway, that's when you first learned about your dad's secret life.
He used to be the original Spider-Man...
(Until a battle with a super-villain resulted in the loss of his right leg.)
Having recently discovered that you also had spider-like powers, you attempted to continue the family tradition.
But your parents aren't pleased.
In fact, your only supporter is your Uncle Phil--
--who, surprise, surprise, was once the costumed hero known as the Green Goblin!
Sheesh! Is it any wonder you're so drawn to the spandex life?!
You're at a crossroad, Miss Parker...
Do you obey your parents, and hang up your webs like a good little girl?
Or--?!

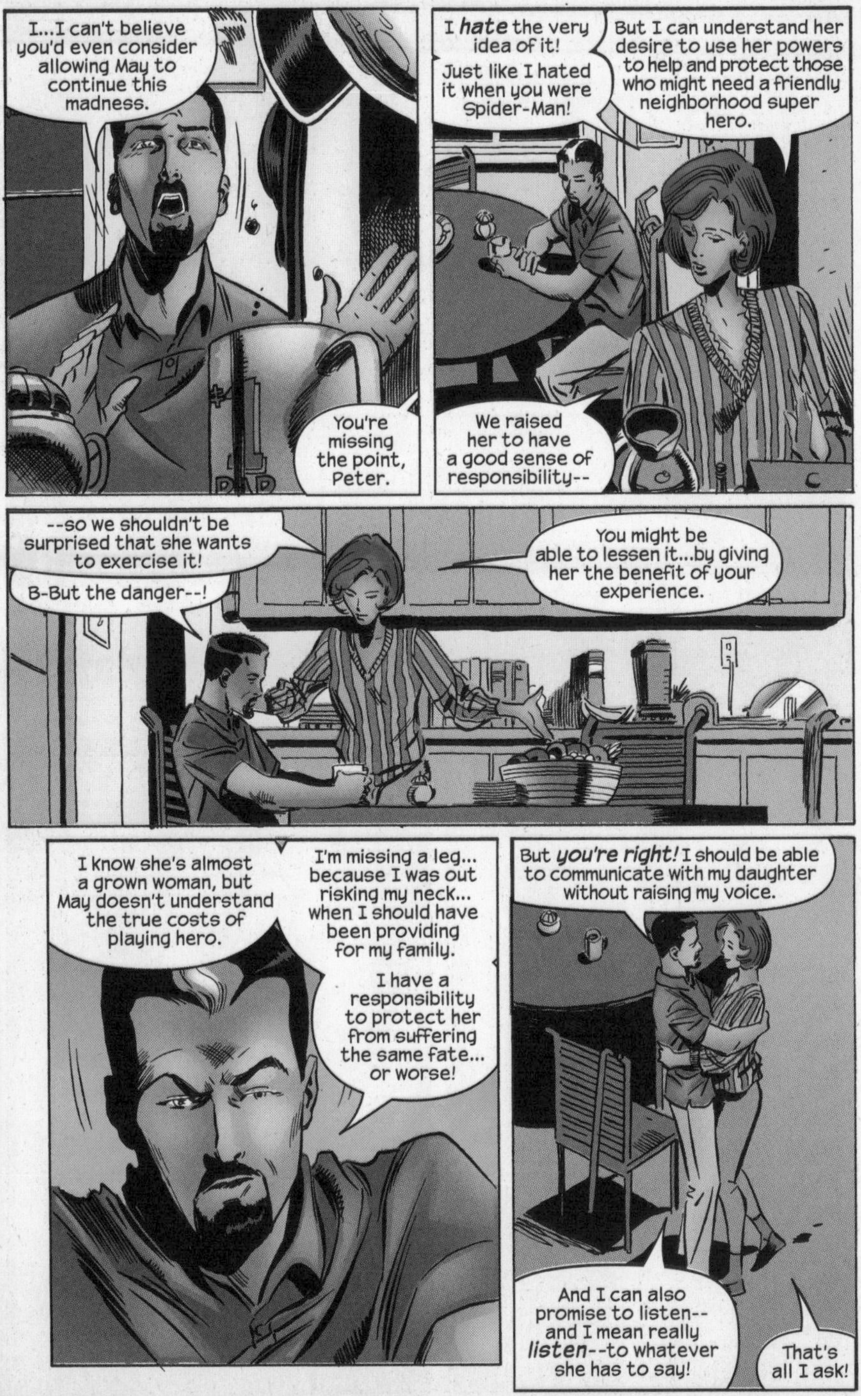

I...I can't believe you'd even consider allowing May to continue this madness.
You're missing the point, Peter.
I *hate* the very idea of it!
Just like I hated it when you were Spider-Man!
But I can understand her desire to use her powers to help and protect those who might need a friendly neighborhood super hero.
We raised her to have a good sense of responsibility--
--so we shouldn't be surprised that she wants to exercise it!
B-But the danger--!
You might be able to lessen it...by giving her the benefit of your experience.
I know she's almost a grown woman, but May doesn't understand the true costs of playing hero.
I'm missing a leg... because I was out risking my neck... when I should have been providing for my family.
I have a responsibility to protect her from suffering the same fate... or worse!
But *you're right!* I should be able to communicate with my daughter without raising my voice.
And I can also promise to listen-- and I mean really *listen*--to whatever she has to say!
That's all I ask!

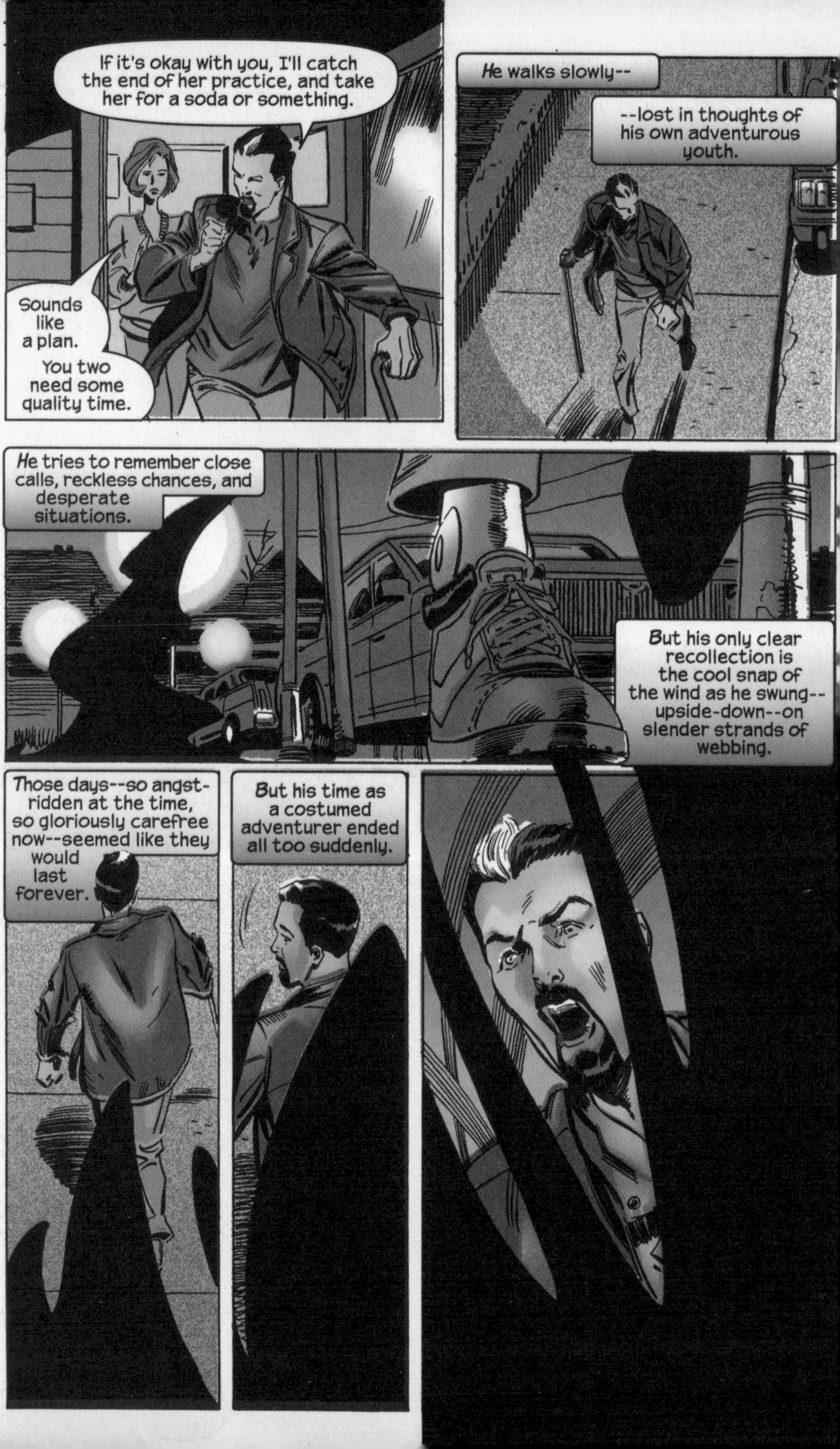
If it's okay with you, I'll catch the end of her practice, and take her for a soda or something.
Sounds like a plan. You two need some quality time.
He walks slowly--
--lost in thoughts of his own adventurous youth.
He tries to remember close calls, reckless chances, and desperate situations.
But his only clear recollection is the cool snap of the wind as he swung--upside-down--on slender strands of webbing.
Those days--so angst-ridden at the time, so gloriously carefree now--seemed like they would last forever.
But his time as a costumed adventurer ended all too suddenly.

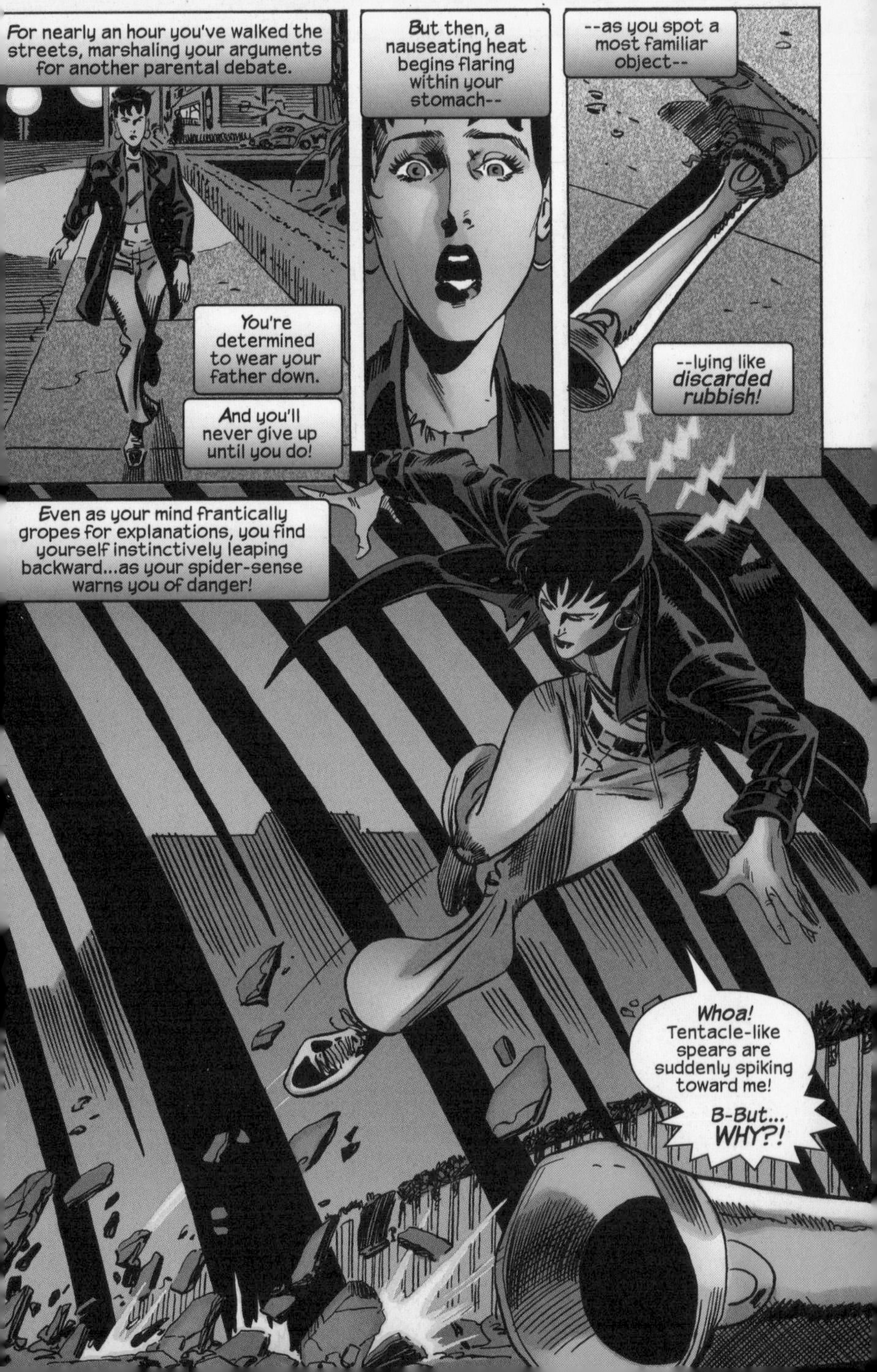
For nearly an hour you've walked the streets, marshaling your arguments for another parental debate.
You're determined to wear your father down.
And you'll never give up until you do!
But then, a nauseating heat begins flaring within your stomach--
--as you spot a most familiar object--
--lying like discarded rubbish!
Even as your mind frantically gropes for explanations, you find yourself instinctively leaping backward...as your spider-sense warns you of danger!
Whoa! Tentacle-like spears are suddenly spiking toward me!
B-But... WHY?!

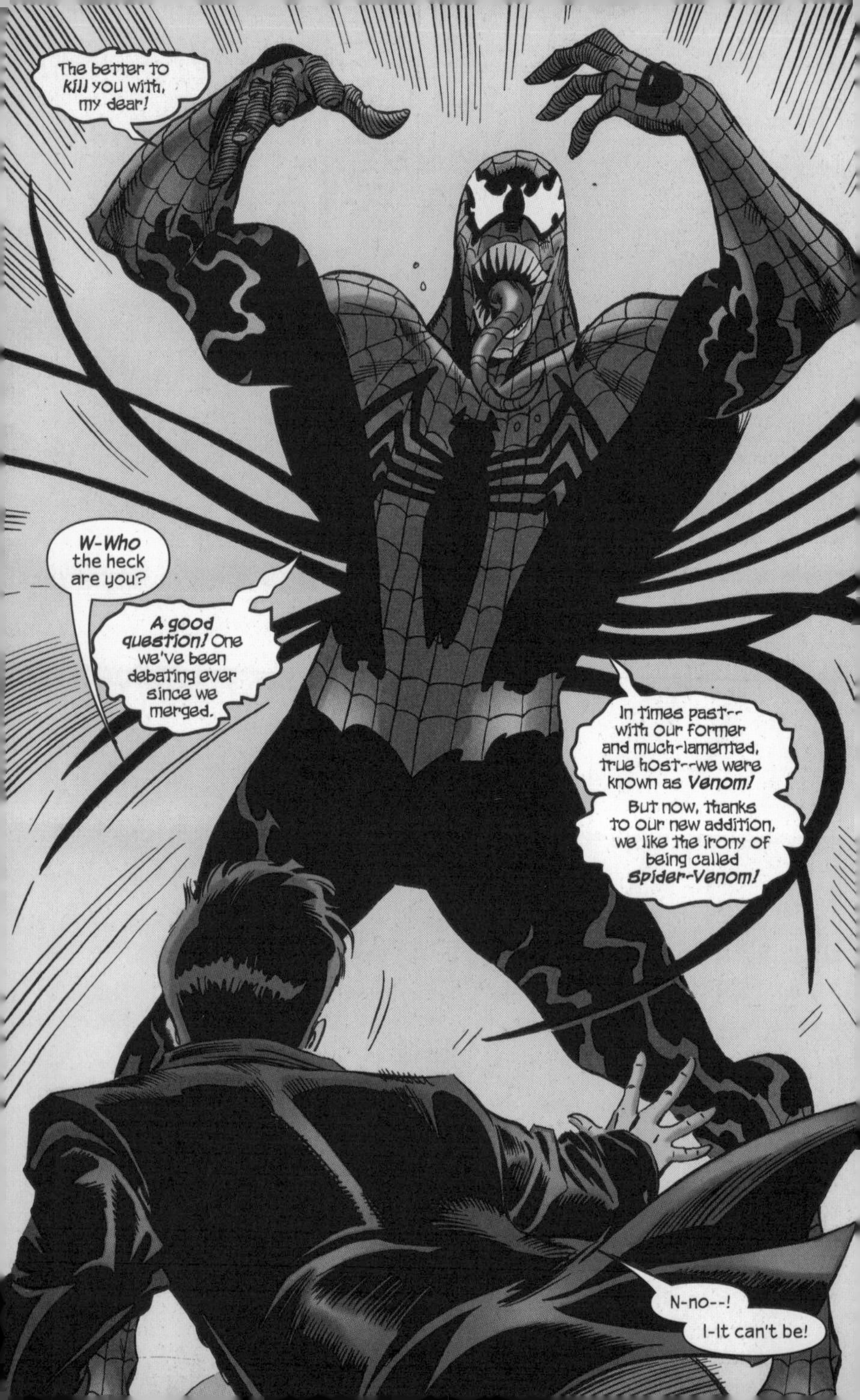
The better to kill you with, my dear!
W-Who the heck are you?
A good question! One we've been debating ever since we merged.
In times past--with our former and much-lamented, true host--we were known as Venom!
But now, thanks to our new addition, we like the irony of being called Spider-Venom!
N-no--!
I-It can't be!

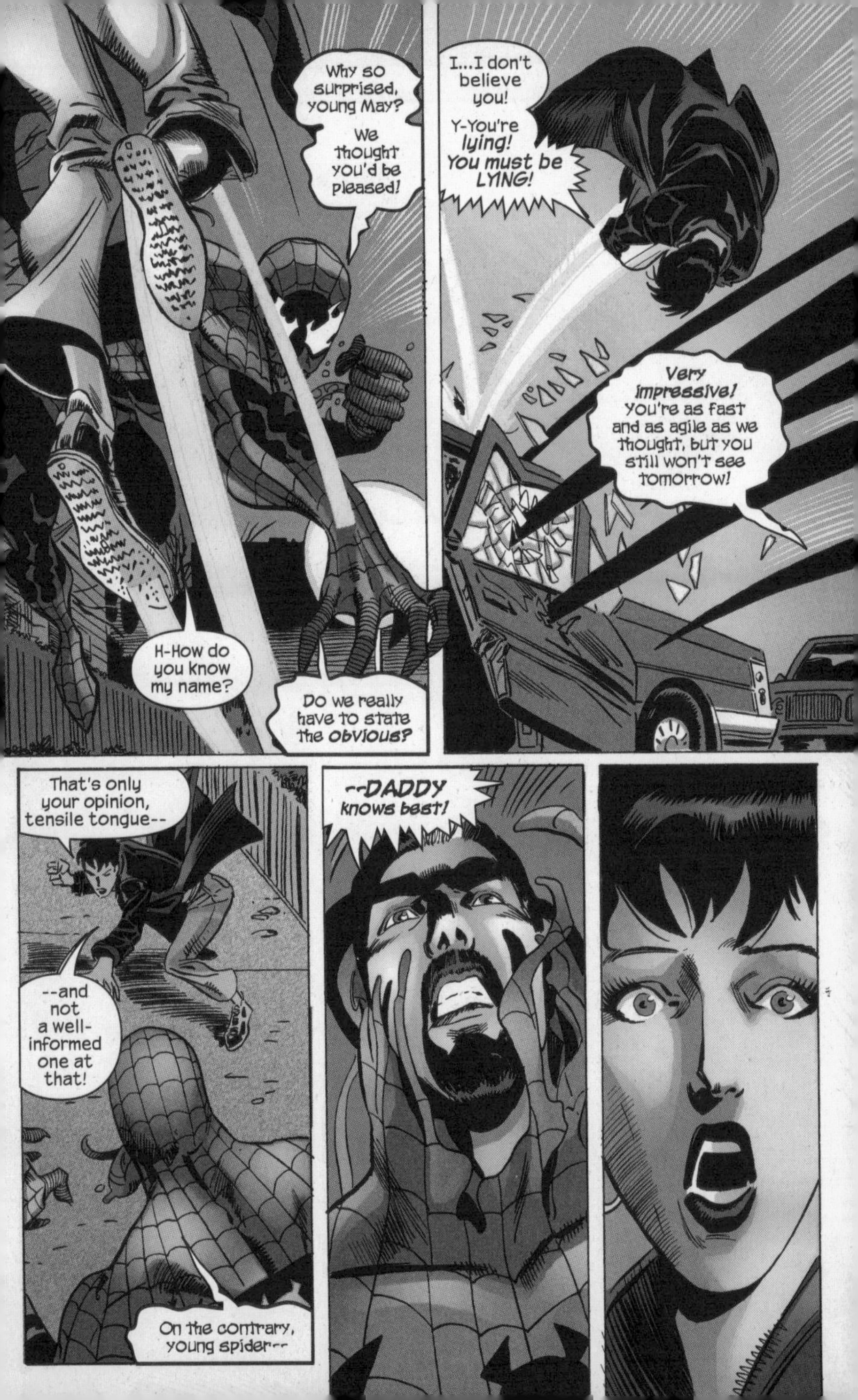

Why so surprised, young May?
We thought you'd be pleased!
H-How do you know my name?
Do we really have to state the *obvious?*
I...I don't believe you!
Y-You're *lying! You must be LYING!*
Very impressive! You're as fast and as agile as we thought, but you still won't see tomorrow!
That's only your opinion, tensile tongue--
--and not a well-informed one at that!
On the contrary, young spider--
--DADDY knows best!

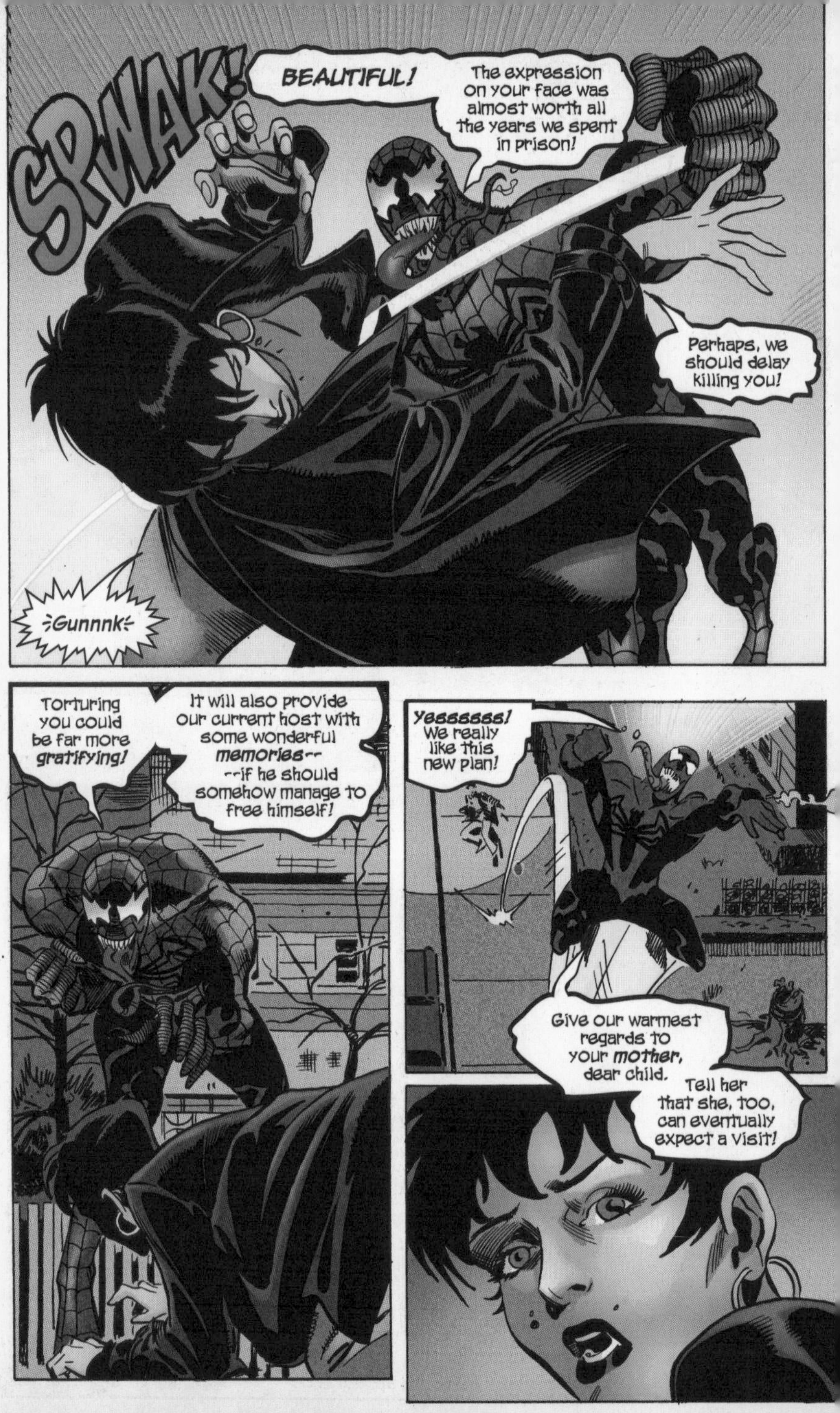
SPWAK!
BEAUTIFUL!
The expression on your face was almost worth all the years we spent in prison!
Perhaps, we should delay killing you!
Gunnnk
Torturing you could be far more gratifying!
It will also provide our current host with some wonderful memories--
--if he should somehow manage to free himself!
Yessssss! We really like this new plan!
Give our warmest regards to your mother, dear child.
Tell her that she, too, can eventually expect a visit!

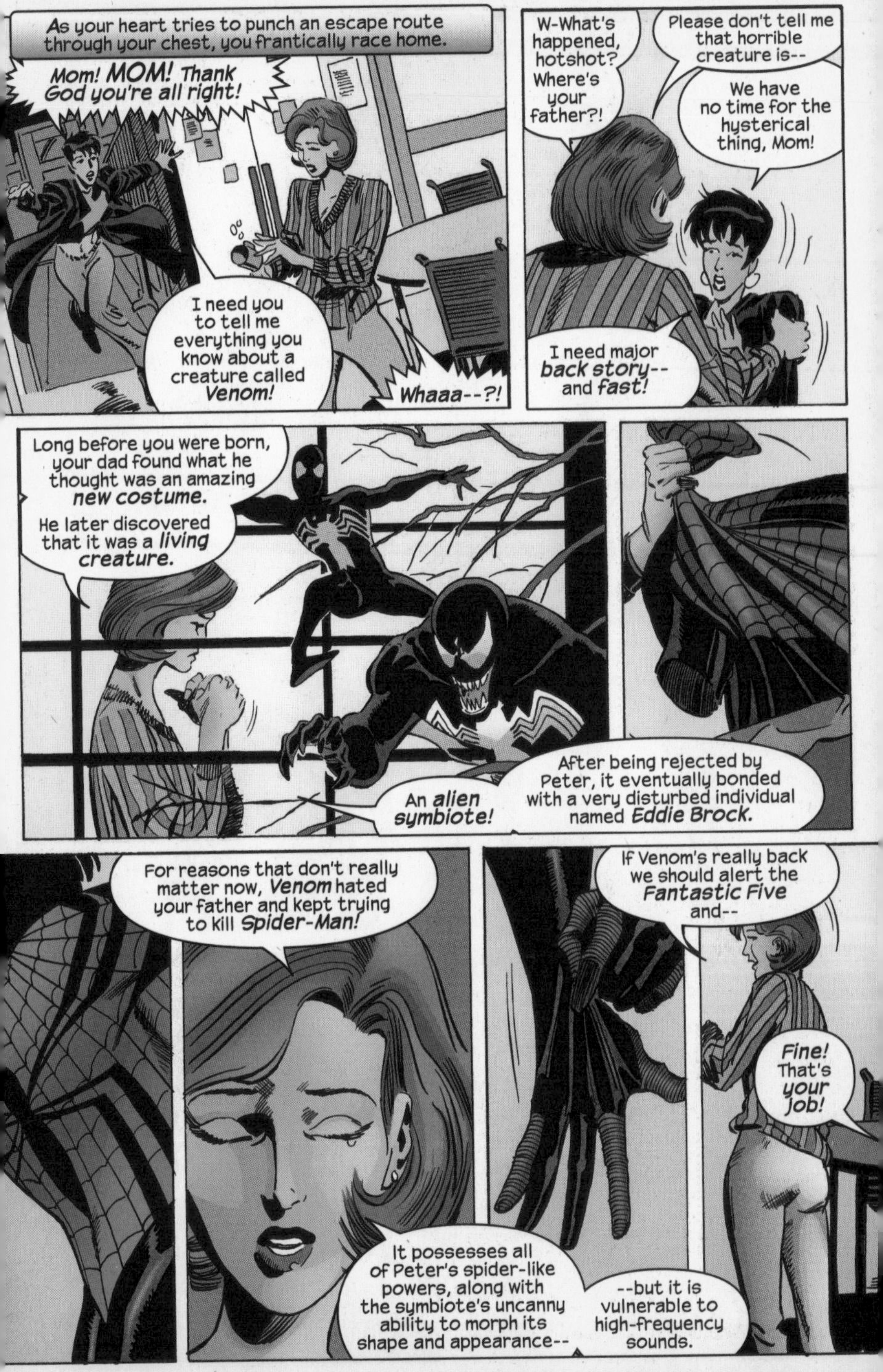

As your heart tries to punch an escape route through your chest, you frantically race home.
Mom! MOM! Thank God you're all right!
I need you to tell me everything you know about a creature called Venom!
Whaaa--?!
W-What's happened, hotshot? Where's your father?!
Please don't tell me that horrible creature is--
We have no time for the hysterical thing, Mom!
I need major back story-- and fast!
Long before you were born, your dad found what he thought was an amazing new costume.
He later discovered that it was a living creature.
An alien symbiote!
After being rejected by Peter, it eventually bonded with a very disturbed individual named Eddie Brock.
For reasons that don't really matter now, Venom hated your father and kept trying to kill Spider-Man!
It possesses all of Peter's spider-like powers, along with the symbiote's uncanny ability to morph its shape and appearance--
--but it is vulnerable to high-frequency sounds.
If Venom's really back we should alert the Fantastic Five and--
Fine! That's your job!

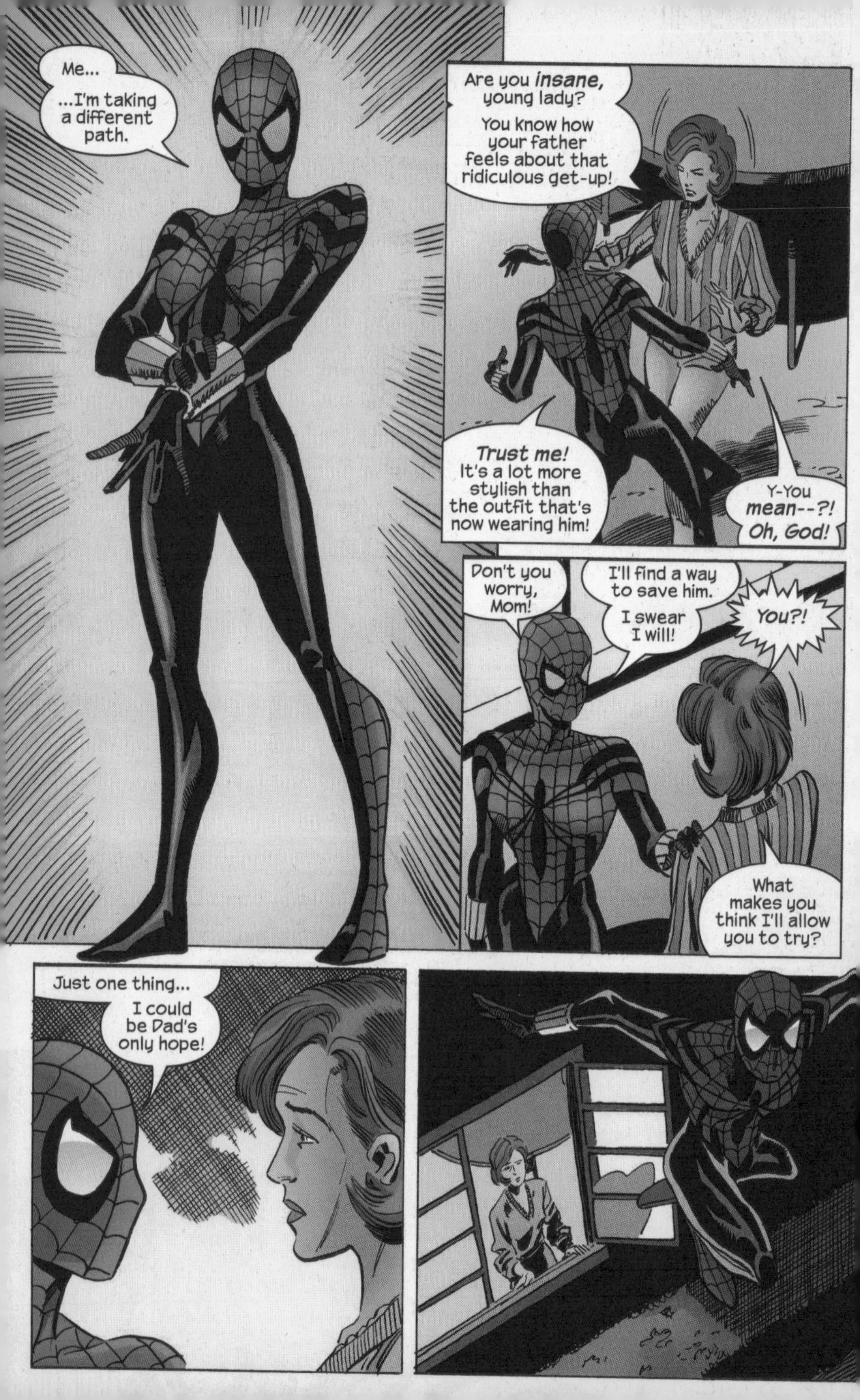
Me...
...I'm taking a different path.
Are you insane, young lady?
You know how your father feels about that ridiculous get-up!
Trust me! It's a lot more stylish than the outfit that's now wearing him!
Y-You mean--?! Oh, God!
Don't you worry, Mom!
I'll find a way to save him.
I swear I will!
You?!
What makes you think I'll allow you to try?
Just one thing...
I could be Dad's only hope!

Even as you web-swing across town, you think about Venom's only weakness--

--and immediately realize that you need the services of a certain someone!

Uncle Phil--?

Be with you in a--!

Oh! Y-You're not--!

You must lead a very interesting life if you have other visitors who enter via the window...but we don't have time to get into that now.

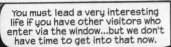

What can I do for you... uhhh... Spider-Girl?

Let's dispense with the verbal games, Uncle Phil.

You know exactly who I am...and I need your help!

Venom has escaped, and he's got my dad!

When you were the Green Goblin, you had some kind of sonic super-power.

Yeah, I used to call it my lunatic laugh.

Lunatic laugh?!? You're kidding, right?

Hey! It sounded better when I was younger.

You want my help? Save the criticism until after you've filled me in.

Deal! But we'd better talk on the fly...

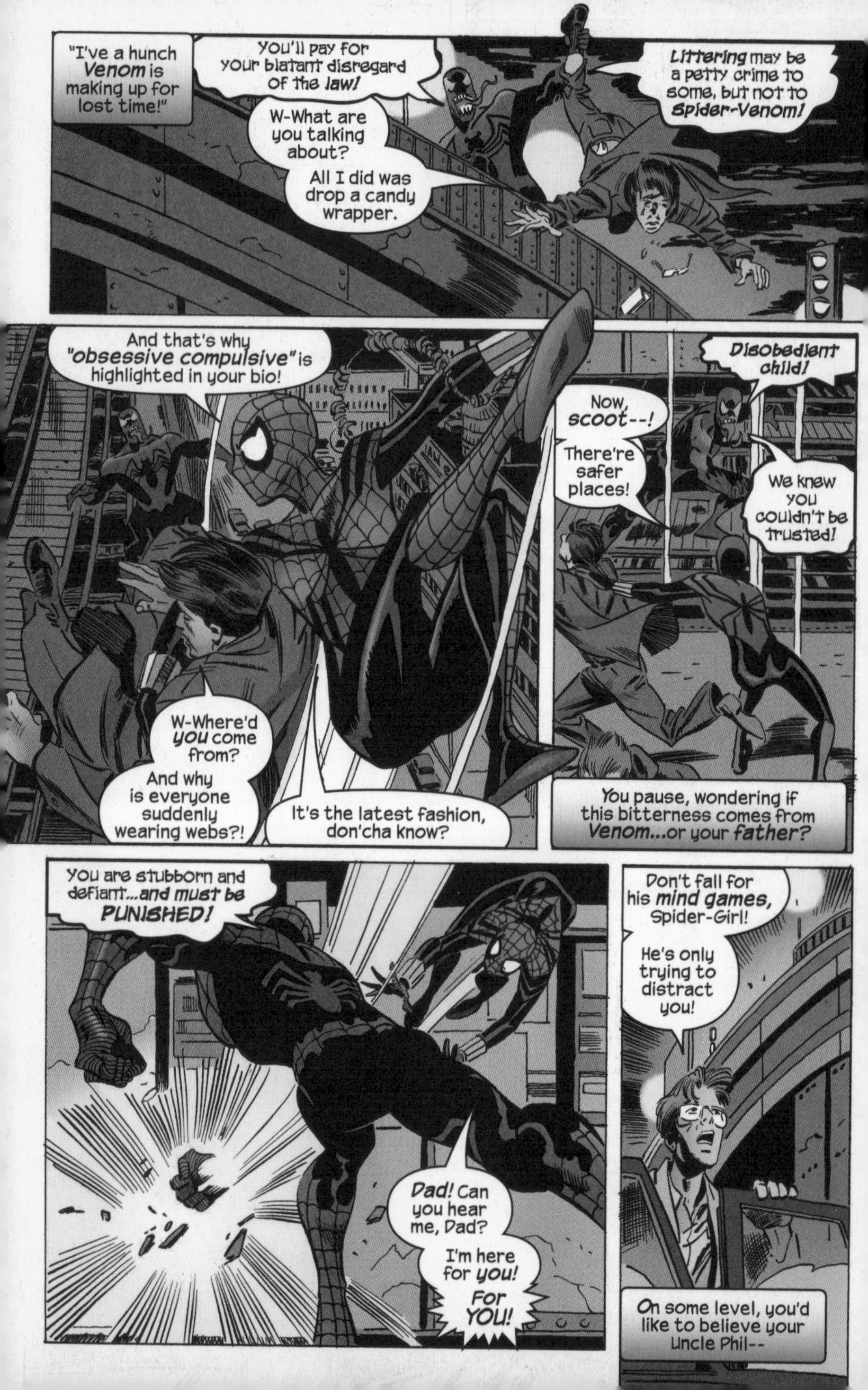
"I've a hunch Venom is making up for lost time!"
You'll pay for your blatant disregard of the law!
W-What are you talking about?
All I did was drop a candy wrapper.
Littering may be a petty crime to some, but not to Spider-Venom!
And that's why "obsessive compulsive" is highlighted in your bio!
W-Where'd you come from?
And why is everyone suddenly wearing webs?!
It's the latest fashion, don'cha know?
Disobedient child!
Now, scoot--!
There're safer places!
We knew you couldn't be trusted!
You pause, wondering if this bitterness comes from Venom...or your father?
You are stubborn and defiant...and must be PUNISHED!
Dad! Can you hear me, Dad?
I'm here for you!
For YOU!
Don't fall for his mind games, Spider-Girl!
He's only trying to distract you!
On some level, you'd like to believe your Uncle Phil--

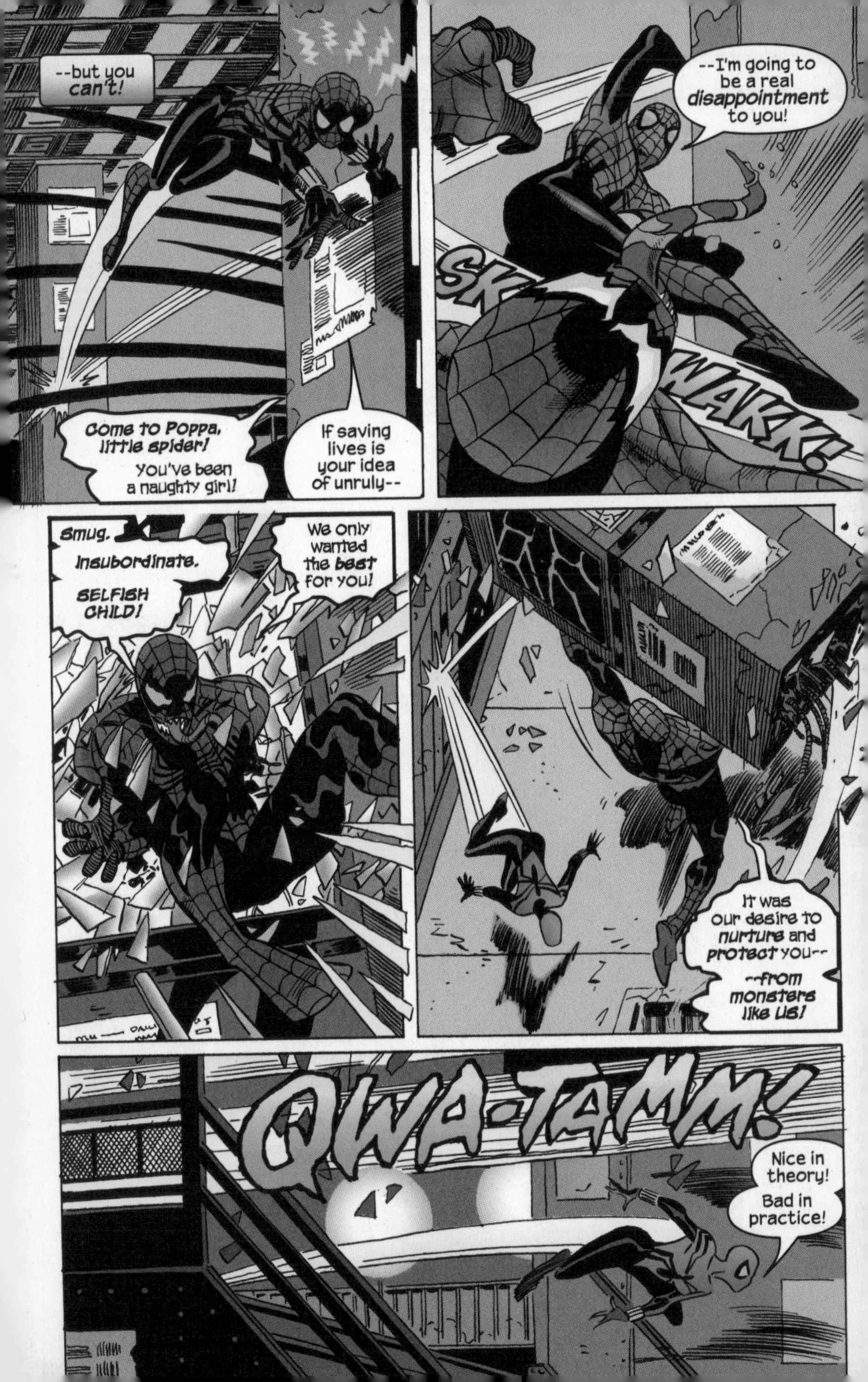
--but you can't!
Come to Poppa, little spider!
You've been a naughty girl!
If saving lives is your idea of unruly--
--I'm going to be a real disappointment to you!
SKWAKK!
Smug.
Insubordinate.
SELFISH CHILD!
We only wanted the best for you!
It was our desire to nurture and protect you--
--from monsters like us!
QWA-TAMM!
Nice in theory!
Bad in practice!

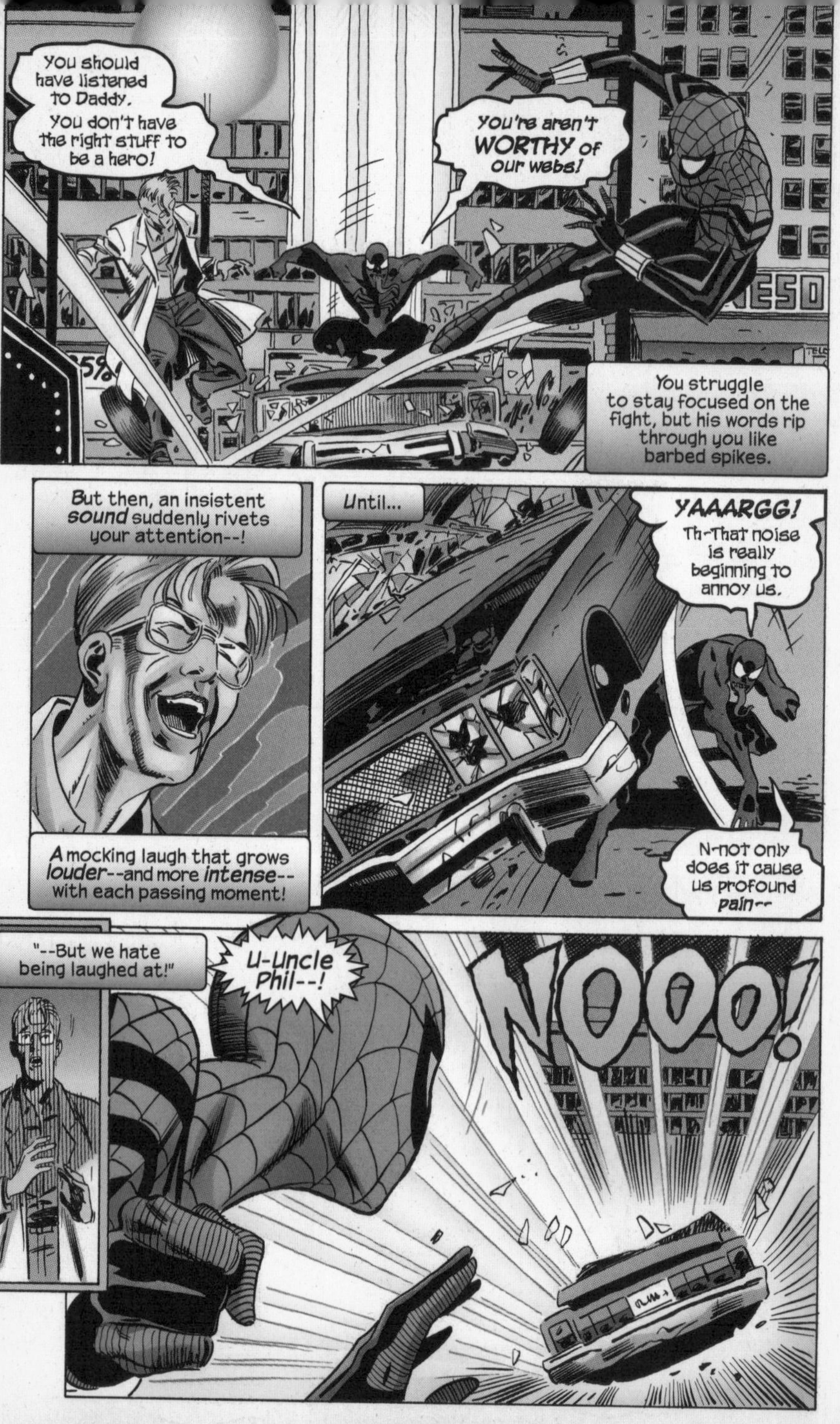

You should have listened to Daddy.
You don't have the right stuff to be a hero!
You're aren't WORTHY of our webs!
You struggle to stay focused on the fight, but his words rip through you like barbed spikes.
But then, an insistent sound suddenly rivets your attention--!
A mocking laugh that grows louder--and more intense--with each passing moment!
Until...
YAAARGG! Th-That noise is really beginning to annoy us.
N-not only does it cause us profound pain--
"--But we hate being laughed at!"
U-Uncle Phil--!
NOOO!

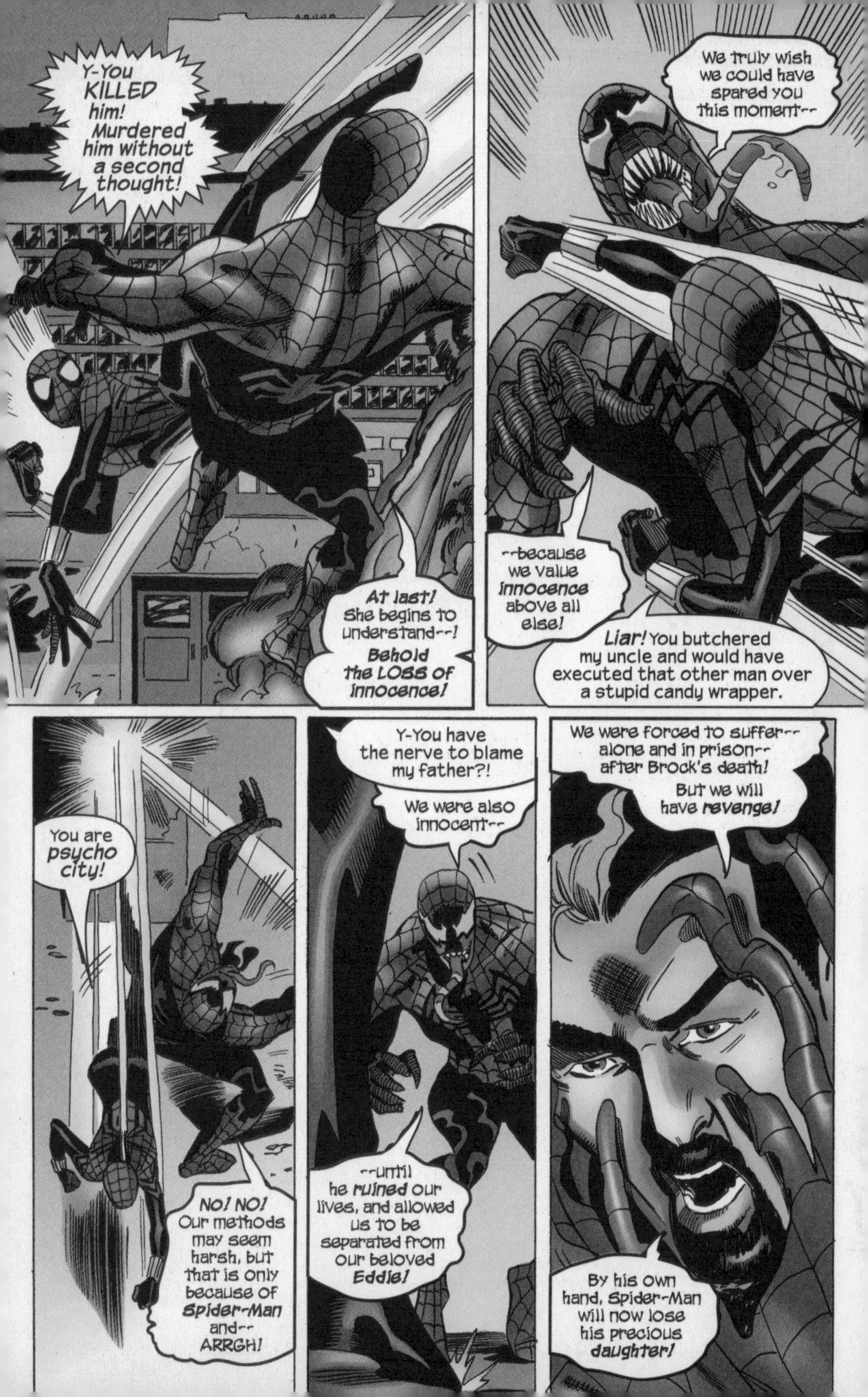

Y-You KILLED him! Murdered him without a second thought!
At last! She begins to understand--! Behold the LOSS of innocence!
We truly wish we could have spared you this moment--
--because we value innocence above all else!
Liar! You butchered my uncle and would have executed that other man over a stupid candy wrapper.
You are psycho city!
NO! NO! Our methods may seem harsh, but that is only because of Spider-Man and-- ARRGH!
Y-You have the nerve to blame my father?!
We were also innocent--
--until he ruined our lives, and allowed us to be separated from our beloved Eddie!
We were forced to suffer-- alone and in prison-- after Brock's death!
But we will have revenge!
By his own hand, Spider-Man will now lose his precious daughter!

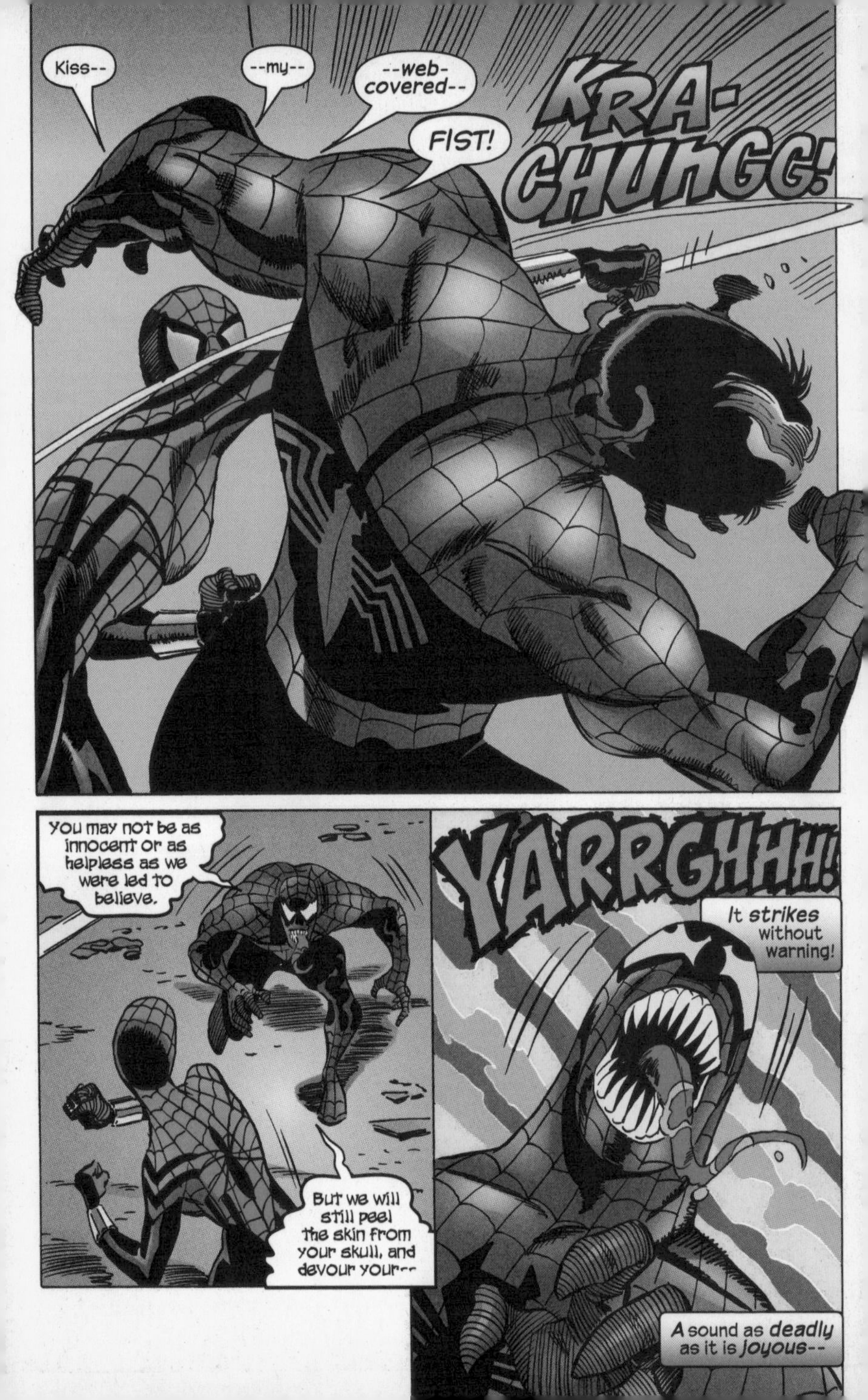
Kiss--
--my--
--web-covered--
FIST!
KRA-CHUNGG!
You may not be as innocent or as helpless as we were led to believe.
But we will still peel the skin from your skull, and devour your--
YARRGHHH!
It strikes without warning!
A sound as deadly as it is joyous--

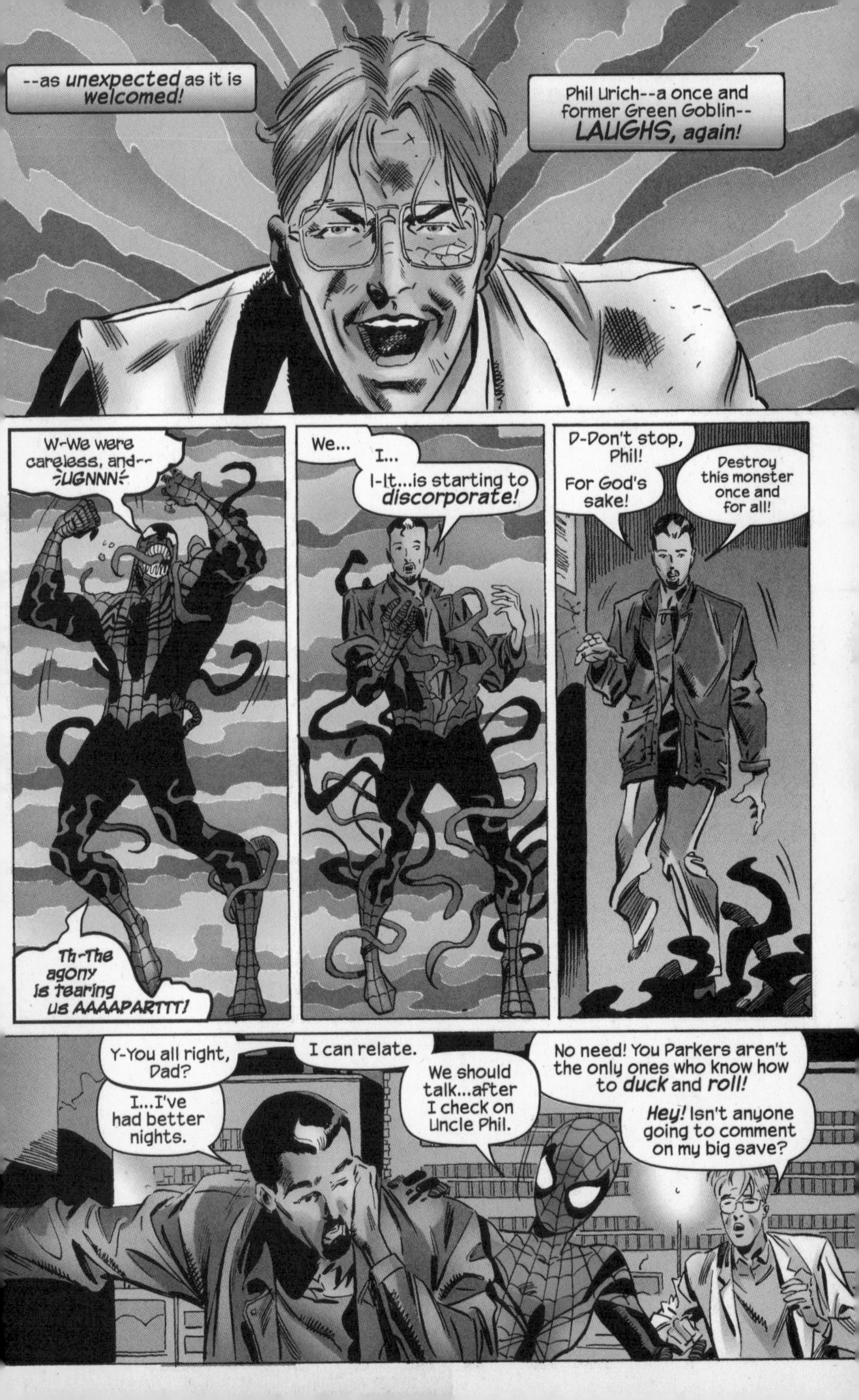

--as unexpected as it is welcomed!
Phil Urich--a once and former Green Goblin--LAUGHS, again!
W-We were careless, and-- UGNNN
Th-The agony is tearing us AAAAPARTTT!
We...
I...
I-It...is starting to discorporate!
D-Don't stop, Phil!
For God's sake!
Destroy this monster once and for all!
Y-You all right, Dad?
I...I've had better nights.
I can relate.
We should talk...after I check on Uncle Phil.
No need! You Parkers aren't the only ones who know how to duck and roll!
Hey! Isn't anyone going to comment on my big save?

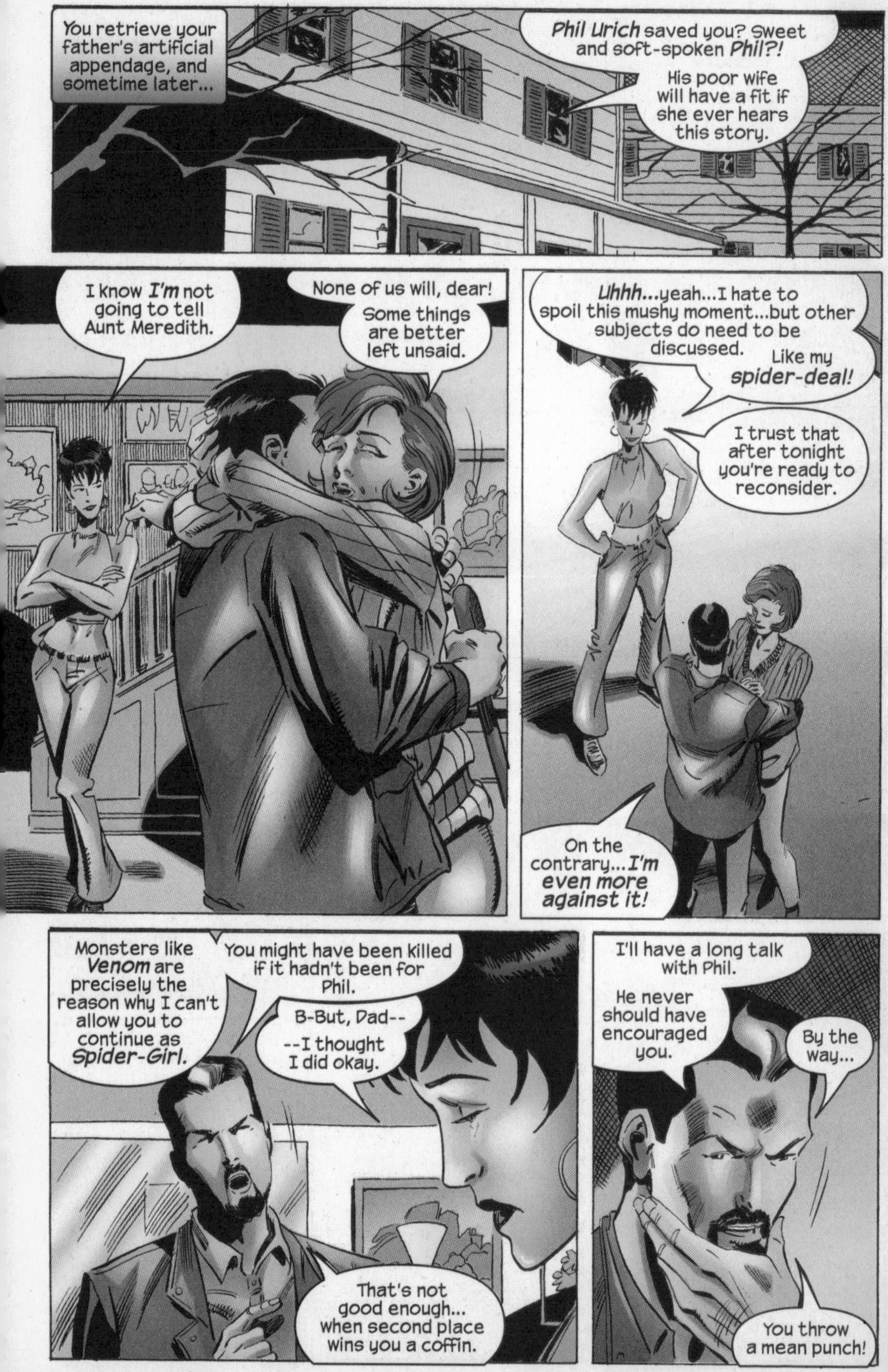
You retrieve your father's artificial appendage, and sometime later...
Phil Urich saved you? Sweet and soft-spoken *Phil?!*
His poor wife will have a fit if she ever hears this story.
I know *I'm* not going to tell Aunt Meredith.
None of us will, dear!
Some things are better left unsaid.
*Uhhh...*yeah...I hate to spoil this mushy moment...but other subjects do need to be discussed.
Like my *spider-deal!*
I trust that after tonight you're ready to reconsider.
On the contrary...*I'm even more against it!*
Monsters like *Venom* are precisely the reason why I can't allow you to continue as *Spider-Girl.*
You might have been killed if it hadn't been for Phil.
B-But, Dad--
--I thought I did okay.
That's not good enough... when second place wins you a coffin.
I'll have a long talk with Phil.
He never should have encouraged you.
By the way...
You throw a mean punch!

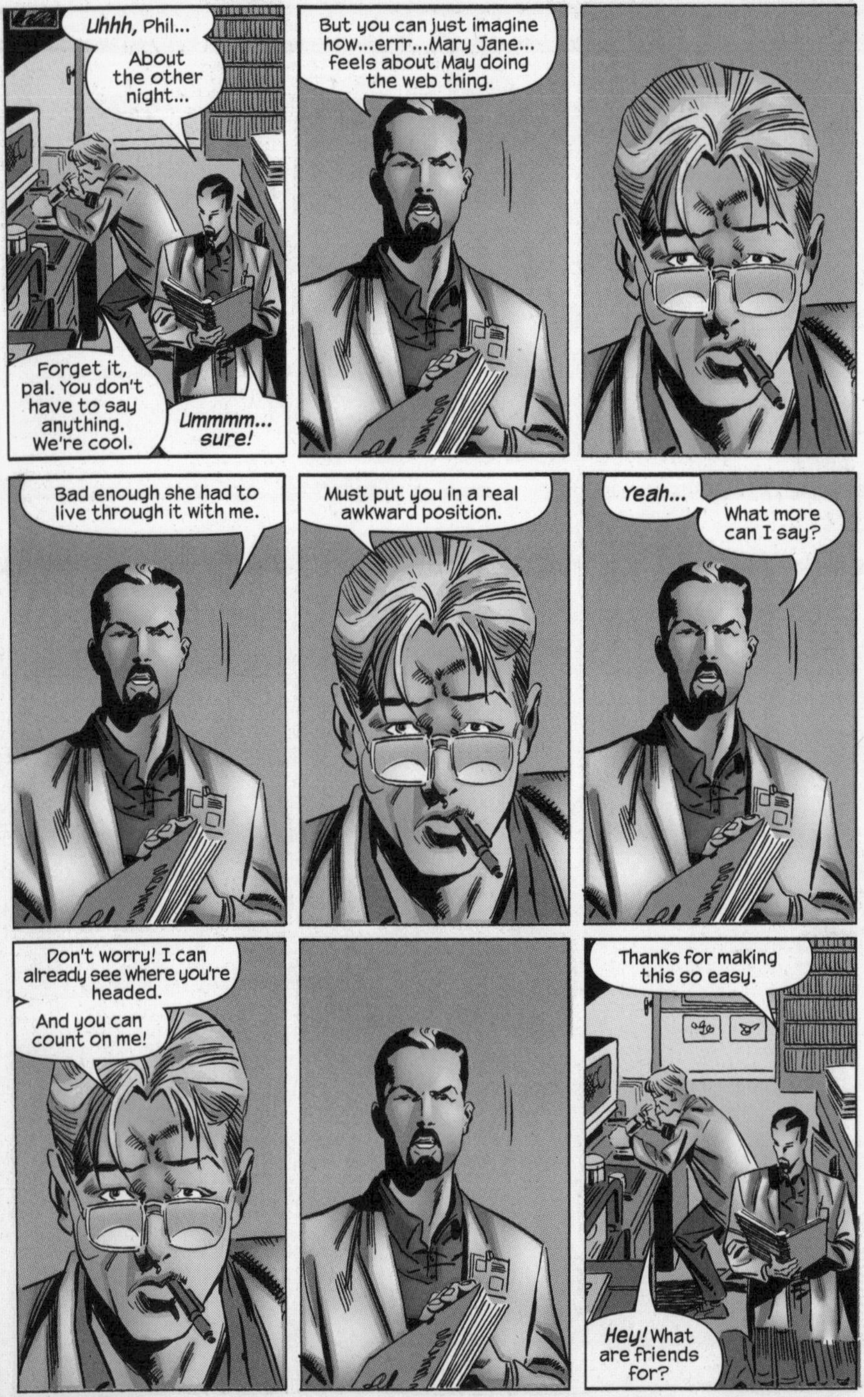

Uhhh, Phil...
About the other night...
Forget it, pal. You don't have to say anything. We're cool.
Ummmm... sure!
But you can just imagine how...errr...Mary Jane... feels about May doing the web thing.
Bad enough she had to live through it with me.
Must put you in a real awkward position.
Yeah...
What more can I say?
Don't worry! I can already see where you're headed.
And you can count on me!
Thanks for making this so easy.
Hey! What are friends for?

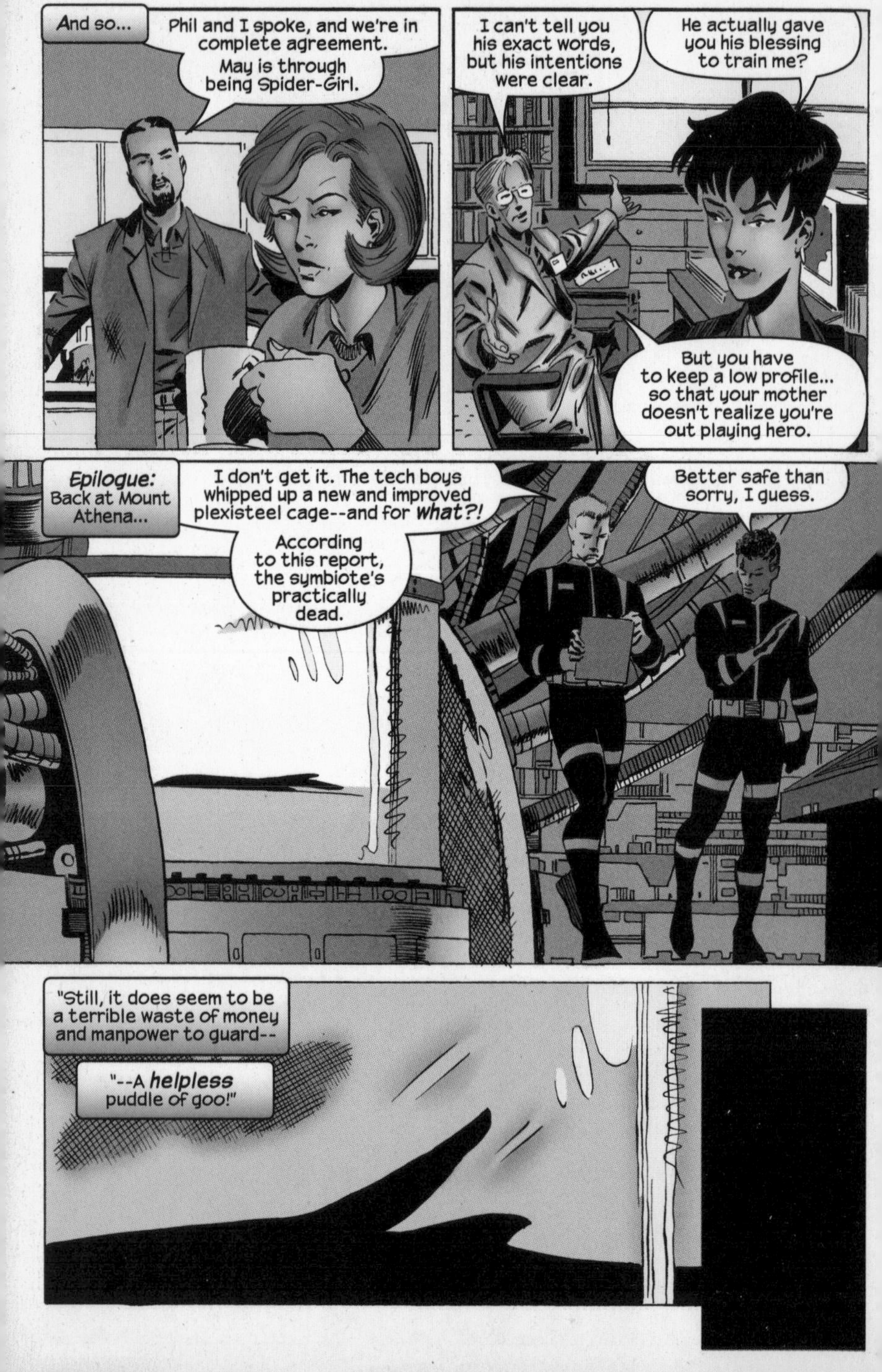
And so...
Phil and I spoke, and we're in complete agreement.
May is through being Spider-Girl.
I can't tell you his exact words, but his intentions were clear.
He actually gave you his blessing to train me?
But you have to keep a low profile... so that your mother doesn't realize you're out playing hero.
Epilogue: Back at Mount Athena...
I don't get it. The tech boys whipped up a new and improved plexisteel cage--and for what?!
According to this report, the symbiote's practically dead.
Better safe than sorry, I guess.
"Still, it does seem to be a terrible waste of money and manpower to guard--
"--A helpless puddle of goo!"